THE VULTURES

A NOVEL

HENRY SETON MERRIMAN

1st WORLD
LIBRARY
Literary Society

The Vultures

Henry Seton Merriman

© 1st World Library, 2009
PO Box 2211
Fairfield, IA 52556
www.1stworldlibrary.com
First Edition

LCCN: 2009923397

Softcover ISBN: 978-1-4218-8846-0
Hardcover ISBN: 978-1-4218-8945-0
eBook ISBN: 978-1-4218-8747-0

Purchase *"The Vultures"*
as a traditional bound book at:
www.1stWorldLibrary.com/purchase.asp?ISBN=978-1-4218-8846-0

1st World Library is a literary, educational organization
dedicated to:

- Creating a free internet library of downloadable ebooks

- Hosting writing competitions and offering book publishing
scholarships.

Interested in more 1st World Library books? contact:
literacy@1stworldlibrary.com
Check us out at: www.1stworldlibrary.com

1st World Library Literary Society

Giving Back to the World

"If you want to work on the core problem, it's early school literacy."

- James Barksdale, former CEO of Netscape

"No skill is more crucial to the future of a child, or to a democratic and prosperous society, than literacy."

- Los Angeles Times

"Literacy... means far more than learning how to read and write... The aim is to transmit... knowledge and promote social participation."

- UNESCO

"Literacy is not a luxury, it is a right and a responsibility. If our world is to meet the challenges of the twenty-first century we must harness the energy and creativity of all our citizens."

- President Bill Clinton

"Parents should be encouraged to read to their children, and teachers should be equipped with all available techniques for teaching literacy, so the varying needs and capacities of individual kids can be taken into account."

- Hugh Mackay

I

ALL AT SEA

Mr. Joseph P. Mangles, at his ease in a deck-chair on the broad Atlantic, was smoking a most excellent cigar. Mr. Mangles was a tall, thin man, who carried his head in the manner curtly known at a girls' school as "poking." He was a clean-shaven man, with bony forehead, sunken cheeks, and an underhung mouth. His attitude towards the world was one of patient disgust. He had the air of pushing his way, chin first, doggedly through life. The weather had been bad, and was now moderating. But Mr. Mangles had not suffered from sea-sickness. He was a dry, hard person, who had suffered from nothing but chronic dyspepsia—had suffered from it for fifty years or so.

"Fine weather," he said. "Women will be coming on deck—hang the fine weather."

And his voice was deep and low like a growl.

"Joseph," said Miss Mangles, "growls over his meals like a dog."

The remark about the weather and the women was addressed to a man who leaned against the rail. Indeed, there was no one else near—and the man made no reply. He was twenty-five or thirty years younger than Mr. Mangles, and looked like an Englishman, but not aggressively so. The large majority of Britons are offensively British. Germans are no better; so it must be racial, this offensiveness. A Frenchman is at his worst, only comically French—a matter of a smile; but Teutonic characteristics are conducive to hostility.

The man who leaned against the rail near to Joseph P. Mangles was six feet high, and rather heavily built, but, like many big men, he seemed to take up no more than his due share of room in this crowded world. There was nothing distinctive about his dress. His demeanor was quiet. When he spoke he was habitually asked to repeat his remark, which he did, with patience, in the same soft, inaudible voice.

There were two men on board this great steamer who were not business men—Joseph P. Mangles and Reginald Cartoner; and, like two ships on a sea of commercial interests, they had drifted together during the four days that had elapsed since their departure from New York. Neither made anything, or sold anything, or had a card in his waistcoat-pocket ready for production at a moment's notice, setting forth name and address and trade. Neither was to be suspected of a desire to repel advances, and yet both were difficult to get on with. For human confidences must be mutual. It is only to God that man can continue telling, telling, telling, and getting never a word in return. These two men had nothing to tell their fellows about themselves; so the other passengers drifted away into those closely linked corporations characteristic of steamer life and left them to themselves—to each other.

And they had never said things to each other—had never, as it were, got deeper than the surface of their daily life.

Henry Seton Merriman

Cartoner was a dreamy man, with absorbed eyes, rather deeply sunk under a strong forehead. His eyelids had that peculiarity which is rarely seen in the face of a man who is a nonentity. They were quite straight, and cut across the upper curve of the pupil. This gave a direct, stern look to dreamy eyes, which was odd. After a pause, he turned slowly, and looked down at his companion with a vague interrogation in his glance. He seemed to be wondering whether Mr. Mangles had spoken. And Mangles met the glance with one of steady refusal to repeat his remark. But Mangles spoke first, after all.

"Yes," he said, "the women will be on deck soon—and my sister Jooly. You don't know Jooly?"

He spoke with a slow and pleasant American accent.

"I saw you speaking to a young lady in the saloon after luncheon," said Cartoner. "She had a blue ribbon round her throat. She was pretty."

"That wasn't Jooly," said Mr. Mangles, without hesitation.

"Who was it?" asked Cartoner, with the simple directness of those who have no self-consciousness—who are absorbed, but not in themselves, as are the majority of men and women.

"My niece, Netty Cahere."

"She is pretty," said Cartoner, with a spontaneity which would have meant much to feminine ears.

"You'll fall in love with her," said Mangles, lugubriously. "They all do. She says she can't help it."

Cartoner looked at him as one who has ears but hears not. He made no reply.

"Distresses her very much," concluded Mangles, dexterously shifting his cigar by a movement of the tongue from the port to the starboard side of his mouth. Cartoner did not seem to be very much interested in Miss Netty Cahere. He was a man having that air of detachment from personal environments which is apt to arouse curiosity in the human heart, more especially in feminine hearts. People wanted to know what there was in Cartoner's past that gave him so much to think about in the present.

The two men had not spoken again when Miss Netty Cahere came on deck. She was accompanied by the fourth officer, a clean-built, clean-shaven young man, who lost his heart every time he crossed the Atlantic. He was speaking rather earnestly to Miss Cahere, who listened with an expression of puzzled protest on her pretty face. She had wondering blue eyes and a complexion of the most delicate pink and white which never altered. She was slightly built, and carried herself in a subtly deprecating manner, as if her own opinion of herself were small, and she wished the world to accept her at that valuation. She made no sign of having perceived her uncle, but nevertheless dismissed the fourth officer, who reluctantly mounted the ladder to the bridge, looking back as he went.

Mr. Mangles threw his cigar overboard.

"She don't like smoke," he growled.

Cartoner looked at the cigar, and absent-mindedly threw his cigarette after it. He had apparently not made up his mind whether to go or stay, when Miss Cahere approached her uncle, without appearing to notice that he was not alone.

"I suppose," she said, "that that was one of the officers of the ship, though he was very young—quite a boy. He was telling me about his mother. It must be terrible to have a near relation a sailor."

She spoke in a gentle voice, and it was evident that she had a heart full of sympathy for the suffering and the poor.

"I wish some of my relations were sailors," replied Mr. Mangles, in his deepest tones. "Could spare a whole crew. Let me introduce my friend, Mr. Cartoner—Miss Cahere."

He completed the introduction with an old-fashioned and ceremonious wave of the hand. Miss Cahere smiled rather shyly on Cartoner, and it was his eyes that turned away first.

"You have not been down to meals," he said, in his gentle, abrupt way.

"No; but I hope to come now. Are there many people? Have you friends on board?"

"There are very few ladies. I know none of them."

"But I dare say some of them are nice," said Miss Cahere, who evidently thought well of human nature.

"Very likely."

And Cartoner lapsed into his odd and somewhat discon- certing thoughtfulness.

Miss Cahere continued to glance at him beneath her dark lashes—dark lashes around blue eyes—with a guileless and wondering admiration. He certainly was a very good-looking man, well set up, with that quiet air which bespeaks good breeding.

"Have you seen the ship on the other side?" she asked, after a pause; "a sailing ship. You cannot see it from here."

As she spoke she made a little movement, as if to show him the spot from whence the ship was visible. Cartoner followed her meekly, and Mr. Mangles, left behind in his deck-chair, slowly sought his cigar-case.

"There," said Miss Cahere, pointing out a sail on the distant horizon. "One can hardly see it now. When I first came on deck it was much nearer. That ship's officer pointed it out to me."

Cartoner looked at the ship without much enthusiasm.

"I think," said Miss Cahere, in a lower voice—she had a rather confidential manner—"I think sailors are very nice, don't you? But... well, I suppose one ought not to say that, ought one?"

"It depends what you were going to say."

Miss Cahere laughed, and made no reply. Her laugh and a glance seemed, however, to convey the comfortable assurance that whatever she had been about to say would not have been applicable to Cartoner himself. She glanced at his trim, upright figure.

"I think I prefer soldiers," she said, thoughtfully.

Cartoner murmured something inaudible, and continued to gaze at the ship he had been told to look at.

"Did you know my uncle before you came on board, or were

you brave enough to force him to speak? He is so silent, you know, that most people are afraid of him. I suppose you had met him before."

"No. It was a mere accident. We were neither of us ill. We were both hungry, and hurried down to a meal. And the stewards placed us next to each other."

Which was a long explanation, without much information in it.

"Oh, I thought perhaps you were in the diplomatic service," said Miss Cahere, carelessly.

For an instant Cartoner's eyes lost all their vagueness. Either Miss Cahere had hit the mark with her second shot, or else he was making a mental note of the fact that Mr. Mangles belonged to that amiable body of amateurs, the American Diplomatic Corps.

Mr. Mangles had naturally selected the leeward side of the deck-house for his seat, and Miss Cahere had brought Cartoner round to the weather side, where a cold Atlantic breeze made the position untenable. Without explanation, and for her own good, he led the way to a warmer quarter. But at the corner of the deck-house a gust caught Miss Cahere, and held her there in a pretty attitude, with her two hands upraised to her hat, looking at him with frank and laughing eyes, and waiting for him to come to her assistance. The same gust of wind made the steamer lurch so that Cartoner had to grasp Miss Cahere's arm to save her from falling.

"Thank you," she said, quietly, and with downcast eyes, when the incident had passed. For in some matters she held old-fashioned notions, and was not one of the modern race of hail-fellow-well-met girls who are friendly in five minutes with men and women alike.

When she came within sight of her uncle, she suddenly hurried towards him, and made an affectionate, laughing attempt to prevent his returning his cigar-case to his jacket pocket. She even took possession of the cigar-case, opened it, and with her own fingers selected a cigar.

"No," she said, firmly, "you are going to smoke again at once. Do you think I did not see you throw away the other? Mr. Cartoner—is it not foolish of him? Because I once said, without reflecting, that I did not care about the smell of tobacco, he never lets me see him smoke now."

As she spoke she laid her hand affectionately on the old man's shoulder and looked down at him.

"As if it mattered whether I like it or not," she said. "And I do like it—I like the smell of your cigars."

Mr. Mangles looked from Cartoner to his niece with an odd smile, which was perhaps the only way in which that lean countenance could express tenderness.

"As if it mattered what I think," she said, humbly, again.

"Always like to conciliate a lady," said Mr. Mangles, in his deep voice.

"Especially when that lady is dependent on you for her daily bread and her frocks," answered Netty, in an affectionate aside, which Cartoner was, nevertheless, able to overhear.

"Where is your aunt Jooly?" inquired the old man, hurriedly. "I thought she was coming on deck."

"So she is," answered Netty. "I left her in the saloon. She is quite well. She was talking to some people."

"What, already?" exclaimed the lady's brother. And Netty nodded her head with a mystic gravity. She was looking towards the saloon stairway, from whence she seemed to expect Miss Mangles.

"My sister Jooly, sir," explained Mr. Mangles to Cartoner, "is no doubt known to you—Miss Julia P. Mangles, of New York City."

Cartoner tried to look as if he had heard the name before. He had lived in the United States during some months, and he knew that it is possible to be famous in New York and quite without honor in Connecticut.

"Perhaps she has not come into your line of country?" suggested Mr. Mangles, not unkindly.

"No—I think not."

"Her line is—at present—prisons."

"I have never been in prison," replied Cartoner.

"No doubt you will get experience in course of time," said Mr. Mangles, with his deep, curt laugh. "No, sir, my sister is a lecturer. She gets on platforms and talks."

"What about?" asked Cartoner.

Mr. Mangles described the wide world, with a graceful wave of his cigar.

"About most things," he answered, gravely; "chiefly about

women, I take it. She is great on the employment of women, and the payment of them. And she is right there. She has got hold of the right end of the stick there. She had found out what very few women know—namely, that when women work for nothing, they are giving away something that nobody wants. So Jooly goes about the world lecturing on women's employment, and pointing out to the public and the administration many ways in which women may be profitably employed and paid. She leaves it to the gumption of the government to discover for themselves that there is many a nice berth for which Jooly P. Mangles is eminently suited, but governments have no gumption, sir. And—"

"Here is Aunt Julie," interrupted Miss Cahere, walking away.

Mr. Mangles gave a short sigh, and lapsed into silence.

As Miss Cahere went forward, she passed another officer of the ship, the second in command, a dogged, heavy man, whose mind was given to the ship and his own career. He must have seen something to interest him in Netty Cahere's face—perhaps he caught a glance from the dark-lashed eyes—for he turned and looked at her again, with a sudden, dull light in his face.

II

SIGNAL HOUSE

Where Gravesend merges into Northfleet—where the spicy odors of chemical-fertilizing works mingle with the dry dust of the cement manufactories which throw their tall chimneys into an ever-gray sky—there stands a house known as the Signal House. Why it is so called no one knows and very few care to inquire. It is presumably a square house of the Jacobean period—presumably because it is so hidden by trees, so wrapped in grimy ivy, so dust-laden and so impossible to get at, that its outward form is no longer to be perceived.

It is within sound of the bells that jingle dismally on the heads of the tram-car horses, plying their trade on the high-road, and yet it is haunted. Its two great iron gates stand on the very pavement, and they are never opened. Indeed, a generation or two of painters have painted them shut, and grime and dirt have laid their seals upon the hinges. A side gate gives entrance to such as come on foot. A door in the wall, up an alley, is labelled "Tradesman's Entrance," but the tradesmen never linger there. No merry milkman leaves the latest gossip with his thin, blue milk on that threshold. The butcher's chariot wheels never tarry at the corner of that alley. Indeed, the local butcher has no chariot. His clients mostly come in a shawl, and take their purchases away with them wrapped in a doubtful newspaper beneath its folds. The better-class buyers wear a cloth cricketing cap, coquettishly attached to a knob of hair by a hat-pin.

The milkman, moreover, is not a merry man, hurrying on his rounds. He goes slowly and pessimistically, and likes to see the halfpenny before he tips his measure.

This, in a word, is a poor district, where no one would live if he could live elsewhere, with the Signal House stranded in the midst of it—a noble wreck on a barren, social shore. For the Signal House was once a family mansion; later it was described as a riverside residence, then as a quaint and interesting demesne. Finally its price fell with a crash, and an elderly lady of weak intellect was sent by her relations to live in it, with two servants, who were frequently to be met in Gravesend in the evening hours, at which time, it is to be presumed, the elderly lady of weak intellect was locked in the Signal House alone. But the house never had a ghost. Haunted houses very seldom have. The ghost was the mere invention of some kitchen-maid.

Haunted or not, the house stood empty for years, until suddenly a foreigner took it—a Russian banker, it was understood. A very nice, pleasant-spoken little gentleman this foreigner, who liked quiet and the river view. He was quite as broad as he was long, though he was not prepos-terously stout. There was nothing mysterious about him. He was well known in the City. He had merely mistaken an undesirable suburb for a desirable one, a very easy mistake for a foreigner to make; and he was delighted at the cheapness of the house, the greenness of the old lawn, the height of the grimy trees within the red brick wall.

He lived there all one summer, and the cement smoke got

Henry Seton Merriman

into his throat in the autumn and gave him asthma, for which complaint he had obviously been designed by Providence, for he had no neck. He used the Signal House occasionally from Saturday till Monday. Then he gave it up altogether, and tried to sell it. It stood empty for some years, while the Russian banker extended his business and lived virtuously elsewhere. Then he suddenly began using the house again as a house of recreation, and brought his foreign servants, and his foreign friends and their foreign servants, to stay from Saturday till Monday.

And all these persons behaved in an odd, Continental way, and played bowls on the lawn at the back of the house on Sundays. The neighbors could hear them but could see nothing, owing to the thickness of the grimy trees and the height of the old brick wall. But no one worried much about the Signal House; for they were a busy people who lived all around, and had to earn their living, in addition to the steady and persistent assuagement of a thirst begotten of cement dust and the pungent smell of bone manure. One or two local amateurs had made sure of the fact that there was nothing in the house that would repay a burglarious investigation, which, added to the fact that the police station is only a few doors off, tended to allay a natural curiosity as to the foreign gentleman's possessions.

When he came he drove in a close cab from Gravesend Station, and usually told the cabman when his services would again be required. He came thus with three friends one summer afternoon, some years ago, and came without luggage. The servants, who followed in a second cab, carried some parcels, presumably of refreshments. These grave gentlemen were, it appeared, about to enjoy a picnic at the Signal House—possibly a tea-picnic in the Russian fashion.

The afternoon was fine, and the gentlemen walked in the

garden at the back of the house. They were walking thus when another cab stopped at the closed iron gate, and the banker hurried, as fast as his build would allow, to open the side door and admit a seafaring man, who seemed to know his bearings.

"Well, mister," he said, in a Northern voice, "another of your little jobs?"

The two men shook hands, and the banker paid the cabman. When the vehicle had gone the host turned to his guest and replied to the question.

"Yes, my fren'," he said, "another of my little jobs. I hope you are well, Captain Cable?"

But Captain Cable was not a man to waste words over the social conventions. He was obviously well—as well as a hard, seafaring life will make a man who lives simply and works hard. He was a short man, with a red face washed very clean, and very well shaven, except for a little piece of beard left fantastically at the base of his chin. His eyes were blue and bright, like gimlets. He may have had a soft heart, but it was certainly hidden beneath a hard exterior. He wore a thick coat of blue pilot-cloth, not because the July day was cold, but because it was his best coat. His hat was carefully brushed and of hard, black felt. It had perhaps been the height of fashion in Sunderland five years earlier. He wore no gloves—Captain Cable drew the line there. As for the rest, he had put on that which he called his shore-going rig.

"And yourself?" he answered, mechanically.

"I am very well, thank you," replied the polite banker, who, it will have been perceived, was nameless to Captain Cable, as he is to the reader. The truth being that his name was so

Henry Seton Merriman

absurdly and egregiously Russian that the plain English tongue never embarked on that sea of consonants. "It is an affair, as usual. My friends are here to meet you, but I think they do not speak English, except your colleague, the other captain, who speaks a little—a very little."

As he spoke he led the way to the garden, where three gentlemen were awaiting them.

"This is Captain Cable," he said, and the three gentlemen raised their hats, much to the captain's discomfiture. He did not hold by foreign ways; but he dragged his hat off and then expectorated on the lawn, just to show that he felt quite at home. He even took the lead in the conversation.

"Tell 'em," he said, "that I'm a plain man from Sun'land that has a speciality, an' that's transshipping cargo at sea, but me hands are clean."

He held them out and they were not, so he must have spoken metaphorically.

The banker translated, addressing himself to one of his companions, rather markedly and with much deference.

"You're speakin' French," interrupted Captain Cable.

"Yes, my fren', I am. Do you know French?"

"Not me," returned Captain Cable, affably. "They're all one to me. They're all damn nonsense."

He was, it seemed, that which is called in these days of blatant patriotism a thorough Englishman, or a true Blue, according to the social station of the speaker.

The gentleman to whom the translation had been addressed smiled. He was a tall and rather distinguished-looking man, with bushy white hair and mustache. His features were square-cut and strong. His eyes were dark, and he had an easy smile. He led the way to some chairs which had been placed near a table at the far end of the lawn beneath a cedar-tree, and his manner had something faintly regal in it, as if in his daily life he had always been looked up to and obeyed without question.

"Tell him that we also are plain men with clean hands," he said.

And the banker replied:

"Oui, mon Prince."

But the interpretation was taken out of his mouth by one of the others, the youngest of the group—a merry-eyed youth, with a fluffy, fair mustache and close-cropped, flaxen hair.

"My father," he said, in perfect English, "says that we also are plain men, and that your hands will not be hurt by touching ours."

He held out his hand as he spoke, and refused to withdraw it until it had been grasped, rather shame-facedly, by Captain Cable, who did not like these effusive foreign ways, but, nevertheless, rather liked the young man.

The banker ranged the chairs round the table, and the oddly assorted group seated themselves. The man who had not yet spoken, and who sat down last, was obviously a sailor. His face was burned a deep brown, and was mostly hidden by a closely cut beard. He had the slow ways of a Northerner, the abashed manner of a merchant skipper on shore. The mark of the other element was so plainly written upon him that Captain Cable looked at him hard and then nodded. Without being invited to do so they sat next to each other at one side of the table, and faced the three landsmen. Again Captain Cable spoke first.

"Provided it's nothing underhand," he said, "I'm ready and willing. Or'nary risks of the sea, Queen's enemies, act o' God—them's my risks! I am uninsured. Ship's my own. I don't mind explosives—"

"There are explosives," admitted the banker.

"Then they must be honest explosives, or they don't go below my hatches. Explosives that's to blow a man up honest, before his face."

"There are cartridges," said the young man who had shaken hands.

"That'll do," said the masterful sailor. And pointing a thick finger towards the banker, added, "Now, mister," and sat back in his chair.

"It is a very simple matter," explained the banker, in a thick, suave voice. "We have a cargo—a greater part of it weight, though there is some measurement—a few cases of light goods, clothing and such. You will load in the river, and all will be sent to you in lighters. There is nothing heavy, nothing large. There is also no insurance, you understand. What falls out of the slings and is lost overside is lost."

The banker paused for breath.

"I understand," said Captain Cable. "It's the same with me and my ship. There is no insurance, no tricking underwriters into unusual risks. It's neck or nothing with me."

And he looked hard at the breathless banker, with whom it was, in this respect, nothing.

"I understand right enough," he added, with an affable nod to the three foreigners.

"You will sail from London with a full general cargo for Malmo or Stockholm, or somewhere where officials are not wide-awake. You meet in the North Sea, at a point to be fixed between yourselves, the *Olaf*, Captain Petersen— sitting by your side."

Captain Cable turned and gravely shook hands with Captain Petersen.

"Thought you was a seafaring man," he said. And Captain Petersen replied that he was "Vair pleased."

"The cargo is to be transshipped at sea, out of sight of land or lightship. But that we can safely leave to you, Captain Cable."

"I don't deny," replied the mariner, who was measuring Captain Petersen out of the corner of his eye, "that I have been there before."

"You can then go up the Baltic in ballast to some small port—just a sawmill, at the head of a fjord—where I shall have a cargo of timber waiting for you to bring back to London. When can you begin loading, captain?"

"To-morrow," replied the captain. "Ship's lying in the river now, and if these gentlemen would like to see her, she's as handy a—"

Henry Seton Merriman

"No, I do not think we shall have time for that!" put in the banker, hastily. "And now we must leave you and Captain Petersen to settle your meeting-place. You have your charts?"

By way of response the captain produced from his pocket sundry folded papers, which he laid tenderly on the table. For the last ten years he had been postponing the necessity of buying new charts of certain sections of the North Sea. He looked round at the high walls and the overhanging trees.

"Hope the wind don't come blustering in here much," he said, apprehensively, as he unfolded the ragged papers with great caution.

The fair-haired young man drew forward his chair, and Cable, seeing the action, looked at him sharply.

"Seafaring man?" he inquired, with a weight of doubt and distrust in his voice.

"Not by profession, only for fun."

"Fun? Man and boy, I've used the sea forty years, and I haven't yet found out where the fun comes in!"

"This gentleman," explained the banker, "his Ex—Mr.—" He paused, and looked inquiringly at the white-haired gentleman.

"Mr. Martin."

"Mr. Martin will be on board the *Olaf* when you meet Captain Petersen in the North Sea. He will act as interpreter. You remember that Captain Petersen speaks no English, and you do not know his language. The two crews, I understand, will be similarly placed. Captain Peterson undertakes to have no one on board speaking English. And your crew, my fren'?"

"My crew comes from Sun'land. Men that only speak English, and precious little of that," replied Captain Cable.

He had his finger on the chart, but paused and looked up, fixing his bright glance on the face of the white-haired gentleman.

"There's one thing—I'm a plain-spoken man myself—what is there for us two—us seafaring men?"

"There is five hundred pounds for each of you," replied the white-haired gentleman for himself, in slow and careful English.

Captain Cable nodded his grizzled head over the chart.

"I like to deal with a gentleman," he said, gruffly.

"And so do I," replied the white-haired foreigner, with a bow.

Captain Cable grunted audibly.

III

A SPECIALTY

A muddy sea and a dirty gray sky, a cold rain and a moaning wind. Short-capped waves breaking to leeward in a little hiss of spray. The water itself sandy and discolored. Far away to the east, where the green-gray and the dirty gray merge into one, a windmill spinning in the breeze—Holland. Near at hand, standing in the sea, the picture of wet and disconsolate solitude, a little beacon, erect on three legs, like a bandbox affixed to a giant easel. It is alight, although it is broad daylight; for it is always alight, always gravely revolving, night and day, alone on this sandbank in the North Sea. It is tended once in three weeks. The lamp is filled; the wick is trimmed; the screen, which is ingeniously made to revolve by the heat of the lamp, is lubricated, and the beacon is left to its solitude and its work.

There must be land to the eastward, though nothing but the spinning mill is visible. The land is below the level of the sea. There is probably an entrance to some canal behind the moving sandbank. This is one of the waste-places of the world—a place left clean on sailors' charts; no one passes that way. These banks are as deadly as many rocks which have earned for themselves a dreaded name in maritime story. For they never relinquish anything that touches them.

They are soft and gentle in their embrace; they slowly suck in the ship that comes within their grasp. Their story is a long, grim tale of disaster. Their treasure is vast and stored beneath a weight, half sand, half water, which must ever baffle the ingenuity of man. Fog, the sailors' deadliest foe, has its home on these waters, rising on the low-lying lands and creeping out to sea, where it blows to and fro for weeks and weeks together. When all the world is blue and sunny, fog-banks lie like a sheet of cotton-wool on these coasts.

"Barrin' fogs—always barrin' fogs!" Captain Cable had said as his last word on leaving the Signal House. "If ye wait a month, never move in a fog in these waters, or ye'll move straight to Davy Jones!"

And chance favored him, for a gale of wind came instead of a fog, one of those May gales that sweep down from the northwest without warning or reason.

At sunset the *Olaf* had crept cautiously in from the west—a high-prowed, well-decked, square-rigged steamer of the old school, with her name written large amidships and her side-lights set aft. Captain Petersen was a cautious man, and came on with the leadsman working like a clock. He was a man who moved slowly. And at sea, as in life, he who moves slowly often runs many dangers which a greater confidence and a little dash would avoid. He who moves slowly is the prey of every current.

Captain Petersen steamed in behind the beacon. He sighted the windmill very carefully, very correctly, very cautiously. He described a half-circle round the bank hidden a few feet below the muddy water. Then he steamed slowly seawards, keeping the windmill full astern and the beacon on his port quarter. When the beacon was bearing southeast he rang the engine-room bell. The steamer, hardly moving before,

Henry Seton Merriman

stopped dead, its bluff nose turned to the wind and the rustling waves. Then Captain Petersen held up his hand to the first mate, who was on the high forecastle, and the anchor splashed over. The *Olaf* was anchored at the head of a submarine bay. She had shoal water all round her, and no vessel could get at her unless it came as she had come. The sun went down, and the red-gray clouds in the stormy west slowly faded into night. There was no land in sight. Even the whirligig windmill was below the horizon now. Only the three-legged beacon stood near, turning its winking, wondering eye round the waste of waters.

Here the *Olaf* rode out the gale that raged all through the night, and in the morning there was no peace, for it still rained and the northwest wind still blew hard. There was no depth of water, however, to make a sea big enough to affect large vessels. The *Olaf* rode easily enough, and only pitched her nose into the yellow sea from time to time, throwing a cloud of spray over the length of her decks, like a bird at its bath.

Soon after daylight the Prince Martin Bukaty came on deck, gay and lively in his borrowed oilskins. His blue eyes laughed in the shadow of the black sou'wester tied down over his eyes, his slight form was lost in the ample folds of Captain Petersen's best oilskin coat.

"It remains to be seen," he said, peering out into the rain and spray, "whether that little man will come to us in this."

"He will come," said Captain Petersen.

Prince Martin Bukaty laughed. He laughed at most things— at the timidity and caution of this Norse captain, at good weather, at bad weather, at life as he found it. He was one of those few and happy people who find life a joy and his fellow-being a huge joke. Some will say that it is easy enough to be gay at the threshold of life; but experience tells that gayety is an inward sun which shines through all the changes and chances of a journey which has assuredly more bad weather than good. The gayest are not those who can be pointed out as the happiest. Indeed, the happiest are those who appear to have nothing to make them happy. Martin Bukaty might, for instance, have chosen a better abode than the stuffy cabin of a Scandinavian cargo-boat and cheerier companions than a grim pair of Norse seamen. He might have sought a bluer sky and a bluer sea, and yet he stood on the dripping deck and laughed. He clapped Captain Petersen on the back.

"Well, we have got here and we have ridden out the worst of it, and we haven't dragged our anchors and nobody has seen us, and that exceedingly amusing little captain will be here in a few hours. Why look so gloomy, my friend?"

Captain Petersen shook the rain from the brim of his sou'wester.

"We are putting our necks within a rope," he said.

"Not your neck—only mine," replied Martin. "It is a necktie that one gets accustomed to. Look at my father! One rarely sees an old man so free from care. How he laughs! How he enjoys his dinner and his wine! The wine runs down a man's throat none the less pleasantly because there is a loose rope around it. And he has played a dangerous game all his life— that old man, eh?"

"It is all very well for you," said Captain Petersen, gravely, turning his gloomy eyes towards his companion. "A prince does not get shot or hanged or sent to the bottom in the high seas."

Henry Seton Merriman

"Ah! you think that," said Prince Martin, momentarily grave. "One can never tell."

Then he broke into a laugh.

"Come!" he said, "I am going aloft to look for that English boat. Come on to the fore-yard. We can watch him come in—that little bulldog of a man."

"If he has any sense he will wait in the open until this gale is over," grumbled Petersen, nevertheless following his companion forward.

"He has only one sense, that man—a sense of infinite fearlessness."

"He is probably afraid—" Captain Petersen paused to hoist himself laboriously on to the rail.

"Of what?" inquired Martin, looking through the ratlines.

"Of a woman."

And Martin Bukaty's answer was lost in the roar of the wind as he went aloft.

They lay on the fore-yard for half an hour, talking from time to time in breathless monosyllables, for the wind was gathering itself together for that last effort which usually denotes the end of a gale. Then Captain Petersen pointed his steady hand almost straight ahead. On the gray horizon a little column of smoke rose like a pillar. It was a steamer approaching before the wind.

Captain Cable came on at a great pace. His ship was very low in the water, and kicked up awkwardly on a following sea. He swung round the beacon on the shoulder of a great wave that turned him over till the rounded wet sides of the steamer gleamed like a whale's back. He disappeared into the haze nearer the land, and presently emerged again astern of the *Olaf*, a black nozzle of iron and an intermittent fan of spray. He was crashing into the seas at full speed—a very different kind of sailor to the careful captain of the *Olaf*. His low decks were clear, and each sea leaped over the bow and washed aft—green and white. As the little steamer came down he suddenly slackened speed, and waved his hand as he stood alone on the high bridge.

Then two or three oilskin-clad figures crept forward into the spray that still broke over the bows. The crew of the *Olaf*, crowding to the rail, looked down on the deeply laden little vessel from the height of their dry and steady deck. They watched the men working quickly almost under water on the low forecastle, and saw that it was good. Captain Cable stood swaying on the bridge—a little, square figure in gleaming oilskins—and said no word. He had a picked crew.

He passed ahead of the *Olaf* and anchored there, paying out cable as if he were going to ride out a cyclone. The steamer had no name visible, a sail hanging carelessly over the stern completely hid name and port of registry. Her forward name-boards had been removed. Whatever his business was, this seaman knew it well.

No sooner was his anchor down than Captain Cable began to lower a boat, and Petersen, seeing the action, broke into mild Scandinavian profanity. "He is going to try and get to us!" he said, pessimistically, and went forward to give the necessary orders. He knew his business, too, this Northern sailor, and when, after a long struggle, the boat containing Captain Cable and two men came within reach, a rope—cleverly thrown—coiled out into the flying scud and fell across the

Henry Seton Merriman

captain's face.

A few minutes later he scrambled on to the deck of the *Olaf* and shook hands with Captain Petersen. He did not at once recognize Prince Martin, who held out his hand.

"Glad to see you, Captain Cable," he said. Cable finished drying the salt water from his face with a blue cotton handkerchief before he shook hands.

"Suppose you thought I wasn't coming," he said, suspiciously.

"No, I knew you would."

"Glad to see me for my own sake?" suggested the captain, grimly smiling.

"Yes, it always does one good to see a man," answered Prince Martin.

"They tell me you're a prince."

"That is all."

The captain measured him slowly with his eyes.

"Makings of a man as well, perhaps," he said, doubtfully. Then he turned to cast an eye over the *Olaf.*

"Tin-kettle of a thing!" he observed, after a pause.

"My little cargo won't be much in her great hold. Hatches are too small. Now, I'm all hatch. Can't open up in this weather. We can turn to and get our running tackle bent. It'll moderate before the evening, and if it does we can work all night. Will your Rile Highnes' be ready to work all night?"

"I shall be ready whenever your High Mightiness is."

The captain gave a gruff laugh.

"Dammy, you're the right sort!" he muttered, looking aloft at the rigging with that contempt for foreign tackle which is essentially the privilege of the British sailor.

Cable gave certain orders, announced that he would send four men on board in the afternoon to bend the running tackle "ship-shape and Bristol fashion," and refused to remain on board the *Olaf* for luncheon.

"We've got a bit of steak," he said, conclusively, and clambered over the side into his boat. In confirmation of this statement the odor of fried onions was borne on the breeze a few minutes later from the small steamer to the large one.

The men from Sunderland came on board during the afternoon—men who, as Captain Cable had stated, had only one language and made singularly small use of that. Music and seamanship are two arts daily practised in harmony by men who have no common language. For a man is a seaman or a musician quite independently of speech. So the running tackle was successfully bent, and in the evening the weather moderated.

There was a half-moon, which struggled through the clouds soon after dark, and by its light the little English steamer sidled almost noiselessly under the shadow of her large companion. Captain Cable's crew worked quickly and quietly, and by nine o'clock that work was begun which was to throw a noose round the necks of Prince Bukaty, Prince Martin, Captain Petersen, and several others.

Henry Seton Merriman

Captain Cable divided the watches so that the work might proceed continuously. The dawn found the smaller steamer considerably lightened, and her captain bright and wakeful at his post. All through the day the transshipping went on. Cases of all sizes and all weights were slung out of the capacious hatches of the one to sink into the dark hold of the other vessel, and there was no mishap. Through the second night the creaking of the blocks never ceased, and soon after daylight the three men who had superintended the work without resting took a cup of coffee together in the cabin of the *Olaf.*

"Likely as not," said Captain Cable, setting down his empty cup, "we three'll not meet again. I have had dealings with many that I've never seen again, and with some that have been careful not to know me if they did see me."

"We can never tell," said Martin, optimistically.

"Of course," the captain went on, "I can hold me tongue. That's agreed—we all hold our tongues, whatever the newspapers may be likely to pay for a word or two. Often enough I've read things in the newspaper that I could put a different name to. And that little ship of mine has had a hand in some queer political pies."

"Yes," answered Martin, with his gay laugh, "and kept it clean all the same."

"That's as may be. And now I'll say good-bye. I'll be calling on your father for my money in three days' time—barrin' fogs. And I'll tell him I left you well. Good-bye, Petersen; you're a handy man. Tell him he's a handy man in his own langwidge, and I'll take it kindly."

Captain Cable shook hands, and clattered out of the cabin in his great sea-boots.

Half an hour later the *Olaf* was alone on that shallow sea, which seemed lonelier and more silent than ever; for when a strong man quits a room he often bequeaths a sudden silence to those he leaves behind.

Henry Seton Merriman

IV

TWO OF A TRADE

"His face reminds one of a sunny graveyard," a witty Frenchwoman had once said of a man named Paul Deulin. And it is probable that Deulin alone could have understood what she meant. Those who think in French have a trick of putting great thoughts into a little compass, and, as the hollow ball of talk is tossing to and fro, it sometimes rings for a moment in a deeper note than many ears are tuned to catch.

The careless word seized the attention of one man who happened to hear it—Reginald Cartoner, a listener, not a talker—and made that man Paul Deulin's friend for the rest of his life. As there is *point de culte sans mystere*, so also there can be no lasting friendship without reserve. And although these two men had met in many parts of the world—although they had in common more languages than may be counted on the fingers—they knew but little of each other.

If one thinks of it, a sunny graveyard, bright with flowers and the gay green of spring foliage, is the shallowest fraud on earth, endeavoring to conceal beneath a specious exterior a thousand tragedies, a whole harvest of lost illusions, a host of grim human comedies. On the other hand, this is a pious fraud; for half the world is young, and will discover the roots of the flowers soon enough.

Cartoner had met Deulin in many strange places. Together they had witnessed queer events. Accredited to a new president of a new republic, they once had made their bow, clad in court dress, and official dignity, to the man whom they were destined to see a month later hanging on his own flagstaff, out over the plaza, from the spare-bedroom window of the new presidency. They had acted in concert; they had acted in direct opposition. Cartoner had once had to tell Deulin that if he persisted in his present course of action the government which he (Cartoner) represented would not be able to look upon it with indifference, which is the language of diplomacy, and means war.

For these men were the vultures of their respective Foreign Offices, and it was their business to be found where the carcass is.

"The chief difference between the gods and men is that man can only be in one place at a time," Deulin had once said to Cartoner, twenty years his junior, in his light, philosophic way, when a turn of the wheel had rendered a long journey futile, and they found themselves far from that place where their services were urgently needed.

"If men could be in two places at the same moment, say once only during a lifetime, their lives would be very different from what they are." Cartoner had glanced quickly at him when he spoke, but only saw a ready, imperturbable smile.

Deulin was a man counting his friends among all nationalities. The captain of a great steamship has perhaps as many acquaintances as may be vouchsafed to one man, and at the

Henry Seton Merriman

beginning of a voyage he has to assure a number of total strangers that he remembers them perfectly. Deulin, during fifty-odd years of his life, had moved through a maze of men, remembering faces as a ship-captain must recollect those who have sailed with him, without attaching a name or being able to allot one saving quality to lift an individual out of the ruck. For it is a lamentable fact that all men and all women are painfully like each other; it is only their faces that differ. For God has made the faces, but men have manufactured their own thoughts.

Deulin had met a few who were not like the others, and one of these was Reginald Cartoner, who was thrown against him, as it were, in a professional manner when Deulin had been twenty years at the work.

"I always cross the road," he said, "when I see Cartoner on the other side. If I did not, he would go past."

This he did in the literal sense the day after Cartoner landed in England on his return from America. Deulin saw his friend emerge from a club in Pall Mall and walk westward, as if he had business in that direction. Like many travellers, the Frenchman loved the open air. Like all Frenchmen, he loved the streets. He was idling in Pall Mall, avoiding a man here and there. For we all have friends whom we are content to see pass by on the other side. Deulin's duty was, moreover, such that it got strangely mixed up with his pleasure, and it often happens that discretion must needs overcome a natural sociability.

Cartoner saw his friend approaching; for Deulin had the good fortune, or the misfortune, to be a distinguished-looking man, with a tall, spare form, a trim white mustache and imperial, and that air of calm possession of his environment which gives to some paupers the manner of a great land-owner. He shook hands in silence, then turned and walked with Cartoner.

"I permit myself a question," he said. "When did you return from Cuba?"

"I landed at Liverpool last night."

Cartoner turned in his abrupt way and looked his companion up and down. Perhaps he was wondering for the hundredth time what might be buried behind those smiling eyes.

"I am in London, as you see," said Deulin, as if he had been asked a question. "I am awaiting orders. Something is brewing somewhere, one may suppose. Your return to London seems to confirm such a suspicion. Let us hope we may have another little… errand together—eh?"

As he spoke, Deulin bowed in his rather grand way to an old gentleman who walked briskly past in the military fashion, and who turned to look curiously at the two men.

"You are dressed in your best clothes," said Deulin, after a pause; "you are going to pay calls."

"I am going to call on one of my old chiefs."

"Then I will ask your permission to accompany you. I, too, have put on a new hat. I am idle. I want something to do. Mon Dieu, I want to talk to a clean and wholesome Englishwoman, just for a change. I know all your old chiefs, my friend. I know where you have been every moment since you made your mark at this business. One watches the quiet men—eh?"

"She will be glad to see you," said Cartoner, with his slow smile.

"Ah! She is always kind, that lady; for I guess where we are going. She might have been a great woman... if she had not been a happy one."

"I always go to see them when I am in town," said Cartoner, who usually confined his conversation to the necessaries of daily intercourse.

"And he—how is he?"

"He is as well as can be expected. He has worked so hard and so long in many climates. She is always anxious about him."

"It is the penalty a woman pays," said Deulin. "To love and to be consumed by anxiety—a woman's life, my friend. Oddly enough, I should have gone there this afternoon, whether I had met you or not. I want her good services— again."

And the Frenchman shrugged his shoulders with a laugh, as if suddenly reminded of some grievous error in his past life.

"I want her to befriend some friends of mine, if she has not done so already. For she knows them, of course. They are the Bukatys. Of course, you know the history of the Bukatys of Warsaw."

"I know the history of Poland," answered Cartoner, looking straight in front of him with reflective eyes. He had an odd way of carrying his head a little bent forward, as if he bore behind his heavy forehead a burden of memories and knowledge of which his brain was always conscious—as a man may stand in the centre of a great library, and become suddenly aware that he has more books than he can ever open and understand.

"Of course you do; you know a host of things. And you know more history that was ever written in books. You know more than I do, and Heaven knows that I know a great deal. For you are a reader, and I never look into a book. I know the surface of things. The Bukatys are in London. I give you that—to put in your pipe and smoke. Father and son. It is not for them that I seek Lady Orlay's help. They must take care of themselves—though they will not do that. It does not run in the family, as you know, who read history books."

"Yes, I know," said Cartoner, pausing before crossing to the corner of St. James's Street, in the manner of a man whose life had not been passed in London streets. For it must be remembered that English traffic is different to the traffic of any other streets in the world.

"There is a girl," pursued the Frenchman. "Families like the Bukatys should kill their girls in infancy. Not that Wanda knows it; she is as gay as a bird, and quite devoted to her father, who is an old ruffian—and my very dear friend."

"And what do you want Lady Orlay to do for Princess Wanda?" inquired Cartoner, with a smile. It was always a marvel to him that Paul Deulin should have travelled so far down the road of life without losing his enthusiasm somewhere by the way.

"That I leave to Lady Orlay," replied Deulin, with an airy wave of his neat umbrella, which imperilled the eyesight of a passing baker-boy, who abused him. Whereupon Deulin turned and took off his hat and apologized.

"Yes," he said, ignoring the incident, "I would not presume to dictate. All I should do would be to present Wanda to her. 'Here is a girl who has the misfortune to be a Bukaty; who has no mother; who has a father who is a plotter and an old ruffian—a Polish noble, in fact—and a brother who is an enthusiast, and as brave as only a prince can be.' I should say, 'You see that circumstances have thrown this girl upon the world, practically alone—on the hard, hard upper-class world—with only one heart to break. It is only men who have a whole row of hearts on a shelf, and, when one is broken, they take down another, made, perhaps, of ambition, or sport, or the love of a different sort of woman—and, vogue la galere, they go on just as well as they did before.'"

"And my accomplished aunt..." suggested Cartoner.

"Would laugh at me, I know that. I would rather have Lady Orlay's laugh than another woman's tears. And so would you; for you are a man of common-sense, though deadly dull in conversation."

As if to prove the truth of this assertion, Deulin was himself silent until they had ascended St. James's Street and turned to the left in Piccadilly; and, sure enough, Cartoner had nothing to say. At last he broke the silence, and made it evident that he had been placidly following the stream of his own thoughts.

"Who is Joseph P. Mangles?" he asked, in his semi-inaudible monotone.

"An American gentleman—the word is applicable in its best sense—who for his sins, or the sins of his forefathers, has been visited with the most terrible sister a man ever had."

"So much I know."

Deulin turned and looked at his companion.

"Then you have met him—that puts another complexion on

your question."

"I have just crossed the Atlantic in the next chair to him."

"And that is all you know about him?"

Cartoner nodded.

"Then Joseph P. Mangles is getting on."

"What is he?" repeated Cartoner.

"He is in the service of his country, my friend, like any other poor devil—like you or me, for instance. He spends half of his time kicking his heels in New York, or wherever they kick their heels in America. The rest of his time he is risking his health, or possibly his neck, wherever it may please the fates to send him. If he had been properly trained, he might have done something, that Joseph P. Mangles; for he can hold his tongue. But he took to it late, as they all do in America. So he has come across, has he? Yes, the storm-birds are congregating, my silent friend. There is something in the wind."

Deulin raised his long, thin nose into the dusty May air and sniffed it.

"Was that girl with them?" he inquired presently—"Miss Netty Cahere?"

"Yes."

"I always make love to Miss Cahere—she likes it best."

Cartoner stared straight in front of him, and made no comment. The Frenchman gave a laugh, which was not entirely pleasant. It was rare that his laugh was harsh, but such a note rang in it now. They did not speak again until they had walked some distance northward of Piccadilly, and stopped before a house with white window-boxes. Several carriages stood at the other side of the road against the square railings.

"Is it her day?" inquired Deulin.

"Yes."

Deulin made a grimace expressive of annoyance.

"And we shall see a number of people we had better not see. But, since we are here, let us go in—with a smile on the countenance, eh? my brave Cartoner."

"And a lie on the tongue."

"There I will meet you, too," replied Deulin, looking into his card-case.

They entered the house, and, as Deulin had predicted, there found a number of people assembled, who noted, no doubt, that they had come together. It was observable that this was not a congregation of fashionable or artistic people; for the women were dressed quietly, and the men were mostly old and white-haired. It was also dimly perceptible that there was a larger proportion of brain in the room than is allotted to the merely fashionable, or to that shallow mixture of the dramatic and pictorial, which is usually designated the artistic world. Moreover, scraps of conversation reached the ear that led the hearer to conclude that the house was in its way a miniature Babel.

The two men separated on the threshold, and Deulin went

forward to shake hands with a tall, white-haired woman, who was the centre of a vivacious group. Over the heads of her guests this lady had already perceived Cartoner, who was making his way more slowly through the crowd. He seemed to have more friends there than Deulin. Lady Orlay at length went to meet Cartoner, and as they shook hands, one of those slight and indefinable family resemblances which start up at odd moments became visible.

"I want you particularly to-morrow night," said the lady; "I have some people coming. I will send a card to your club this evening."

And she turned to say good-bye to a departing guest. Deulin was at Cartoner's elbow again.

"Here," he said, taking him by the sleeve and speaking in his own tongue, "I wish to present you to friends of mine. Prince Pierre Bukaty," he added, stopping in front of a tall, old man, with bushy, white hair, and the air of a mediaeval chieftain, "allow me to present my old friend Cartoner."

The two men shook hands without other greeting than a formal bow. Deulin still held Cartoner by the sleeve, and gently compelled him to turn towards a girl who was looking round with bright and eager eyes. She had a manner full of energy and spirit, and might have been an English girl of open air and active tastes.

"Princess Wanda," said the Frenchman, "my friend Mr. Cartoner."

The eager eyes came round to Cartoner's face, of which the gravity seemed suddenly reflected in them.

"He is the best linguist in Europe," said Deulin, in a gay

whisper; "even Polish; he speaks with the tongue of men and of angels."

And he himself spoke in Polish.

Princess Wanda met Cartoner's serious eyes again, and in that place, where human fates are written, another page of those inscrutable books was folded over.

V

AN OLD ACQUAINTANCE

Prince Bukaty was an affable old man, with a love of good wine and a perfect appreciation of the humorous. Had he been an Englishman, he would have been an honest squire of the old Tory type, now fast fading before facilities for foreign travel and a cheap local railway service. But he was a Pole, and the fine old hatred which should have been bestowed upon the Radicals fell to the lot of the Russians, and the contempt hurled by his British prototype upon Dissent was cast upon Commerce as represented in Poland by the thrifty German *emigre.*

The prince carried his bluff head with that air which almost invariably bespeaks a stormy youth, and looked out over mankind from his great height as over a fine standing crop of wild oats. As a matter of fact, he had grown to manhood in the years immediately preceding those wild early sixties, when all Europe was at loggerheads, and Poland seething in its midst, as lava seethes in the crater of a volcano.

The prince had been to England several times. He had friends in London. Indeed, he possessed them in many parts of the world, and, oddly enough, he had no enemies. To his credit be it noted that he was not an exile, which is usually another name for a scoundrel. For he who has no abiding city generally considers himself exempt from the duties of citizenship.

"They do not take me seriously," he said to his intimate friends; "they do not honor me by recognizing me as a dangerous person; but we shall see."

And the Prince Bukaty was thus allowed to go where he listed, and live in Warsaw if he so desired. Perhaps the secret of this lay in the fact that he was poor; for a poor man has few adherents. In the olden times, when the Bukatys had been rich, there were many professing readiness to follow him to the death—which is the way of the world. "You have but to hold up your hand," cries the faithful follower. But wise men know that the hand must have something in it. The prince had been young and impressionable when Poland was torn to pieces, when that which for eight centuries had been one of the important kingdoms of the world was wiped off the face of Europe, like writing off a slate. He was not a ruffian, as Deulin had described him; but he was a man who had been ruffled, and nothing could ever smooth him.

He was too frank by nature to play a hopeless game with the cunning and the savor of spite which hopeless games require. If he liked a man, he said so; if he disliked one, he was equally frank about it. He liked Cartoner on the briefest of brief introductions, and said so.

"It is difficult to find a man in London who speaks anything but English, and of anything but English topics. You are the narrowest people in the world—you Londoners. But you are no Londoner; I beg your pardon. Well, then, come and see me to-morrow. We are in a hotel in Kensington—will you come? That is the address."

And he held out a card with a small gold crown emblazoned in the corner, after the mode of eastern Europe. Cartoner reflected for a moment, which was odd in a man whose decisions were usually arrived at with lightning speed. For he had a slow tongue and a quick brain. There are few better equipments with which to face the world.

"Yes," he said at length; "it will give me much pleasure."

The prince glanced at him curiously beneath his bushy eyebrows. What was there to need reflection in such a small question?

"At five o'clock," he said. "We can give you a cup of the poisonous tea you drink in this country."

And he went away laughing heartily at the small witticism. People whose lives are anything but a joke are usually content with the smallest jests.

It was scarcely five o'clock the next day when Cartoner was conducted by a page-boy to the Bukatys' rooms in the quiet old hotel in Kensington. The Princess Wanda was alone. She was dressed in black. There is in some Varsovian families a heritage of mourning to be worn until Poland is reinstated. She was slightly but strongly made. Like her father and her brother, there was a suggestion of endurance in her being, such as is often found in slightly made persons.

"I came as early as I could," said Cartoner, and, as he spoke, the clock struck.

The princess smiled as she shook hands, and then perceived that she had not been intended to show amusement. Cartoner had merely made a rather naive statement in his low monotone. She thought him a little odd, and glanced at him again. She changed color slightly as she turned towards a chair. He was quite grave and honest.

"That is kind of you," she said, speaking English without the least suspicion of accent; for she had had an English governess all her life. "My father will take it to mean that you wanted to come, and are not only taking pity on lonely foreigners. He will be here in a minute. He has just been called away."

"It was very kind of him to ask me to call," replied Cartoner.

There was a simple directness in his manner of speech which was quite new to the Princess Wanda. She had known few Englishmen, and her own countrymen had mostly the manners of the French. She had never met a man who conveyed the impression of purpose and of the habit of going straight towards his purpose so clearly as this. Cartoner had not come to pay an idle visit. She wondered why he had come. He did not rush into conversation, and yet his silence had no sense of embarrassment in it. His hair was turning gray above the temples. She could see this as he took a chair near the window. He was probably ten years older than herself, and gave the impression of experience and of a deep knowledge of the world. From living much alone he had acquired the habit of wondering whether it was worth while to say that which came into his mind—which is a habit fatal to social success.

"Monsieur Deulin dined with us last night," said the princess, following the usual instinct that silence between strangers is intolerable. "He talked a great deal of you."

"Ah, Deulin is a diplomatist. He talks too much."

"He accuses you of talking too little," said Wanda, with

some spirit.

"You see, there are only two methods of leaving things unsaid, princess."

"Which is diplomacy?" she suggested.

"Which is diplomacy."

"Then I think you are both great artists," she said, with a laugh, as the door opened and her father entered the room.

"I only come to ask you a question—a word," said the prince. "Heavens! your English language! I have a man down-stairs—a question of business—and he speaks the oddest English. Now what is the meaning of the word jettison?"

Cartoner gave him the word in French.

"Ah!" cried the prince, holding up his two powerful hands, "of course. How foolish of me not to guess. In a moment I will return. You will excuse me, will you not? Wanda will give you some tea."

And he hurried out of the room, leaving Cartoner to wonder what a person so far removed above commerce could have to do with the word jettison.

The conversation returned to Deulin. He was a man of whom people spoke continually, and had spoken for years. In fact, two generations had found him a fruitful topic of conver- sation without increasing their knowledge of him. If he had only been that which is called a public man, a novelist or a singer, his fortune would have been easy. All his advertising would have been done for him by others. For there was in him that unknown quantity which the world must needs think magnificent.

"I want you to tell me all you know about him," said the princess in her brisk way. "He is the only old man I have ever seen whose thoughts have not grown old too. And, of course, one wonders why. He is the sort of person who might do anything surprising. He might fall in love and marry, or something like that, you know. Papa says he is married already, and his wife is in a mad asylum. He says there is a tragedy. But I don't. He has no wife—unless he has two."

"I know nothing of that side of his life. I only know his career."

"I do not care about his career," said the princess, lightly. "I go deeper than careers."

She looked at Cartoner with a wise nod and a shrewd look in her gay, blue eyes.

"A man's career is only the surface of his life."

"Then some men's lives are all surface," said Cartoner.

Wanda gave a little, half-pitying, half-contemptuous jerk of her head.

"Some men have the soul of an omnibus-horse," she replied.

Cartoner reflected for a moment, looking gravely the while at this girl, who seemed to know so much of life and to have such singularly clear and decisive views upon it.

"What would you have them do beyond going on when required and stopping when expedient—and avoiding collisions?" he inquired.

"I should like them to break the omnibus up occasionally," she answered, "and take a wrong turning sometimes, just to see if a little happiness lay that way."

"Yes," he laughed. "You are a Pole and a Bukaty. I knew it as soon as I saw you."

"One must do something. We were talking of such things last night, and Monsieur Deulin said that his ideal combination in a man was an infinite patience and a sudden premeditated recklessness."

"Now you have come down to a mere career again," said Cartoner.

"Not necessarily."

The prince came into the room again at this moment.

"What are you people discussing," he asked, "so gravely?"

He spoke in French, which was the language that was easiest to him, for he had been young when it was the fashion in Poland to be French.

"I do not quite know," answered Cartoner, slowly. "The princess was giving me her views."

"I know," retorted the old man, with his rather hollow laugh. "They are long views, those views of hers."

Cartoner was still standing near the window. He turned absently and looked out, down into the busy street. There he saw something which caused him intense surprise, though he did not show it; for, like any man of strong purpose, his face had but one expression, and that of thoughtful attention. He saw Captain Cable, of the *Minnie*, crossing the street, having just quitted the hotel. This was the business acquaintance of Prince Bukaty's, who had come to speak of jettison.

Cartoner knew Captain Cable well, and his specialty in maritime skill. He had seen war waged before now with material which had passed in and out of the *Minnie's* hatches.

The prince did not refer again to the affairs that had called him away. The talk naturally turned to the house where they had first met, and Wanda mentioned that her father and she were going to the reception given by the Orlays that evening.

"You're going, of course?" said the prince.

"Yes, I am going."

"You go to many such entertainments?"

"No, I go to very few," replied Cartoner, looking at Wanda in his speculative way.

Then he suddenly rose and took his leave, with a characteristic omission of the usual "Well, I must be off," or any such catch-word. He certainly left a great deal unsaid which this babbling world expects.

He walked along the crowded streets, absorbed in his own thoughts, for some distance. Then he suddenly emerged from that quiet shelter, and accepted the urgent invitation of a hansom-cab driver to get into his vehicle.

"Westminster Bridge," he said.

He quitted the cab at the corner of the bridge, and walked quickly down to the steamboat-landing.

"Where do you want to go to?" inquired the gruff, seafaring ticket-clerk.

"As far as I can," was the reply.

A steamer came almost at once, and Cartoner selected a quiet seat over the rudder. He must have known that the *Minnie* was so constructed that she could pass under the bridges, for he began to look for her at once. It was six o'clock, and a spring tide was running out. All the passenger traffic was turned to the westward, and a friendly deck-hand, having leisure, came and gave Cartoner his views upon cricket, in which, as was natural in one whose life was passed on running water, his whole heart seemed to be absorbed. Cartoner was friendly, but did not take advantage of this affability to make inquiries about the *Minnie*. He knew, perhaps, that there is no more suspicious man on earth than a river-side worker.

The steamer raced under the bridges, and at last shot out into the Pool, where a few belated barges were drifting down stream. A number of steamers lay at anchor, some working cargo, others idle. The majority were foreigners, odd-shaped vessels, with funnels like a steam threshing-machine, and gayly painted deck-houses.

In one quiet corner, behind a laid-up excursion-boat and a file of North Sea fish-carriers, lay the *Minnie*, painted black, with nothing brighter than a deep brown on her deck-house, her boats painted a shabby green. She might have been an overgrown tug or a superannuated fish-carrier.

Cartoner landed at the Cherry Orchard Pier, and soon found

a boatman to take him to the *Minnie*.

"Just took the skipper on board a few minutes ago, sir," he said. "He must have come down by the boat before yours."

A few minutes later Cartoner stood on the deck of the *Minnie*, and banged with his fist on the cover of the cabin gangway, which was tantamount to ringing at Captain Cable's front door.

The sailor's grim face appeared a moment later, emerging like the face of a hermit-crab from its shell. The frown slowly faded, and the deep, unwashed wrinkles took a kindlier curve.

"It's you, Mr. Cartoner," he said. "Glad to see you."

"I was passing in a steamer," answered Cartoner, quietly, "and recognized the *Minnie*."

"I take it friendly of you, Mr. Cartoner, remembering the rum time you and me had together. Come below. I've got a drop of wine somewhere stowed away in a locker."

VI

THE VULTURES

"I suppose," Miss Mangles was saying—"I suppose, Joseph, that Lady Orlay has been interested in the work without our knowing it?"

"It is possible, Jooly—it is possible," replied Mr. Joseph P. Mangles, looking with a small, bright, speculative eye out of the window of his private sitting-room in a hotel in Northumberland Avenue.

Miss Mangles was standing behind him, and held in her hand an invitation-card notifying that Lady Orlay would be at home that same evening from nine o'clock till midnight.

"This invitation," said the recipient, "accompanied as it is by a friendly note explaining that the shortness of the invitation lies in the fact that we only arrived the day before yesterday, seems to point to it, Joseph. It seems to indicate that England is prepared to give me a welcome."

"On the face of it, Jooly, it would seem—just that."

Mr. Mangles continued to gaze with a speculative eye into Northumberland Avenue. If, as Cartoner had suggested, the

Henry Seton Merriman

profession of which Mr. Joseph P. Mangles was a tardy ornament, needed above all things a capacity for leaving things unsaid, the American diplomatist was not ignorant in his art. For he did not inform his sister that the invitation to which she attached so flattering a national importance owed its origin to an accidental encounter between himself and Lord Orlay—a friend of his early senatorial days—in Pall Mall the day before.

Miss Mangles stood with the card in her hand and reflected. No woman and few men would need to be told, moreover, the subject of her thoughts. Of what, indeed, does every woman think the moment she receives an invitation?

"Jooly," Mr. Mangles had been heard to say behind that lady's back—"Jooly is an impressive dresser when she tries."

But the truth is that Jooly did not always try. She had not tried this morning, but stood in the conventional hotel room dressed in a black cloth garment which had pleats down the front and back and a belt like a Norfolk jacket. Miss Mangles was large and square-shouldered. She was a rhomboid, in fact, and had that depressing square-and-flat waist which so often figures on the platform in a great cause. Her hair was black and shiny and straight; it was drawn back from her rounded temples by hydraulic pressure. Her mouth was large and rather loose; it had grown baggy by much speaking on public platforms—a fearsome thing in a woman. Her face was large and round and white. Her eyes were dull. Long ago there must have been depressing moments in the life of Julia P. Mangles—moments spent in front of her mirror. But, like the woman of spirit that she was, she had determined that, if she could not be beautiful, she could at all events be great.

One self-deception leads to another. Miss Mangles sat down and accepted Lady Orlay's invitation in the full and perfect conviction that she owed it to her greatness.

"Are they abstainers?" she asked, reflectively, going back in her mind over the causes she had championed.

"Nay," replied Joseph, winking gravely at a policeman in Northumberland Avenue.

"Perhaps Lord Orlay is open to conviction."

"If you tackle Orlay, you'll find you've bitten off a bigger bit than you can chew," replied Joseph, who had a singular habit of lapsing into the vulgarest slang when Julia mounted her high horse in the presence of himself only. When others were present Mr. Mangles seemed to take a sort of pride in this great woman. Let those explain the attitude who can.

Lady Orlay's entertainments were popularly said to be too crowded, and no one knew this better than Lady Orlay.

"Let us ask them all and be done with them," she said; and had said it for thirty years, ever since she had begun a social existence with no other prospects than that which lay in her husband's brain—then plain Mr. Orlay. She had never "done with them," had never secured that peaceful domestic leisure which had always been her dream and her husband's dream, and would never secure it. For these were two persons, now old and white-haired and celebrated, who lived in the great world, and had a supreme contempt for it.

The Mangleses were among the first to arrive, Julia in a dress of rich black silk, with some green about it, and a number of iridescent beetle-wings serving as a relief. Miss Netty Cahere was a vision of pink and self-effacing quietness.

"We shall know no one," she said, with a shrinking movement of her shoulders as they mounted the stairs.

"Not even the waiters," replied Joseph Mangles, in his lugubrious bass, glancing into a room where tea and coffee were set out. "But they will soon know us."

They had not been in the room, however, five minutes before an acquaintance entered it, tall and slim, like a cheerful Don Quixote, with the ribbon of a great order across his shirt-front. He paused for a moment near Lord and Lady Orlay, and his entrance caused, as it usually did, a little stir in the room. Then he turned and greeted Joseph Mangles. Over the large, firm hand of that gentleman's sister he bowed in silence.

"I have nothing to say to that great woman," he sometimes said. "She is so elevated that my voice will not reach her."

Deulin then turned to where Miss Cahere had been standing. But she had moved away a few paces, nearer to a candelabrum, under which she was now standing, and a young officer in full German uniform was openly admiring her, with a sort of wonder on his foolish, Teutonic face.

"Ah! I expected you had forgotten me," she said, when Deulin presented himself.

"Believe me—I have tried," he replied, with great earnestness; but the complete innocence of her face clearly showed that she did not attach any deep meaning to his remark.

"You must see so many people that you cannot be expected to remember them all."

"I do not remember them all, mademoiselle—only a very,

very few."

"Then tell me, who is that lovely girl you bowed to as you came into the room?"

"Is there another in the room?" inquired Deulin, looking around him with some interest.

"Over there, with the fair hair, dressed in black."

"Ah! talking to Cartoner. Yes. Do you think her beautiful?"

"I think she is perfectly lovely. But somehow she does not look like one of us, does she?" And Miss Cahere lowered her voice in a rather youthful and inexperienced way.

"She is not like one of us, Miss Cahere," replied Deulin.

"Why?"

"Because we are plebeians, and she is a princess."

"Oh, then she is married?" exclaimed Miss Cahere, and her voice fell three semitones on the last word.

"No. She is a princess in her own right. She is a Pole."

Miss Cahere gave a little sigh.

"Poor thing," she said, looking at the Princess Wanda, with a soft light of sympathy in her gentle eyes.

"Why do you pity her?" asked Deulin, glancing down sharply.

"Because princesses are always obliged to marry royalties, are they not—for convenience, I mean—not from... from inclination, like other girls?"

And Miss Cahere's eyelids fluttered, but she did not actually raise her eyes towards her interlocutor. An odd smile flickered for an instant on Deulin's lips.

"Ah!" he said, with a sharp sigh—and that was all. He bowed, and turned away to speak to a man who had been waiting at his elbow for some minutes. This also was a Frenchman, who seemed to have something special to report, for they walked aside together.

It was quite late in the evening before Deulin succeeded in his efforts to get a few moments' speech with Lady Orlay. He found that unmatched hostess at leisure in the brief space elapsing between the arrival of the latest and the departure of the earliest.

"I was looking for you," she said; "you, who always know where everybody is. Where is Mr. Mangles? An under-secretary was asking for him a moment ago."

"Mangles is listening to the music in the library—comparatively happy by himself behind a barricade of flowers."

"And that preposterous woman?"

"That preposterous woman is in the refreshment-room."

Thus they spoke of the great lecturer on Prison Wrongs.

"You have seen the Bukatys?" inquired Lady Orlay. "I called on them the moment I received your note from Paris. They are here to-night. I have never seen such a complexion. Is it characteristic of Poland?"

"I think so," replied Deulin, with unusual shortness, looking away across the room.

Lady Orlay's clever eyes flashed round for a moment, and she looked grave. It was as if she had pushed open the door of another person's room.

"I like the old man," she said, with a change of tone. "What is he?"

"He is a rebel."

"Proscribed?"

"No—they dare not do that. He was a great man in the sixties. You remember how in the great insurrection an unfailing supply of arms and ammunition came pouring into Poland over the Austrian frontier—more arms than the national government could find men for."

"Yes, I remember that."

"That is the man," said Deulin, with a nod of his head in the direction of the Prince Bukaty, who was talking and laughing near at hand.

"And the girl—it is very sad—I like her very much. She is gay and brave."

"Ah!" said Deulin, "when a woman is gay and brave—and young—Heaven help us."

"Thank you, Monsieur Deulin."

"And when she is gay and brave, and... old... milady—God keep her," he said with a grave bow.

"I liked her at once. I shall be glad to do anything I can, you know. She has a great capacity for making friends."

"She has already made a few—this evening," put in the Frenchman, with a significant gesture of his gloved hand.

"Ah!"

"Not one who can hurt her, I think. I can see to that. The usual enemy—of a pretty girl—that is all."

He broke off with a sudden laugh. Once or twice he had laughed like that, and his manner was restless and uneasy. In a younger man, or one less experienced and hardened, the observant might have suspected some hidden excitement. Lady Orlay turned and looked at him curiously, with the frankness of a friendship which had lasted nearly half a century.

"What is it?"

He laughed—but he laughed uneasily—and spread out his hands in a gesture of bewilderment.

"What is what?"

Lady Orlay looked at her fan reflectively as she opened and closed it.

"Reginald Cartoner has turned up quite suddenly," she said. "Mr. Mangles has arrived from Washington. You are here from Paris. A few minutes ago old Karl Steinmetz, who still watches the nations en amateur, shook hands with me. This Prince Bukaty is not a nonentity. All the Vultures are assembling, Paul. I can see that. I can see that my husband sees it."

"Ah! you and yours are safe now. You are in the backwater—you and Orlay—quietly moored beneath the trees."

"Finally," continued Lady Orlay, without heeding the interruption, "you come to me with a light in your eye which I have seen there only once or twice during nearly fifty years. It means war, or something very like it—the Vultures."

She gave a little shiver as she looked round the room. After a short silence Deulin rose suddenly and held out his hand.

"Good-bye," he said. "You are too discerning. Good-bye."

"You are going—?"

"Away," he answered, with a wave of the hand descriptive of space. "I must go and pack my trunks."

Lady Orlay had not moved when Mr. Mangles came up to say good-night. Miss Julia P. Mangles bowed in a manner which she considered impressive and the world thought ponderous. Netty Cahere murmured a few timid words of thanks.

"We shall hope to see you again," said Lady Orlay to Mr. Mangles.

"'Fraid not," he answered; "we're going to travel on the Continent."

"When do you start?" asked her ladyship.

"To-morrow morning."

"Another one," muttered Lady Orlay, watching Mr. Mangles

Henry Seton Merriman

depart. And her brief reverie was broken into by Reginald Cartoner.

"You have come to say good-bye," she said to him.

"Yes."

"You are going away again?"

"Yes."

"And you will not tell me where you are going."

"I cannot," answered Cartoner.

"Then I will tell you," said Lady Orlay, who, as Paul Deulin had said, was very experienced and very discerning.

"You are going to Russia, all of you."

VII

AT THE FRONTIER

Daylight was beginning to contend with the brilliant electric illumination of the long platform as that which is called the Warsaw Express steamed into Alexandrowo Station. There are many who have never heard of Alexandrowo, and others who know it only too well.

How many a poor devil has dropped from the footboard of the train just before these electric lights were reached—to take his chance of crossing the frontier before morning—history will never tell! How many have succeeded in passing in and out of that dread railway station with a false passport and a steady face, beneath the searching eye of the officials, Heaven only knows! There is no other way of passing Alexandrowo—of getting in or out of the kingdom of Poland—but by this route. Before the train is at a standstill at the platform each one of the long corridor carriages is boarded by a man in the dirty white trousers, the green tunic and green cap, the top-boots, and the majesty of Russian law. Here, whatever time of day or night, winter or summer, it is always as light as day, thanks to an unsparing use of electricity. There are always sentries on the outer side of the train. The platform is a prison-yard—the waiting rooms are prison-yards.

Henry Seton Merriman

With a passport in perfect order, vised for here and there and everywhere, with good clothes, good luggage, and nothing contraband in baggage or demeanor, Alexandrowo is easy enough. Obedience and patience will see the traveller through. There is no fear of his being left in the huge station, or of his going anywhere but to his avowed and rightful destination. But with a passport that is old or torn, with a visa which bears any but a recent date, with a restless eye or a hunted look, the voyager had better take his chance of dropping from the footboard at speed, especially if it be a misty night.

Like sheep, the passengers are driven from the train in which not so much as a newspaper is left. Only the sleeping-car is allowed to go through, but it is emptied and searched. The travellers are penned within a large room where the luggage is inspected, and they are deprived of their passports. When the customs formalities are over they are allowed to find the refreshment-room, and there console themselves with weak tea in tumblers until such time as they are released.

The train on this occasion was a full one, and the great inspection-room, with its bare walls and glaring lights, crammed to overflowing. The majority of the travellers seemed, as usual, to be Germans. There were a few ladies. And two men, better dressed than the others, had the appearance of Englishmen. They drifted together—just as the women drifted together and the little knot of shady characters who hoped against hope that their passports were in order. For the most part, no one spoke, though one German commercial traveller protested with so much warmth that an examination of his trunks was nothing but an intrusion on the officer's valuable time that a few essayed to laugh and feel at their ease.

Reginald Cartoner, who had been among the first to quit

Lady Orlay's, was an easy first across the frontier. He had twelve hours' start of anybody, and was twenty-four hours ahead of all except Paul Deulin, whose train had steamed into Berlin Station as the Warsaw Express left it. He seemed to know the ways of Alexandrowo, and the formalities to be observed at the frontier, but he was not eager to betray his knowledge. He obeyed with a silent patience the instructions of the white-aproned, black-capped porter who had a semi-official charge of him. He made no attempt to escape an examination of his luggage, and he avoided the refreshment-room tea.

Cartoner glanced at the man, whose appearance would seem to indicate that he was a fellow-countryman, and made sure that he did not know him. Then he looked at him again, and the other happened to turn his profile. Cartoner recognized the profile, and drew away to the far corner of the exami-nation-room. But they drifted together again—or, perhaps, the younger man made a point of approaching. It was, at all events, he who, when all had been marshalled into the refreshment-room, drew forward a chair and sat down at the table where Cartoner had placed himself.

He ordered a cup of coffee in Russian, and sought his cigarette-case. He opened it and laid it on the table in front of Cartoner. He was a fair young man, with an energetic manner and the clear, ruddy complexion of a high-born Briton.

"Englishman?" he said, with an easy and friendly nod.

"Yes," answered Cartoner, taking the proffered cigarette. His manner was oddly stiff.

"Thought you were," said the other, who, though his clothes were English and his language was English, was nevertheless not quite an Englishman. There was a sort of eagerness in his look, a picturesque turn of the head—a sense, as it were, of the outwardly pictorial side of existence. He moved his chair, in order to turn his back on a Russian officer who was seated near, and did it absently, as if mechanically closing his eye to something unsightly and conducive to discomfort. Then he turned to his coffee with a youthful spirit of enjoyment.

"All this would be mildly amusing," he said, "at say any other hour of the twenty-four, but at three in the morning it is rather poor fun. Do you succeed in sleeping in these German schlafwagens?"

"I can sleep anywhere," replied Cartoner, and his companion glanced at him inquiringly. It seemed that he was sleepy now, and did not wish to talk.

"I know Alexandrowo pretty well," the other volunteered, nevertheless, "and the ways of these gentlemen. With some of them I am quite on friendly terms. They are inconceivably stupid; as boring as—the multiplication-table. I am going to Warsaw; are you? I fancy we have the sleeping-car to ourselves. I live in Warsaw as much as anywhere."

He paused to feel in his pocket, not for his cigarettes this time, but for a card.

"I know who you are," said Cartoner, quietly: "I recognized you from your likeness to your sister. I was dancing with her forty-eight hours ago in London."

"Wanda?" inquired the other, eagerly. "Dear old Wanda! How is she? She was the prettiest girl in the room, I bet."

He leaned across the table.

"Tell me," he said, "all about them. But, first, tell me your name. Wanda writes to me nearly every day, and I hear about all their friends—the Orlays and the others. What is your name? She is sure to have made mention of it in her letters."

"Reginald Cartoner."

"Ah! I have heard of you—but not from Wanda."

He paused to reflect.

"No," he added, rather wonderingly, after a pause. "No, she never mentioned your name. But, of course, I know it. It is better known out of England than in your own country, I fancy. Deulin—you know Deulin?—has spoken to us of you. No doubt we have dozens of other friends in common. We shall find them out in time. I am very glad to meet you. You say you know my name—yes, I am Martin Bukaty. Odd that you should have recognized me from my likeness to Wanda. I am very glad you think I am like her. Dear old Wanda! She is a better sort than I am, you know."

And he finished with a frank and hearty laugh—not that there was anything to laugh at, but merely because he was young, and looked at life from a cheerful standpoint.

Cartoner sipped his coffee, and looked reflectively at his companion over the cup. "Cartoner," Paul Deulin had once said to a common friend, "weighs you, and naturally finds you wanting." It seemed that he was weighing Prince Martin Bukaty now.

"I saw your father also," he said, at length. "He was kind enough to ask me to call, which I did."

"That was kind of you. Of course we know no one in

London—no one, I mean, who speaks anything except English. That is a thing which is never quite understood on the Continent—that if you go to London you must speak English. If you cannot, you had better hang yourself and be done with it, for you are practically in solitary confinement. My father does not easily make friends—you must have been very civil to him."

"According to my lights, I was," admitted Cartoner.

Martin laughed again. It is a gay heart that can be amused at three in the morning.

"The truth is," continued Martin, in his quick and rather heedless way, "that we Poles are under a cloud in Europe now. We are the wounded man by the side of the road from Jerusalem down to Jericho, and there is a tendency to pass by on the other side. We are a nation with a bad want, and it is nobody's business to satisfy it. Everybody is ready, however, to admit that we have been confoundedly badly treated."

He tossed off his coffee as he spoke, and turned in his chair to nod an acknowledgment to the profound bows of a gold-laced official who had approached him, and who now tendered an envelope, with some murmured words of politeness.

"Thank you—thank you," said Prince Martin, and slipped the envelope within his pocket.

"It is my passport," he explained to Cartoner, lightly. "All the rest of you will receive yours when you are in the train. Mine is the doubtful privilege of being known here, and being a suspected character. So they are doubly polite and doubly watchful. As for you, at Alexandrowo you rejoice in a happy obscurity. You will pass in with the crowd, I suppose."

"I always try to," replied Cartoner. Which was strictly true.

"You see," went on Martin, not too discreetly, considering their environments, "we cannot forget that we were a great nation before there was a Russian Empire or an Austrian Empire or a German Empire. We are a landlady who has seen better days; who has let her lodgings to three foreign gentlemen who do not pay the rent—who make us clean their boots and then cast them at our heads."

The doors of the great room had now been thrown open, and the passengers were passing slowly out to the long, deserted platform. It was almost daylight now, and the train was drawn up in readiness to start, with a fresh engine and new officials. The homeliness of Germany had vanished, giving place to that subtle sense of discomfort and melancholy which hangs in the air from the Baltic to the Pacific coast.

"I hope you will stay a long time in Warsaw," said Martin, as they walked up the platform. "My father and sister will be coming home before long, and will be glad to see you. We will do what we can to make the place tolerable for you. We live in the Kotzebue, and I have a horse for you when you want it. You know we have good horses in Warsaw, as good as any. And the only way to see the country is from the saddle. We have the best horses and the worst roads."

"Thanks, very much," replied Cartoner. "I, of course, do not know how long I shall stay. I am not my own master, you understand. I never know from one day to another what my movements may be."

"No," replied Martin, in the absent tone of one who only half hears. "No, of course not. By-the-way, we have the races coming on. I hope you will be here for them. In our small way, it is the season in Warsaw now. But, of course, there are difficulties—even the races present difficulties—there is the military element."

He paused and indicated with a short nod the Russian officer who was passing to his carriage in front of them.

"They have the best horses," he explained. "They have more money than we have. We have been robbed, as you know. You, whose business it is."

He turned, with his foot on the step of the carriage. He was so accustomed to the recognition of his rank that he went first without question.

"Yes," he said, with a laugh, "I had quite forgotten that it is your business to know all about us."

"I have tried to remind you of it several times," answered Cartoner, quietly.

"To shut me up, you mean?" asked the younger man.

"Yes."

Martin was standing at the door of Cartoner's compartment. He turned away with a laugh.

"Good-night," he said. "Hope you will get some more sleep. We shall meet again in a few hours."

He closed the sliding door, and as the train moved slowly out of the station Cartoner could hear the cheerful voice—of a rather high timbre—in conversation with the German attendant in the corridor. For, like nearly all his countrymen, Prince Martin was a man of tongues. The Pole is compelled by circumstances to learn several languages: first, his own;

then the language of the conqueror, either Russian or German, or perhaps both. For social purposes he must speak the tongue of the two countries that promised so much for Poland and performed so little—England and France.

Cartoner sat on the vacant seat in his compartment, which had not been made up as a bed, and listened thoughtfully to the pleasant tones. It was broad daylight now, and the flat, carefully cultivated land was green and fresh. Cartoner looked out of the window with an unseeing eye, and the sleeping-carriage lumbered along in silence. The Englishman seemed to have no desire for sleep, though, not being an impressionable man, he was usually able to rest and work, fast and eat at such times as might be convenient. He was considered by his friends to be a rather cold, steady man, who concealed under an indifferent manner an almost insatiable ambition. He certainly had given way to an entire absorption in his profession, and in the dogged acquirement of one language after another as occasion seemed to demand.

He had been, it was said, more than usually devoted to his profession, even to the point of sacrificing friendships which, from a social and possibly from an ambitious point of view, could not have failed to be useful to him. Martin Bukaty was not the first man whom he had kept at arm's-length. But in this instance the treatment had not been markedly successful, and Cartoner was wondering now why the prince had been so difficult to offend. He had refused the friendship, and the effect had only been to bring the friend closer. Cartoner sat at the open window until the sun rose and the fields were dotted here and there with the figures of the red-clad peasant women working at the crops. At seven o'clock he was still sitting there, and soon after Prince Martin Bukaty, after knocking, drew back the sliding door and came into the compartment, closing the door behind him.

"I have been thinking about it," he said, in his quick way, "and it won't do, you know—it won't do. You cannot appear in Warsaw as our friend. It would never do for us to show special attention to you. Anywhere else in the world, you understand, I am your friend, but not in Warsaw."

"Yes," said Cartoner, "I understand."

He rose as he spoke, for Prince Martin was holding out his hand.

"Good-bye," he said, in his quiet way, and they shook hands as the train glided into Warsaw Station.

In the doorway Martin turned and looked back over his shoulder.

"All the same, I don't understand why Wanda did not mention your name to me. She might have foreseen that we should meet. She is quick enough, as a rule, and has already saved my father and me half a dozen times."

He waited for an answer, and at length Cartoner spoke.

"She did not know that I was coming," he said.

VIII

IN A REMOTE CITY

The Vistula is the backbone of Poland, and, from its source
in the Carpathians to its mouth at Dantzic, runs the whole
length of that which for three hundred years was the leading
power of eastern Europe. At Cracow—the tomb of many
kings—it passes half round the citadel, a shallow, sluggish
river; and from the ancient capital of Poland to the present
capital—Warsaw—it finds its way across the great plain,
amid the cultivated fields, through the quiet villages of
Galicia and Masovia.

Warsaw is built upon two sides of the river, the ancient town
looking from a height across the broad stream to the suburb
of Praga. In Praga—a hundred years ago—the Russians,
under Suvaroff, slew thirteen thousand Poles; in the river
between Praga and the citadel two thousand were drowned.
Less than forty years ago a crowd of Poles assembled in the
square in front of the castle to protest against the tyranny of
their conquerors. They were unarmed, and when the Russian
soldiery fired upon them they stood and cheered, and refused
to disperse. Again, in cold blood, the troops fired, and the
Warsaw massacre continued for three hours in the streets.

Warsaw is a gay and cheerful town, with fine streets and

good shops, with a cold, gray climate, and a history as grim as that of any city in the world save Paris. Like most cities, Warsaw has its principal street, and, like all things Polish, this street has a terrible name—the Krakowski Przedmiescie. It is in this Krakowski Faubourg that the Hotel de l'Europe stands, where history in its time has played a part, where kings and princes have slept, where the Jew Hermani was murdered, where the bodies of the first five victims of the Russian soldiery were carried after the massacre and there photographed, and, finally, where the great light from the West—Miss Julie P. Mangles—alighted one May morning, looking a little dim and travel-stained.

"Told you," said Mr. Mangles to his sister, who for so lofty a soul was within almost measurable distance of snappishness—"told you you would have nothing to complain of in the hotel, Jooly."

But Miss Mangles was not to be impressed or mollified. Only once before had her brother and niece seen this noble woman in such a frame of mind—on their arrival at the rising town of New Canterbury, Massachusetts, when the deputation of Women Workers and Wishful Waiters for the Truth failed to reach the railway depot because they happened on a fire in a straw-hat manufactory on their way, and heard that the newest pattern of straw hat was to be had for the picking up in the open street.

There had been no deputation at Warsaw Station to meet Miss Mangles. London had not recognized her. Berlin had shaken its official head when she proposed to visit its plenipotentiaries, and hers was the ignoble position of the prophet—not without honor in his own country—who cannot get a hearing in foreign parts.

"This is even worse than I anticipated," said Miss Mangles,

watching the hotel porters in a conflict with Miss Netty Cahere's large trunks.

"What is worse, Jooly?"

"Poland!" replied Miss Mangles, in a voice full of foreboding, and yet with a ring of determination in it, as if to say that she had reformed worse countries than Poland in her day.

"I allow," said Mr. Mangles, slowly, "that at this hour in the morning it appears to be a one-horse country. You want your breakfast, Jooly?"

"Breakfast will not put two horses to it, Joseph," replied Miss Mangles, looking not at her brother, but at the imposing hotel concierge with a bland severity indicative of an intention of keeping him strictly in his place.

Miss Netty quietly relieved her aunt of the small impedimenta of travel, with a gentle deference which was better than words. Miss Cahere seemed always to know how to say or do the right thing, or, more difficult still, to keep the right silence. Either this, or the fact that Miss Mangles was conscious of having convinced her hearers that she was as expert in the lighter swordplay of debate as in the rolling platform period, somewhat alleviated the lady's humor, and she turned towards the historic staircase, which had run with the blood of Jew and Pole, with a distinct air of condescension.

"Tell me," said Mr. Joseph Mangles to the concierge, in a voice of deep depression which only added to the incongruity of his French, "what languages you speak."

"Russian, French, Polish, German, English—"

"That'll do to go on with," interrupted Mangles, in his own tongue. "We'll get along in English. My name is Mangles."

Whereupon the porter bowed low, as to one for whom first-floor rooms and a salon had been bespoken, and waved his hand towards the stairs, where stood a couple of waiters.

Of the party, Miss Cahere alone appeared cool and composed and neat. She might, to judge from her bright eyes and delicate complexion, have slept all night in a comfortable bed. Her hat and her hair had the appearance of having been arranged at leisure by a maid. Miss Netty had on the surface a little manner of self-depreciating flurry which sometimes seemed to conceal a deep and abiding calm. She had little worldly theories, too, which she often enunciated in her confidential manner; and one of these was that one should always, in all places and at all times, be neat and tidy, for no one knows whom one may meet. And, be it noted in passing, there have been many successful human careers based upon this simple rule.

She followed the waiter up-stairs with that soft rustle of the dress which conveys even in the obtuse masculine mind a care for clothes and the habit of dealing with a good dressmaker. At the head of the stairs she gave a little cry of surprise, for Paul Deulin was coming along the broad corridor towards her, swinging the key of his bedroom and nonchalantly humming an air from a recent comic opera. He was, it appeared, as much at home here as in London or Paris or New York.

"Ah, mademoiselle!" he said, standing hat in hand before her, "who could have dreamed of such a pleasure—here and at this moment—in this sad town?"

"You seemed gay enough—you were singing," answered

Miss Cahere.

"It was a sad little air, mademoiselle, and I was singing flat. Perhaps you noticed it?"

"No, I never know when people are singing flat or not. I have no ear for music. I only know when I like to hear a person's voice. I have no accomplishments, you know," said Netty, with a little humble drawing-in of the shoulders.

"Ah!" said Deulin, with a gesture which conveyed quite clearly his opinion that she had need of none. And he turned to greet Miss Mangles and her brother.

Miss Mangles received him coldly. Even the greatest of women is liable to feminine moments, and may know when she is not looking her best. She shook hands, with her platform bow—from the waist—and passed on.

"Hallo!" said Joseph Mangles. "Got here before us? Thought you'd turn up. Dismal place, eh?"

"You have just arrived, I suppose?" said Deulin.

"Oh, please don't laugh at us!" broke in Netty. "Of course you can see that. You must know that we have just come out of a sleeping-car!"

"You always look, mademoiselle, as if you had come straight from heaven," answered Deulin, looking at Miss Cahere, whose hand was at her hair. It was pretty hair and a pretty, slim, American hand. But she did not seem to hear, for she had turned away quickly and was speaking to her uncle. Deulin accompanied them along the corridor, which is a long one, for the Hotel de l'Europe is a huge quadrangle.

"You startled me by your sudden appearance, you know," she said, turning again to the Frenchman, which was probably intended for an explanation of her heightened color. She was one of those fortunate persons who blush easily—at the right time. "I am sure Uncle Joseph will be pleased to have you in the same hotel. Of course, we know no one in Warsaw. Have you friends here?"

"Only one," replied Deulin—"the waiter who serves the Zakuska counter down-stairs. I knew him when he was an Austrian nobleman, travelling for his health in France. He does not recognize me now."

"Will you stay long?"

"I did not intend to," replied Deulin, "when I came out of my room this morning."

"But you and Mr. Cartoner have Polish friends, have you not?" asked Netty.

"Not in Warsaw," was the reply.

"Suppose we shall meet again," broke in Joseph Mangles at this moment, halting on the threshold of the gorgeous apartment. He tapped the number on the door in order to draw Deulin's attention to it. "Always welcome," he said. "Funny we should meet here. Means mischief, I suppose."

"I suppose it does," answered Deulin, looking guilelessly at Netty.

He took his leave and continued his way down-stairs. Out in the Krakowski Faubourg the sun was shining brightly and the world was already astir, while the shops were opening and buyers already hurrying home from the morning markets. It is a broad street, with palaces and churches on either side. Every palace has its story; two of them were confiscated by the Russian government because a bomb, which was thrown from the pavement, might possibly have come from one of the windows. Every church has rung to the strains of the forbidden Polish hymn—"At Thy altar we raise our prayer; deign to restore us, O Lord, our free country." Into almost all of them the soldiers have forced their way to make arrests.

Paul Deulin walked slowly up the faubourg towards the new town. The clocks were striking the hour. He took off his hat, and gave a little sigh of enjoyment of the fresh air and bright sun.

"Just Heaven, forgive me!" he said, with upturned eyes. "I have already told several lies, and it is only eight o'clock. I wonder whether I shall find Cartoner out of bed?"

He walked on in a leisurely way, brushing past Jew and Gentile, gay Cossack officers, and that dull Polish peasant who has assuredly lived through greater persecution than any other class of men. He turned to the right up a broad street and then to the left into a narrower, quieter thoroughfare, called the Jasna. The houses in the Jasna are mostly large, with court-yards, where a few trees struggle for existence. They are let out in flats, or in even smaller apartments, where quiet people live—professors, lawyers, and other persons, who have an interest within themselves and are not dependent on the passer-by for entertainment.

Into one of these large houses Deulin turned, and gave his destination to the Russian doorkeeper as he passed the lodge. This was the second floor, and the door was opened by a quick-mannered man, to whom the Frenchman nodded familiarly.

Henry Seton Merriman

"Is he up yet?" he inquired, and called the man by his Christian name.

"This hour, monsieur," replied the servant, leading the way along a narrow corridor. He opened a door, and stood aside for Deulin to pass into a comfortably furnished room, where Cartoner was seated at a writing-table.

"Good-morning," said the Frenchman. As he passed the table he took up a book and went towards the window, where he sat down in a deep arm-chair. "Don't let me disturb you," he continued. "Finish what you are doing."

"News?" inquired Cartoner, laying aside his pen. He looked at Deulin gravely beneath his thoughtful brows. They were marvellously dissimilar—these friends.

"Bah!" returned Deulin, throwing aside the book he had picked up—Lelewel's *History of Poland*, in Polish. "I trouble for your future, Cartoner. You take life so seriously—you, who need not work at all. Even uncles cannot live forever, and some day you will be in a position to lend money to poor devils of French diplomatists. Think of that!"

He reflected for a moment.

"Yes," he said, after a pause, "I have news of all sorts—news which goes to prove that you are quite right to take an apartment instead of going to the hotel. The Mangles arrived here this morning—Mangles frere, Mangles soeur, and Miss Cahere. I say, Cartoner—" He paused, and examined his own boots with a critical air.

"I say, Cartoner, how old do you put me?"

"Fifty."

"All that, mon cher?—all that? Old enough to play the part of an old fool who excels all other fools."

Cartoner took up his pen again. He had suddenly thought of something to put down, and in his odd, direct way proceeded to write, while Deulin watched him.

"I say," said the Frenchman at length, and Cartoner paused, pen in hand—"what would you think of me if I fell in love with Netty Cahere?"

"I should think you a very lucky man if Netty Cahere fell in love with you," was the reply.

The Frenchman shrugged his shoulders.

"Yes," he said. "I have known you a good many years, and have gathered that that is your way of looking at things. You want your wife to be in love with you. Odd! I suppose it is English. Well, I don't know if there is any harm done, but I certainly had a queer sensation when I saw Miss Cahere suddenly this morning. You think her a nice girl?"

"Very nice," replied Cartoner, gravely.

Deulin looked at him with an odd smile, but Cartoner was looking at the letter before him.

"What I like about her is her quiet ways," suggested Deulin, tentatively.

"Yes."

Then they lapsed into silence, while Cartoner thought of his letter. Deulin, to judge from a couple of sharp sighs which caught him unawares, must have been thinking of Netty

Cahere. At length the Frenchman rose and took his leave, making an appointment to dine with Cartoner that evening.

Out in the street he took off his hat to high heaven again.

"More lies!" he murmured, humbly.

IX

THE SAND-WORKERS

At the foot of the steep and narrow Bednarska—the street running down from the Cracow Faubourg to the river—there are always many workers. It is here that the bathing-houses and the boat-houses are. Here lie the steamers that ply slowly on the shallow river. Here, also, is a trade in timber where from time to time one of the smaller rafts that float from the Carpathians down to Dantzic is moored and broken up. Here, also, are loafers, who, like flies, congregate naturally near the water.

A few hundred yards higher up the river, between the Bednarska and the spacious Jerozolimska Alley, many carts and men work all day in the sand which the Vistula deposits along her low banks. The Jerozolimska starts hopefully from the higher parts of the city—the widest, the newest, the most Parisian street in the town, Warsaw's only boulevard—down the hill, as if it expected to find a bridge at the bottom. But there is no bridge there, and the fine street dwindles away to sandy ruts and a broken tow-path. Here horses struggle vainly to drag heavy sand-carts from the ruts, while their drivers swear at them and the sand-workers lean on their spades and watch. A cleaner sand is dredged from the middle or brought across in deep-laden punts from the many banks

Henry Seton Merriman

that render navigation next to impossible—a clean, hard sand, most excellent for building purposes.

It was the hour of the mid-day dinner—for Polish hours are the hours of the early Victorian meals. Horses and men were alike at rest. The horses nibbled at the thin grass, while the men sat by the water and ate their gray bread, which only tastes of dampness and carraway-seeds. It was late autumn, and the sun shone feebly through a yellow haze. The scene was not exhilarating. The Vistula, to put it plainly, is a dismal river. Poland is a dismal country. A witty Frenchman, who knew it well, once said that it is a country to die for, but not to live in.

It was only natural that the workmen should group together for their uninteresting meal. The sand-bank offered a comfortable seat. Their position was in a sense a strategetical one. They were in full view of the bridge and of the high land behind them, but no one could approach within half a mile unperceived.

"Yes," one of the workmen was saying, "those who know say that there will inevitably be a kingdom of Poland again. Some day. And if some day, why not now? Why not this time?"

His hearers continued to eat in silence. Some were slightly built, oval-faced men—real Poles; others had the narrower look of the Lithuanian; while a third type possessed the broad and placid face that comes from Posen. Some were born to this hard work of the sand-hills; others had that look in the eyes, that carriage of the head, which betokens breeding and suggests an ancestral story.

"The third time, they say, is lucky," answered a white-haired man, at length. He was a strong man, with the lines of hunger cut deeply in his face. The work was nothing to him. He had labored elsewhere. The others turned and looked at him, but he said no more. He glanced across the river towards the spires of Praga pointing above the brown trees. Perhaps he was thinking of those other times, which he must have seen fifty and twenty years ago. His father must have seen Praga paved with the dead bodies of its people. He must have seen the river run sluggish with the same burden. He may have seen the people shot down in the streets of Warsaw only twenty years before. His eyes had the dull look which nearly always betokens some grim vision never forgotten. He seemed a placid old man, and was known as an excellent worker, though cruel to his horses.

He who had first spoken—a boatman known as Kosmaroff—was a spare man, with a narrow face and a long, pointed chin, hidden by a neat beard. He was not more than thirty-five years old, and presented no outward appearance of having passed through hardships. His manner was quick and vivacious, and when he laughed, which was not infrequent, his mouth gave an odd twist to the left. The corner went upwards towards the eye. His smile was what the French call a pale smile. At times, but very rarely, a gleam of recklessness passed through his dark eyes. He had been a raftsman, and was reputed to be the most daring of those little-known watermen at flood-times and in the early thaw. He glanced towards the old man as if hoping that more was coming.

"Yes, it will be the third time," he said, when the other had lapsed into a musing silence, "though few of us have seen it with our own eyes. But we have other means of remembering. We have also the experience of our forefathers to guide us—though we cannot say that our forefathers have told us—"

Henry Seton Merriman

He broke off with a short laugh. His grandfather had died at Praga; his father had gone to Siberia to perish there.

"We shall time it better," he said, "than last time. We have men watching the political world for us. The two emperors are marked as an old man is marked by those who are named in his will. If anything happened to Bismarck, if Austria and Russia were to fall out, if the dogs should quarrel among themselves—the three dogs that have torn Poland to pieces! Anything would do! They knew the Crimean War was coming. England and France were so slow. And they threw a hundred thousand men into Warsaw before they turned to the English. That showed what they thought of us!"

The others listened, looking patiently at the river. The spirit of some was broken. There is nothing like hunger for breaking the spirit. Others looked doubtful, for one reason or another. These men resembled a board of directors—some of them knew too little, others too much. It seemed to be Kosmaroff's mission to keep them up to a certain mark by his boundless optimism, his unquestioning faith in a good cause.

"It is all very well for you," said one, a little fat man with beady eyes. Fat men with beady eyes are not usually found in near proximity to danger of any sort—"you, who are an aristocrat, and have nothing to lose!"

Kosmaroff ate his bread with an odd smile. He did not look towards the speaker. He knew the voice perhaps, or he knew that the great truth that a man's character is ever bubbling to his lips, and every spoken word is a part of it running over.

"There are many who can be aristocrats some day—with a little good-fortune," he said, and the beady eyes brightened.

"I lost five at Praga," muttered an elderly man, who had the subdued manner of the toiler. "That is enough for me."

"It is well to remember Praga," returned Kosmaroff, in a hard monotone. "It is well to remember that the Muscovites have never kept their word! There is much to remember!"

And a murmur of unforgetfulness came from the listeners. Kosmaroff glanced sideways at two men who sat shoulder to shoulder staring sullenly across the river.

"I may be an aristocrat by descent," he said, "but what does that come to? I am a raftsman. I work with my hands, like any other. To be a Polish aristocrat is to have a little more to give. They have always done it. They are ready to do it again. Look at the Bukatys and a hundred others, who could go to France and live there peaceably in the sunshine. I could do it myself. But I am here. The Bukatys are here. They will finish by losing everything—the little they have left—or else they will win everything. And I know which they will do. They will win! The prince is wise. Prince Martin is brave; we all know that!"

"And when they have won will they remember?" asked one of the two smaller men, throwing a brown and leathery crust into the river.

"If they are given anything worth remembering they will not forget it. You may rely on that. They know what each gives—whether freely or with a niggard hand—and each shall be paid back in his own coin. They give freely enough themselves. It is always so with the aristocrats; but they expect an equal generosity in others, which is only right!"

The men sat in a row facing the slow river. They were toil-worn and stained; their clothing was in rags. But beneath their sandy hair more than one pair of eyes gleamed from time to time with a sudden anger, with an intelligence made for higher things than spade and oar. As they sat there they were like the notes of a piano, and Kosmaroff played the instrument with a sure touch that brought the fullest vibration out of each chord. He was a born leader; an organizer not untouched perchance by that light of genius which enables some to organize the souls of men.

Nor was he only a man of words, as so many patriots are. He was that dangerous product, a Pole born in Siberia. He had served in a Cossack regiment. The son of convict No. 2704, he was the mere offspring of a number—a thing not worth accounting. In his regiment no one noticed him much, and none cared when he disappeared from it. And now here he was back in Poland, with a Russian name for daily use and another name hidden in his heart that had blazed all over Poland once. Here he was, a raftsman plying between Cracow and Warsaw, those two hot-beds of Polish patriotism—a mere piece of human driftwood on the river. He had made the usual grand tour of Russia's deadliest enemies. He had been to Siberia and Paris and London. He might have lived abroad, as he said, in the sunshine; but he preferred Poland and its gray skies, manual labor, and the bread that tastes of dampness. For he believed that a kingdom which stood in the forefront for eight centuries cannot die. There are others who cherish the same belief.

"This time," he went on, after a pause, "I have news for you. We are a little nearer. It is our object to be ready, and then to wait patiently until some event in Europe gives us our opportunity. Last time they acted at the wrong moment. This time we shall not do that, but we shall nevertheless act with decision when the moment arrives. We are a step nearer to readiness, and we owe it to Prince Martin Bukaty again. He is never slow to put his head in the noose, and laughs with the rope around his neck. And he has succeeded again, for he has the luck. We have five thousand rifles in Poland—"

He paused and looked down the line of grimy faces, noting that some lighted up and others drooped. The fat little man with the beady eyes blinked as he stared resolutely across the river.

"In Warsaw!" he added, significantly. "So, if there are any who think that the cause is a dead one, they had better say so now—and take the consequences." He concluded rather grimly, with his one-sided smile.

No one seemed disposed to avail himself of this invitation.

"And there is ammunition enough," continued Kosmaroff, "to close the account of every Muscovite in Warsaw!"

His voice vibrated as he spoke, with the cold and steady hatred of the conquered; but on his face there only rested the twisted smile.

"I tell you this," he went on, "because I am likely to go to Cracow before long, and so that you may know what is expected of you. Certain events may be taken beforehand as a sure signal for assembly—such as the death of either emperor, of the King of Prussia, or of Bismarck, the declaration of war by any of the great powers. There is always something seething on the Indian frontier, and one day the English will awake. The Warsaw papers will not have the news; but the *Czas* and the other Cracow journals will tell you soon enough, and you can all see the Galician papers when you want to, despite their censors and their police!"

A contemptuous laugh from the fat man confirmed this statement. This was his department. In many men cunning takes the place of courage.

At this moment the steam-whistle of the iron-works farther up the river boomed out across the plain. The bells of the city churches broke out into a clanging unanimity as to the time of day, and all the workers stirred reluctantly. The dinner-hour was over.

Kosmaroff rose to his feet and stretched himself—a long, lithe, wiry figure.

"Come," he said. "We must go back to work."

He glanced from face to face, and any looking with under-standing at his narrow countenance, his steady, dark eyes, and clean-cut nose must have realized that they stood in the presence of that rare and indefinable creation—a strong man.

X

A WARNING

It is a matter of history that the division of Poland into three saved many families from complete ruin. For some suffered confiscation in the kingdom of Poland and saved their property in Galicia; others, again in Posen had estates in Masovia, which even Russian justice could not lay hands upon—that gay justice of 1832, which declared that, in protesting against the want of faith of their conquerors, the Poles had broken faith. The Austrian government had sympathized with the discontent of those Poles who had fallen under Russian sway, while in Breslau it was permitted to print and publish plain words deemed criminal in Cracow and Warsaw. The dogs, in a word, behaved as dogs do over their carrion, and, having secured a large portion, kept a jealous eye on their neighbor's jaw.

The Bukatys had lost all in Poland except a house or two in Warsaw, but a few square miles of fertile land in Galicia brought in a sufficiency, while Wanda had some property in the neighborhood of Breslau bequeathed to her by her mother. The grim years of 1860 and 1861 had worn out this lady, who found the peace that passeth man's understanding while Poland was yet in the horrors of a hopeless guerilla warfare.

Henry Seton Merriman

"Russia owes me twenty years of happiness and twenty million rubles," the old prince was in the habit of saying, and each year on the anniversary of his wife's death he reckoned up afresh this debt. He mentioned it, moreover, to Russian and Pole alike, with that calm frankness which was somehow misunderstood, for the administration never placed him among the suspects. Poland has always been a plain-speaking country, and the Poles, expressing themselves in the roughest of European tongues, a plain-spoken people. They spoke so plainly to Henry of Valois when he was their king that one fine night he ran away to mincing France and gentler men. When, under rough John Sobieski, they spoke with their enemy in the gate of Vienna, their meaning was quite clear to the Moslem understanding.

The Prince Bukaty had a touch of that rough manner which commands respect in this smooth age, and even Russian officials adopted a conciliatory attitude towards this man, who had known Poland without one of their kind within her boundaries.

"You cannot expect an old man such as I to follow all the changes of your petty laws, and to remember under which form of government he happens to be living at the moment!" he had boldly said to a great personage from St. Petersburg, and the observation was duly reported in the capital. It was, moreover, said in Warsaw that the law had actually stretched a point or two for the Prince Bukaty on more than one occasion. Like many outspoken people, he passed for a barker and not a biter.

It does not fall to the lot of many to live in a highly civilized town and submit to open robbery. Prince Bukaty lived in a small palace in the Kotzebue street, and when he took his morning stroll in the Cracow Faubourg he passed under the shadow of a palace flying the Russian flag, which palace was his, and had belonged to his ancestors from time imme-morial. He had once made the journey to St. Petersburg to see in the great museum there the portraits of his fathers, the books that his predecessors had collected, the relics of Poland's greatness, which were his, and the greatness thereof was his.

"Yes," he answered to the loquacious curator, "I know. You tell me nothing that I do not know. These things are mine. I am the Prince Bukaty!"

And the curator of St. Petersburg went away, sorrowful, like the young man who had great possessions.

For Russia had taken these things from the Bukatys, not in punishment, but because she wanted them. She wanted offices for her bureaucrats on the Krakowski Przedmiescie, in Warsaw, so she took Bukaty Palace. And to whom can one appeal when Caesar steals?

Poland had appealed to Europe, and Europe had expressed the deepest sympathy. And that was all!

The house in the Kotzebue had the air of an old French town-house, and was, in fact, built by a French architect in the days of Stanislaus Augustus, when Warsaw aped Paris. It stands back from the road behind high railings, and, at the farther end of a paved court-yard, to which entrance is gained by two high gates, now never opened in hospitality, and only unlocked at rare intervals for the passage of the quiet brougham in which the prince or Wanda went and came. The house is just round the corner of the Kotzebue, and therefore faces the Saski Gardens—a quiet spot in this most noisy town. The building is a low one, with a tiled roof and long windows, heavily framed, of which the smaller panes and thick woodwork suggest the early days of window-glass. Inside, the house is the house of a poor man. The carpets are worn thin; the furniture, of a sumptuous design, is carefully patched and mended. The atmosphere has that mournful scent of better days—now dead and past. It is the odor of monarchy, slowly fading from the face of a world that reeks of cheap democracy.

The air of the rooms—the subtle individuality which is impressed by humanity on wood and texture—suggested that older comfort which has been succeeded by the restless luxury of these times.

The prince was, it appeared, one of those men who diffuse tranquillity wherever they are. He had moved quietly through stirring events; had acted without haste in hurried moments. For the individuality of the house must have been his. Wanda had found it there when she came back from the school in Dresden, too young to have a marked individuality of her own. The difference she brought to the house was a certain brightness and a sort of experimental femininity, which reigned supreme until her English governess came back again to live as a companion with her pupil. Wanda moved the furniture, turned the house round on its staid basis, and made a hundred experiments in domestic economy before she gave way to her father's habits of life. Then she made that happiest of human discoveries, which has the magic power of allaying at one stroke the eternal feminine discontent which has made the world uneasy since the day that Eve idled in that perfect garden—she found that she was wanted in the world!

The prince did not tell her so. Perhaps his need of her was too obvious to require words. He had given his best years to Poland, and now that old age was coming, that health was failing and wealth had vanished, Poland would have none of him.

There was no Poland. At this moment Wanda burst upon him, so to speak, with a hundred desires that only he could fulfil, a hundred questions that only he could answer. And, as wise persons know, to fulfil desires and answer questions is the best happiness.

Father and daughter lived a quiet life in the house that was called a palace by courtesy only. For Martin was made of livelier stuff, and rarely stayed long at home. He came and went with a feverish haste; was fond of travel, he said, and the authorities kept a questioning eye upon his movements.

There are two doors to the Bukaty Palace. As often as not, Martin made use of the smaller door giving entrance to the garden at the back of the house, which garden could also be entered from an alley leading round from the back of the bank, which stands opposite the post-office in the busier part of Kotzebue Street.

He came in by this door one evening and did not come alone, for he was accompanied by a man in working-clothes. The streets of Warsaw are well lighted and well guarded by a most excellent police, second only as the Russians are to the police of London. It is therefore the custom to go abroad at night as much as in the day, and the Krakowski is more crowded after dark than during the afternoon. Kosmaroff had walked some distance behind Prince Martin in the streets. Martin unlocked the gate of the garden and passed in, leaving the gate open with the key in the lock. In a minute Kosmaroff followed, locked the gate after him, and gave the key back to its owner on the steps of the garden door of the house, where Martin was awaiting him, latch-key in hand. They did it without comment or instruction, as men carry out a plan frequently resorted to.

Martin led the way into the house, along a dimly lighted

corridor, to a door which stood ajar. Outside the night was cold; within were warmth and comfort. Martin went into the long room. At the far end, beneath the lamp and near an open wood fire, the prince and Wanda were sitting. They were in evening dress, and the prince was dozing in his chair.

"I have brought Kos to see you," said Martin, and, turning, he looked towards the door. The convict's son, the convict, came forward with that ease which, to be genuine, must be quite unconscious. He apparently gave no thought to his sandy and wrinkled top-boots, from which the original black had long since been washed away by the waters of the Vistula. He wore his working-clothes as if they were the best habit for this or any other palace. He took Wanda's hand and kissed it in the old-world fashion, which has survived to this day in Poland. But the careless manner in which he raised her fingers to his lips would have showed quite clearly to a competent observer that neither Wanda nor any other woman had ever touched his heart.

"You will excuse my getting up," said the prince. "My gout is bad to-night. You will have something to eat?"

"Thank you, I have eaten," replied Kosmaroff, drawing forward a chair.

Martin put the logs together with his foot, and they blazed up, lighting with a flickering glow the incongruous group.

"He will take a glass of port," said the prince, turning to Wanda, and indicating the decanter from which, despite his gout, he had just had his after-dinner wine.

Wanda poured out the wine and handed it to Kosmaroff, who took it with a glance and a quick smile of thanks, which seemed to indicate that he was almost one of the family.

And, indeed, they were closely related, not only in the present generation, but in bygone days. For Kosmaroff represented a family long since deemed extinct.

"I have come," he said, "to tell you that all is safe. Also to bid you good-bye. As soon as I can get employment I shall go down to Thorn to stir them up there. They are lethargic at Thorn."

"Ah!" laughed the prince, moving his legs to a more comfortable position, "you young men! You think everybody is lethargic. Don't move too quickly. That is what I always preach."

"And we are ready enough to listen to your preaching," answered Kosmaroff. "You will admit that I came here to-night in obedience to your opinion that too much secrecy is dangerous because it leads to misunderstandings. Plain speaking and clear understanding was the message you sent me—the text of your last sermon."

With his quick smile Kosmaroff touched the rim of the prince's wineglass, which stood at his elbow, and indicated by a gesture that he drank his health.

"That was not my text—that was Wanda's," answered the prince.

"Ah!" said Kosmaroff, looking towards Wanda. "Is that so? Then I will take it. I believe in Wanda's views of life. She has a vast experience."

"I have been to Dresden and to London," answered Wanda, "and a woman always sees much more than a man."

"Always?" asked Kosmaroff, with his one-sided smile.

"Always."

But Kosmaroff had turned towards the prince in his quick, jerky way.

"By-the-way," he asked, "what is Cartoner doing in Warsaw?"

"Cartoner—the Englishman who speaks so many languages? We met him in London," answered the prince. "Who is he? Why should he not be here?"

"I will tell you who he is," answered Kosmaroff, with a sudden light in his eyes. "He is the man that the English send when they suspect that something is going on which they can turn to good account. He has a trick of finding things out— that man. Such is his reputation, at all events. Paul Deulin is another, and he is here. He is a friend of yours, by-the-way; but he is not dangerous, like Cartoner. There is an American here, too. His instructions are Warsaw and Petersburg. There is either something moving in Russia or else the powers suspect that something may move in Poland before long. These men are here to find out. They must find out nothing from us."

The prince shrugged his shoulders indifferently. He did not attach much importance to these foreigners.

"Of course," went on Kosmaroff, "they are only watchers. But, as Wanda says, some people see more than others. The American, Mangles, who has ladies with him, will report upon events after they have happened. So will Deulin, who is an idler. He never sees that which will give him trouble. He does not write long despatches to the Quai d'Orsay, because he knows that they will not be read there. But Cartoner is different. There are never any surprises for the English in matters that Cartoner has in hand. He reports on events before they have happened, which is a different story. I merely warn you."

As he spoke, Kosmaroff rose, glancing at the clock.

"There are no instructions?"

"None," answered the prince. "Except the usual one—patience!"

"Ah yes," replied Kosmaroff, "we shall be patient."

He did not seem to think that it might be easier to be patient in this comfortable house than on the sand-hills of the Vistula in the coming winter months.

"But be careful," he added, addressing Martin more particularly, "of this man Cartoner. He will not betray, but he will know—you understand. And no one must know!"

He shook hands with Martin and Wanda and then with the prince.

"You met him in London, you say?" he said to the prince. "What did you think of him?"

"I thought him—a quiet man."

"And Wanda?" continued Kosmaroff, lightly, turning to her—"she who sees so much. What did she think of him?"

"I was afraid of him!"

XI

AN AGREEMENT TO DIFFER

The Saxon Gardens are in the heart of Warsaw, and, in London, would be called a park. At certain hours the fashionable world promenades beneath the trees, and at all times there is a thoroughfare across from one quarter of the town to another.

Wanda often sat there in the morning or walked slowly with her father at such times as the doctor's instructions to take exercise were still fresh upon his memory. There are seats beneath the trees, overlooking the green turf and the flowers so dear to the Slavonian soul. Later in the morning these seats are occupied by nurses and children, as in any other park in any other city. But from nine to ten Wanda had the alleys mostly to herself.

The early autumn had already laid its touch upon the trees, and the leaves were brown. The flowers, laboriously tended all through the brief, uncertain summer, had that forlorn look which makes autumn in Northern latitudes a period of damp depression. Wanda had gone out early, and was sitting at the sunny side of the broad alley that divides the gardens in two from end to end. She was waiting for Martin, who had been called back at the door of the palace and had promised to follow in a few minutes. He had a hundred engagements during the day, a hundred friends among those unfortunate scions of noble houses who will not wear the Russian uniform, who cannot by the laws of their caste engage in any form of commerce, and must not accept a government office—who are therefore idle, without the natural Southern sloth that enables Italians and Spaniards to do nothing gracefully all day long. Wanda was wiser than Martin. Girls generally are infinitely wiser than young men. But the wisdom ceases to grow later in life, and old men are wiser than old women. Wanda was, in a sense, Martin's adviser, mentor, and friend. She had, as he himself acknowledged, already saved him from dangers into which his natural heedlessness and impetuosity would have led him. As to the discontent in which all Poland was steeped, which led the princes and their friends into many perils, Wanda had been brought up to it, just as some families are brought up to consumption and the anticipation of an early death.

In her eminently practical, feminine way of looking at things, Wanda was much more afraid of Martin running into debt than into danger. Debt and impecuniosity would be so inconvenient at this time, when her father daily needed some new comfort, and daily depended for his happiness more and more upon his port wine and that ease which is only to be enjoyed by an easy mind.

Wanda was thinking of these things in the Saski Gardens, and hardly heeded the passers-by, though—for the feminine instincts were strong in her—she looked with softer eyes on the children than she did on the Jew who hurried past, with bent back and a bowed head, from the richer quarter of the town to his own mysterious purlieus of the Franoiszkanska. The latter, perhaps, recalled the thoughts of Martin and his heedlessness; the former made her think of—she knew not what.

She was looking towards the colonnade that marks the site of the King of Saxony's palace, when Cartoner came through the archway into the garden. She recognized him even at this distance, for his walk was unlike that of the nervous, quick-moving Pole or the lurking Jew. It was more like the gait of a Russian; but all the Russians in Warsaw wear a uniform. That is why they are there. There was a suggestion of determination in the walk of this Englishman.

He came down the wide alley towards her, and then suddenly perceived her. She saw this without actually looking at him, and knew the precise moment when he first caught sight of her. It was presumably upon experience that Wanda based her theory that women see twice as much as men. She saw him turn, without hesitation, away from her down a narrower alley leading to the right. It was his intention to avoid her. But the only turning he could take was that leading to the corner of Kotzebue Street, and Martin was at the other end of it, coming towards him. Cartoner was thus caught in the narrow alley. Wanda sat still and watched the two men. She suddenly knew in advance what would happen, as it is often vouchsafed to the human understanding to know at a moment's notice what is coming; and she had a strange, discomforting sense that these minutes were preordained—that Martin and Cartoner and herself were mere puppets in the hands of Fate, and must say and do that which has been assigned to them in an unalterable scheme of succeeding events.

She watched the two men meet and shake hands, in the English fashion, without raising their hats. She could see Cartoner's movements to continue his way, and Martin's detaining hand slipped within the Englishman's arm.

"What does it matter?" Martin was saying. "There is no one to see us here, at this hour in the morning. We are quite safe.

There is Wanda, sitting on the seat, waiting for me. Come back with me."

And Wanda could divine the words easily enough from her brother's attitude and gestures. It ought to have surprised her that Cartoner yielded, for it was unlike him. He was so much stronger than Martin—so determined, so unyielding. And yet she felt no surprise when he turned and came towards her with Martin's hand still within his arm. She knew that it was written that he must come; divined vaguely that he had something to say to her which it was safer to say than to leave to be silently understood and perhaps misunderstood. She gave an impatient sigh. She had always ruled her father and brother and the Palace Bukaty, and this sense of powerlessness was new to her.

While they approached, Martin continued to talk in his eager, laughing way, and Cartoner smiled slowly as he listened.

"I saw you," he said to Wanda, as he took off his hat, "and went the other way to avoid you."

And, having made this plain statement, he stood silently looking at her. He looked into her eyes, and she met his odd, direct gaze without embarrassment.

"Cartoner and I," Prince Martin hastened to explain, "travelled from Berlin together, and we agreed then that, much as we might desire it, it would be inconvenient for me to show him that attention which one would naturally want to show to an Englishman travelling in Poland. That is why he went the other way when he saw you."

Wanda looked at Cartoner with her quick, shrewd smile. It would have been the obvious thing to have confirmed this explanation. But Cartoner kept silent. He had acquired, it seemed, the fatal habit—very rare among men and almost unknown in women—of thinking before he spoke. Which habit is deadly for that which is called conversation, because if one decides not to give speech to the obvious and the unnecessary and the futile there is in daily intercourse hardly anything left.

"You see," said Martin, who always had plenty to say for himself, "in this province of Russia we are not even allowed to choose our own friends."

"Even in a free country one does not pick one's friends out, like the best strawberries from a basket," said Wanda.

"Not a question to be arranged beforehand," put in Cartoner.

"Not even by the governor-general of Poland?" asked Wanda, looking thoughtfully at the falling leaves which a sudden gust of wind had showered round them.

"Not even by the Czar."

"Who, I am told, means well!" said Martin, ironically, and with a gay laugh, for irony and laughter may be assimilated by the young. "Poor man! It must be terrible to know that people are saying behind one's back that one means well! I hope no one will ever say that of me."

Wanda had sat down again, and was stirring the dead leaves with her walking-stick.

"Martin and I are going for a tramp," she said. "We like to get away from the noise and the dust—and the uniforms."

But Martin sat down beside her and made room for Cartoner.

"We attract less attention than if we stand," he explained. And Cartoner took the seat offered. "Such hospitality as our circumstances allow us to offer you," commented the young prince, gayly, "a clean stone seat on the sunny side of a public garden."

"But let us understand each other," put in Wanda, in her practical way, and looked from one man to the other with those gay, blue eyes that saw so much, "since we are conspirators."

"The better we understand each other the better conspirators we shall be," said Cartoner.

"I notice you don't ask, 'What is the plot?'" said Wanda.

"The plot is simple enough," answered Martin, for Cartoner said nothing, and looked straight in front of him. He did not address one more than the other, but explained the situation, as it were, for the benefit of all whom it might concern. He had lighted a cigarette—a little Russian affair, all gold lettering and mouthpiece, and as he spoke he jerked the ash from time to time so that it should not fly and incommode his sister.

"Rightly or wrongly, we are suspected of being malcontents. The Bukatys have in the past been known to foster that spirit of Polish nationality which it has been the endeavor of three great countries to suppress for nearly a century. Despite Russia, Prussia, and Austria there is still a Polish language and a Polish spirit; despite the Romanoffs, the Hapsburgs, and the Hohenzollerns there are still a few old Lithuanian and Ruthenian families extant. And rightly or wrongly, those in authority are kind enough to blame, among others, the Bukatys for these survivals. Weeds, it seems, are hard to kill. Whether we are really to blame or not is of no consequence.

It does not matter to the dog whether he deserves his bad name or not—after he is hanged. But it is not good to be a Bukaty and live in Poland just now, though some of us manage to have a good time despite them all—eh, Wanda?"

And he laid his hand momentarily on his sister's arm. But she did not answer. She desired before all things that clear understanding which was part of her creed of life, and she glanced quickly from side to side for fear some interruption should approach.

"Mr. Cartoner, on the other hand," he continued, in his airy way, "is a most respectable man—in the employ of his country. That is what damns Mr. Cartoner. He is in the employ of his country. And he has a great reputation, to which I take off my hat."

And he saluted gayly Cartoner's reputation.

"It would never do," continued Martin, "for us, the suspects, to be avowedly the friend of the man who is understood to be an envoy in some capacity of his government. Whether he is really such or not is of no consequence. It matters little to the dog, you remember."

"But what are we to do?" asked Wanda, practically. "Let us have a clear understanding. Are we to pass each other in the streets?"

"No," answered Cartoner, speaking at length, without hesitation and without haste—a man who knew his own mind, and went straight to the heart of the question. "We must not meet in the streets."

"That may not be as easy as it sounds," said Wanda, "in a small city like Warsaw. Are you so long-sighted that you can always make sure of avoiding us?"

"I can, at all events, try," answered Cartoner, simply. After a pause (the pauses always occurred when it happened, so to say, to be Cartoner's turn to speak) he rose from the stone seat, which was all that the Bukatys could offer him in Warsaw. "I can begin at once," he said, gravely. And he took off his hat and went away.

It was done so quickly and quietly that Wanda and Martin were left in silence on the seat, watching him depart. He went the way he had come, down the broad walk towards the colonnade, and disappeared between the pillars of that building.

"A man of action, and not of words," commented Martin, who spoke first. "I like him. Come, let us go for our walk."

And Wanda said nothing. They rose and went away without speaking, though they usually had plenty to say to each other. It almost seemed that Cartoner's silence was contagious.

He, for his part, went into the Faubourg and crossed to the river side of that wide street. It thus happened that he missed seeing Mr. Joseph Mangles, sunning himself upon the more frequented pavement, and smoking a contemplative cigar. Mr. Mangles would have stopped him had they met. Paul Deulin was not far behind Mr. Mangles, idling past the shops, which could scarcely have had much interest for the Parisian.

"Ah!" said the Frenchman to himself, "there is our friend Reginald. He is in one of his silent humors. I can see that from this distance."

He turned on the pavement and watched Cartoner, who was walking rather slowly.

"If any woman ever marries that man," the Frenchman said to himself, "she will have to allow a great deal to go without saying. But, then, women are good at that."

And he continued his leisurely contemplation of the dull shop-windows.

Cartoner walked on to his rooms in the Jasna, where he found letters awaiting him. He read them, and then sat down to write one which was not an answer to any that he had received. He wrote it carefully and thoughtfully, and when it was written sealed it. For in Warsaw it is well to seal such letters as are not intended to be read at the post-office. And if one expects letters of importance, it is wiser not to have them sent to Poland at all, for the post-office authorities are kind enough to exercise a parental censorship over the travellers' correspondence.

Cartoner's letter was addressed to an English gentleman at his country house in Sussex, and it asked for an immediate recall from Poland. It was a confession, for the first time, that the mission entrusted to him was more than he could undertake.

XII

CARTONER *VERSUS* FATE

It has been said that on the turf, and under it, all men are equal. It is, moreover, whispered that the crooked policy of Russia forwards the cause of horseracing at Warsaw by every means within its power, on the theory that even warring nationalities may find themselves reconciled by a common sport. And this dream of peace, pursued by the successor of that Czar who said to Poland: "Gentlemen—no dreams," seems in part justified by the undeniable fact that Russians and Poles find themselves brought nearer together on the race-course than in any other social function in Warsaw.

"Come," cried Paul Deulin, breaking in on the solitude of Cartoner's rooms after lunch one day towards the end of October. "Come, and let us bury the hatchet, and smoke the cigarette of peace before the grand-stand at the Mokotow. Everybody will be there. All Poland and his wife, all the authorities and their wives, and these ladies will peep sideways at each other, and turn up their noses at each other's toilets. To such has descended the great strife in eastern Europe."

"You think so."

"Yes, I think so, or I pretend to think so, which comes to the same thing, and makes it a more amusing world for those who have no stake in it. Come with me, and I will show you this little world of Warsaw, where the Russians walk on one side and the Poles pass by on the other; where these fine Russian officers glance longingly across the way, only too ready to take their hearts there and lose them—but the Czar forbids it. And, let me tell you, there is nothing more dangerous in the world than a pair of Polish eyes."

He broke off suddenly; for Cartoner was looking at him with a speculative glance, and turned away to the window.

"Come," he said. "It is a fine day—St. Martin's summer. It is Sunday, but no matter. All you Englishmen think that there is no recording angel on the Continent. You leave him behind at Dover."

"Oh, I have no principles," said Cartoner, rising from his chair, and looking round absent-mindedly for his hat.

"You would be no friend of mine if you had. There is no moderation in principles. If a man has any at all, he always has some to spare for his neighbors. And who wants to act up to another man's principles? By-the-way, are you doing any good here, Cartoner?"

"None."

"Nor I," pursued Deulin; "and I am bored. That is why I want you to come to the races with me. Besides, it would be more marked to stay away than to go—especially for an Englishman and a Frenchman, who lead the world in racing."

"That is why I am going," said Cartoner.

"Then you don't like racing?"

"Yes, I am very fond of it," answered the Englishman, in the same absent voice, as he led the way towards the door.

In the Jasna they found a drosky, where there is always one to be found at the corner of the square, and they did not speak during the drive up the broad Marszalkowska to the rather barren suburb of the Mokotow (where bricks and mortar are still engaged in emphasizing the nakedness of the land), for the simple reason that speech is impossible while driving through the streets of the worst-paved city in Europe. Which is a grudge that the traveller may bear against Russia, for if Poland had been a kingdom she would assuredly have paved the streets of her capital.

The race-course is not more than fifteen minutes' drive from the heart of the town, and all Warsaw was going thither this sunny afternoon. At the entrance a crowd was slowly working its way through the turnstiles, and Deulin and Cartoner passed in with it. They had the trick, so rare among travellers, of doing this in any country without attracting undue attention.

It was a motley enough throng. There were Polish ladies and gentlemen in the garb of their caste, which is to-day the same all the world over, though in some parts of Ruthenia and Lithuania one may still come across a Polish gentleman of the old school in his frogged coat and top-boots. German tradesmen and their families formed here and there one of those domesticated and homely groups which the Fatherland sends out into the world's trading centres. And moving amid these, as quietly and unobtrusively as possible, the Russian officers, who virtually had the management of the course— tall, fair, clean men, with sunburned faces and white skins— energetic, refined, and strong. They were mostly in white tunics with gold shoulder-straps, blue breeches, and much gold lace. Here and there a Cossack officer moved with long, free strides in his dressing-gown of a coat, heavily ornamented with silver, carrying high his astrakhan cap, and looking round him with dark eyes that had a gleam of something wild and untamed in them. It was a meeting-ground of many races, one of the market-places where men may greet each other who come from different hemispheres and yet owe allegiance to one flag: are sons of the empire which to-day gathers within one ring-fence the north, the south, the east, and the west.

"France amuses me, England commands my respect, but Russia takes my breath away," said Deulin, elbowing his way through the medley of many races. On all sides one heard different languages—German, the sing-song Russian—the odd, exclamatory tongue which three emperors cannot kill.

"And Germany?" inquired Cartoner, in his low, curt voice.

"Bores me, my friend."

He was pushing his way gently through into the paddock, where a number of men were congregated, but no ladies.

"The Fatherland," he added, "the heavy Fatherland! I killed a German once, when I was in the army of the Loire—a most painful business."

He was still shaking his head over this reminiscence when they reached the gateway of the paddock. He was passing through it when, without turning towards him, he grasped Cartoner's arm.

"Look!" he said, "look!"

There was a sudden commotion in the well-dressed crowd in the paddock, and above the gray coats and glossy hats the tossing colors of a jockey. The head of a startled horse and two gleaming shoes appeared above the heads of men for a moment. A horse had broken away with its jockey only half in the saddle.

The throng divided, and dispersed in either direction like sheep before a dog—all except one man, who, walking with two sticks, could not move above a snail's pace.

Then, because they were both quick men, with the instincts and a long practice of action in moments calling for a rapid decision, Deulin and Cartoner ran forward. But they could not save the catastrophe which they knew was imminent. The horse advanced with long, wild strides, and knocked the crippled old man over as if he were a ninepin. He came on at a gallop now, the jockey leaning forward and trying to catch a broken bridle, his two stirrups flying, his cap off. The little man was swearing in English. And he had need to, for through the paddock gate the crowd was densely packed and he was charging into it on a maddened horse beyond control.

Deulin was nearer, and therefore the first to get to the horse; but Cartoner's greater weight came an instant later, and the horse's head was down.

"Let go! let go!" cried the jockey through his teeth, as Cartoner and Deulin, one on each side, crammed the stirrups over his feet. "Let go! I'll teach him!"

And they obeyed him, for the horse interested them less than the Prince Bukaty, lying half-stunned on the turf. They were both at his side in a moment and saw him open his eyes.

"I am unhurt," he said. "Help me up. No! sh—h! No, nothing

is broken; it is that confounded gout. No, I cannot rise yet! Leave me for a minute. Go, one of you, and tell Wanda that I am unhurt. She is in box No. 18, in the grand-stand."

He spoke in French, to Deulin more particularly.

"Go and tell her," said the Frenchman, over his shoulder, in English. "Some busy fool has probably started off by this time to tell her that her father is killed. You will find us in the club-house when you come back."

So Cartoner went to the grand-stand to seek Wanda there, in the face of all Warsaw, with his promise to avoid her still fresh in his memory. As he approached he saw her in the second tier of boxes. She was dressed in black and white, as she nearly always was. It was only the Russians and the Germans who wore gay colors. He could see the surprise on her face and in Martin's eyes as he approached, and knew that there were a hundred eyes watching him, a hundred ears waiting to catch his words when he spoke.

"Princess," he said, "the prince has had a slight accident, and has sent me to tell you that he is unhurt, in case you should hear any report to the contrary. He was unable to avoid a fractious horse, and was knocked down. Mr. Deulin is with him, and they have gone to the club pavilion."

He spoke rather slowly in French, so that all within ear-shot could understand and repeat.

"Shall we go to him?" asked Wanda, rising.

"Only to satisfy yourself. I assure you he is unhurt, princess, and would come himself were he able to walk."

Wanda rose, and turned to take her cloak from the back of

her chair.

"Will you take us to him, monsieur?" she said.

And the three quitted the grand-stand together in a rather formal silence. The next race was about to start, and the lawn, with its forlorn, autumnal flower-beds, was less crowded now as they walked along it towards the paddock.

"It was very good of you to come and tell us," said Martin, in English, "with the whole populace looking on. It will do you no good, you know, to do a kindness to people under a cloud. I suppose it was true what you said about the prince being unhurt?"

"Almost," answered Cartoner. "He is rather badly shaken. I think you will find it necessary to go home, but there is no need for anxiety."

"Oh no!" exclaimed Martin. "He is a tough old fellow. You cannot come in here, you know, Wanda. It is against the Jockey Club laws, even in case of accidents."

He stood at the gate of the club enclosure as he spoke.

"Wait here," he said, "with Cartoner, and I will be back in a few minutes."

So Cartoner and Wanda were left in the now deserted paddock, while the distant roar of voices announced that the start for the next race had been successfully accomplished.

Wanda looked rather anxiously towards the little square pavilion into which her brother was hurrying, and Cartoner only looked at Wanda. He waited till she should speak, and she did not appear to have anything to say at that moment.

Perhaps in this one case that clear understanding of which she was such a pronounced advocate was only to be compassed by silence, and not by speech. The roar of voices behind them came nearer and nearer as the horses approached the winning-post. The members of the club stood rigid beneath the pavilion awning, some with field-glasses, others with knitted brows and glittering eyes. All eyes were turned in one direction, except Wanda's and Cartoner's.

Then, when the race was over and the roar had subsided, Martin came hurrying back, and one glance at his face told them that there was no need for anxiety.

"He is laughing in there over a glass of cognac. He refuses absolutely to go home, and he wants me to help him up the stairs. He will sit under the awning, he says. And we are to go back to the grand-stand," Martin said, as he approached.

"See," he added, pointing to the paddock where the crowd was hurrying to gather round the winning horse. "See, it is already a thing of the past. And he wants it to be so. He wants no fuss made about it. It is no good advertising the fact of the existence of a dog with a bad name, eh? Thank you all the same, Cartoner, for your good offices. You and Deulin, they say, averted a catastrophe. The incident is over, my dear Wanda. It is forgotten by all except us. Wait here a minute and I will come back to you."

With a nod to Cartoner, as if to say, "I leave her to your care," he turned and left them again.

Then at length Wanda spoke.

"You see," she said, "you are not so strong as—"

"As what?" he asked, seeing that she sought a word.

"As Fate, I suppose," she answered, and her eyes were grave as she looked across the mournful level land towards the west, where the sun was sinking below parallel bars of cloud to the straight line of the horizon. Sunset over a plain is one of nature's tragic moments.

"Is it Fate?" she asked, with a sudden change of manner.

"Even Fate can be hampered in its movements, princess," answered Cartoner.

"By what?"

"By action. I have written for my recall."

He was looking towards the pavilion. It seemed that it was he, and not his companion, who was now anxious for Martin to return. Wanda was still looking across the course towards the sinking sun.

"You have asked to be recalled from Warsaw?" she said.

"Yes."

"Then," she said, after a pause, "it would have been better for you if we had not met at Lady Orlay's, in London. Monsieur Deulin once said that you had never had a check in your career. This is the first check. And it has come through— knowing us."

Cartoner made no answer, but stood watching the door of the pavilion with patient, thoughtful eyes.

"You cannot deny it," she said.

And he did not deny it.

Then she turned her head, and looked at him with clever, speculative keenness.

"Why have you asked for your recall?" she asked, slowly.

And still Cartoner made no answer. He was without rival in the art of leaving things unsaid. Then Martin came to them, laughing and talking. And across the course, amid the tag-rag and bobtail of Warsaw, the eyes of the man called Kosmaroff watched their every movement.

XIII

THE WHEELS OF CHANCE

When Martin and Wanda returned to the grand-stand they found the next box to theirs, which had hitherto been empty, occupied by a sedate party of foreigners. Miss Mangles had come to the races, not because she cared for sport, but because she had very wisely argued in her mind that one cannot set about to elevate human nature without a knowledge of those depths to which it sometimes descends.

"And this," she said, when she had settled herself on the chair commanding the best view, "this is the turf."

"That," corrected Mr. Mangles, pointing down to the lawn with his umbrella, "is the turf. This is the grand-stand."

"The whole," stated Miss Mangles, rather sadly, and indicating with a graceful wave of her card, which was in Russian and therefore illegible to her, the scene in general, "the whole constitutes the turf."

Joseph P. Mangles sat corrected, and looked lugubriously at Netty, who was prettily and quietly dressed in autumnal tints, which set off her delicate and transparent complexion to perfection. Her hair was itself of an autumnal tint, and her eyes of the deep blue of October skies.

"And these young men are on it," concluded Miss Mangles, with her usual decision. One privilege of her sex she had not laid aside—the privilege of jumping to conclusions. Netty glanced beneath her dark lashes in the direction indicated by Miss Mangles's inexorable finger; but some of the young men happening to look up, she instantly became interested in the Russian race-card which she could not read.

"It is very sad," she said.

Miss Mangles continued to look at the young men severely, as if making up her mind how best to take them in hand.

"Don't see the worst of 'em here," muttered Mr. Mangles, dismally. "It isn't round about the grand-stand that young men come to grief—on the turf. That contingent is waiting to be called up into the boxes, and reformed—by the young women."

Netty looked gently distressed. At times she almost thought Uncle Joseph inclined to be coarse. She looked across the lawn with a rather wistful expression, eminently suited to dark blue eyes. The young men below were still glancing up in her direction, but she did not seem to see them. At this moment Wanda and Martin returned to their box. Wanda was preoccupied, and sat down without noticing the new-comers. Several ladies leaned over the low partitions and asked questions, which were unintelligible to Netty, and the news was spread from mouth to mouth that the Prince Bukaty was not hurt.

Joseph P. Mangles looked at the brother and sister beneath his heavy brows. He knew quite well who they were, but did not consider himself called upon to transmit the information.

"Even the best people seem to lend their countenance to this," said Miss Mangles, in an undertone.

"You are right, Jooly."

But Miss Mangles did not hear. She was engaged in bowing to Paul Deulin, who was coming up the steps. She was rather glad to see him, for the feeling had come over her that she was quite unknown to all these people. This is a feeling to which even the greatest are liable, and it is most unpleasant. For the heart of the celebrated is apt to hunger for the nudge of recognition and the surreptitious sidelong glance which convey the gratifying fact that one has been recognized. Paul Deulin would serve to enlighten these benighted people, and some little good might yet be done by a distinct and dignified attitude of disapproval towards the turf.

"One would scarcely expect to see you here, Mr. Deulin," she said, shaking hands, with a playful shake of the head.

"Since you are here," he answered, "there can be no harm. It is only a garden-party, after all."

And he bowed over Netty's head with an empressement which would have conveyed to any one more versed in the ways of men the reason why he had come.

"Do you bet, Mr. Deulin?" inquired Jooly.

"Never, unless I am quite sure," he answered.

"There is," observed Miss Mangles, who was inclined to be gracious—"there is perhaps less harm in that."

"And less risk," explained Deulin gravely. "But surely," he said, in a lower tone, turning to Netty, "you know the

Princess Wanda? Did you not meet her at Lady Orlay's?"

Netty had already displayed some interest in Martin Bukaty, which was perhaps indiscreet. For a young man's vanity is singularly alert, and he was quite ready to return the interest with interest, so to speak.

"Yes," she replied, "we met her at Lady Orlay's. But I think she does not remember—though she seemed to recollect Mr. Cartoner, whom she met at the same time."

Deulin looked at her with his quick smile as he nodded a little, comprehending nod, and Netty's eyes looked into his innocently.

"Be assured," he answered, "that she has not seen you, or she would not fail to remember you. You are sitting back to back, you observe. The princess is rather distrait with thoughts of her father, who has just had a slight mishap."

He bent forward as he spoke and touched Wanda on the shoulder.

"Wanda," he said, "this young lady remembers meeting you in London."

Wanda turned and, rising, held her hand over the low barrier that divided the two boxes.

"Of course," she said, "Miss Cahere. You must excuse my sitting down so near to you without seeing you. I was thinking of something else."

"I hardly expect you to recollect me," Netty hastened to say. "You must have met so many people in London. Is it not odd that so many who were at Lady Orlay's that night should be in Warsaw to-day?"

"Yes," answered Wanda, rather absently. "Are there many?"

"Why, yes. Mr. Deulin was there, and yourself and the prince and we three and—Mr. Cartoner."

She looked round as she spoke for Cartoner, but only met Martin Bukaty's eyes fixed upon her with open admiration. When speaking she had much animation, and her eyes were bright.

"I am sure you are here with your brother. The likeness is unmistakable. I hope the prince is not hurt?" she said, in her little, friendly, confidential way to Wanda.

"No, he is not hurt, thank you. Yes, that is my brother. May I introduce him? Martin. Miss Cahere—my brother."

And the introduction was effected, which was perhaps what Netty wanted. She did not take much notice of Martin, but continued to talk to Wanda.

"It must be so interesting," she said, "to live in Warsaw and to be able to help the poor people who are so down-trodden."

"But I do nothing of that sort," replied Wanda. "It is only in books that women can do anything for the people of their country. All I can do for Poland is to see that one old Polish gentleman gets what he likes for dinner, and to housekeep generally—just as you do when you are at home, no doubt."

"Oh," protested Netty, "but I am not so useful as that. That is what distresses me. I seem to be of no use to anybody. And I am sure I could never housekeep."

And some faint line of thought, suggested perhaps by the last remark, made her glance in passing at Martin. It was so quick that only Martin saw it. At all events, Paul Deulin appeared to be looking rather vacantly in another direction.

"I suppose Miss Mangles does all that when you are at home?" said Wanda, glancing towards the great woman, who was just out of ear-shot.

"My dear Wanda," put in Deulin, in a voice of gravest protest, "you surely do not expect that of a lady who housekeeps for all humanity. Miss Mangles is one of our leaders of thought. I saw her so described in a prominent journal of Smithville, Ohio. Miss Mangles, in her care for the world, has no time to think of an individual household."

"Besides," said Netty, "we have no settled home in America. We live differently. We have not the comfort of European life."

And she gave a little sigh, looking wistfully across the plain. Martin noticed that she had a pretty profile, and the tenderest little droop of the lips.

At this moment a race, the last on the card, put a stop to further conversation, and Netty refused, very properly, to deprive Martin of the use of his field-glasses.

"I can see," she said, in her confidential way, "well enough for myself with my own eyes."

And Martin looked into the eyes, so vaunted, with much interest.

"I am sure," she said to Wanda, when the race was over, "that I saw Mr. Cartoner a short time ago. Has he gone?"

"I fancy he has," was the reply.

"He did not see us. And we quite forgot to tell him the number of our box. I only hope he was not offended. We saw a great deal of him on board. We crossed the Atlantic in the same ship, you know."

"Indeed!"

"Yes. And one becomes so intimate on a voyage. It is quite ridiculous."

Deulin, leaning against the pillar at the back of the box, was thoughtfully twisting his grizzled mustache as he watched Netty. There was in his attitude some faint suggestion of an engineer who has set a machine in motion and is watching the result with a contemplative satisfaction.

Martin was reluctantly making a move. One or two carriages were allowed to come to the gate of the lawn, and of these one was Prince Bukaty's.

"Come, Wanda," said Martin. "We must not keep him waiting. I can see him, with his two sticks, coming out of the club enclosure."

"I will go with you to make sure that he is none the worse," said Deulin, "and then return to the assistance of these ladies."

He did not speak as they moved slowly through the crowd. Nor did he explain to Wanda why he had reintroduced Miss Cahere. He stood watching the carriages after they had gone.

"The gods forbid," he said, piously, to himself, "that I should attempt to interfere in the projects of Providence! But it is well that Wanda should know who are her friends and who her enemies. And I think she knows now, my shrewd princess."

And he bowed, bareheaded, in response to a gay wave of the hand from Wanda as the carriage turned the corner and disappeared. He turned on his heel, to find himself cut off from the grand-stand by a dense throng of people moving rather confusedly towards the exit. The sky was black, and a shower was impending.

"Ah, well!" he muttered, philosophically, "they are capable of taking care of themselves."

And he joined the throng making for the gates. It appeared, however, that he gave more credit than was merited; for Netty was carried along by a stream of people whose aim was a gate to the left of the great gate, and though she saw the hat of her uncle above the hats of the other men, she could not make her way towards it. Mr. Mangles and his sister passed out of the large gateway, and waited in the first available space beyond it. Netty was carried by the gentle pressure of the crowd to the smaller gate, and having passed it, decided to wait till her uncle, who undoubtedly must have seen her, should come in search of her. She was not uneasy. All through her life she had always found people, especially men, ready, nay, anxious, to be kind to her. She was looking round for Mr. Mangles when a man came towards her. He was only a workman in his best suit of working clothes. He had a narrow, sunburned face, and there was in his whole being a not unpleasant suggestion of the seafaring life.

"I am afraid," he said, in perfect English, as he raised his cap, "that you have lost the rest of your party. You are also in the wrong course, so to speak. We are the commoner people here, you see. Can I help you to find your father?"

"Thank you," answered Netty, without concealing her surprise. "I think my uncle went out of the larger gate, and it seems impossible to get at him. Perhaps—"

"Yes," answered Kosmaroff, "I will show you another way with pleasure. Then that tall gentleman is not your father?"

"No. Mr. Mangles is my uncle," replied Netty, following her companion.

"Ah, that is Mr. Mangles! An American, is he not?"

"Yes. We are Americans."

"A diplomatist?"

"Yes, my uncle is in the service."

"And you are at the Europe. Yes, I have heard of Mr. Mangles. This way; we can pass through this alley and come to the large gate."

"But you—you are not a Pole? It is so kind of you to help me," said Netty, looking at him with some interest. And Kosmaroff, perceiving this interest, slightly changed his manner.

"Ah! you are looking at my clothes," he said, rather less formally. "In Poland things are not always what they seem, mademoiselle. Yes, I am a Pole. I am a boatman, and keep my boat at the foot of Bednarska Street, just above the bridge. If you ever want to go on the river, it is pleasant in the evening, you and your party, you will perhaps do me the great honor of selecting my poor boat, mademoiselle?"

"Yes, I will remember," answered Netty, who did not seem

to notice that his glance was, as it were, less distant than his speech.

"I knew at once—at once," he said, "that you were English or American."

"Ah! Then there is a difference—" said Netty, looking round for her uncle.

"There is a difference—yes, assuredly."

"What is it?" asked Netty, with a subtle tone of expectancy in her voice.

"Your mirror will answer that question," replied Kosmaroff, with his odd, one-sided smile, "more plainly than I should ever dare to do. There is your uncle, mademoiselle, and I must go."

Mr. Mangles, perceiving the situation, was coming forward with his hand in his pocket, when Kosmaroff took off his cap and hurried away.

"No," said Netty, laying her hand on Mr. Mangle's arm, "do not give him anything. He was rather a superior man, and spoke a little English."

XIV

SENTENCED

Like the majority of Englishmen, Cartoner had that fever of the horizon which makes a man desire to get out of a place as soon as he is in it. The average Englishman is not content to see a city; he must walk out of it, through its suburbs and beyond them, just to see how the city lies.

Before he had been long in Warsaw, Cartoner hired a horse and took leisurely rides out of the town in all directions. He found suburbs more or less depressing, and dusty roads innocent of all art, half-paved, growing wider with the lapse of years, as in self-defence the foot-passengers encroached on the fields on either side in search of a cleaner thoroughfare. To the north he found that the great fort which a Russian emperor built for Warsaw's good, and which in case of emergency could batter the city down in a few hours, but could not defend it from any foe whatever. Across the river he rode through Praga, of grimmest memory, into closely cultivated plains. But mostly he rode by the riverbanks, where there are more trees and where the country is less uniform. He rode more often than elsewhere southward by the Vistula, and knew the various roads and paths that led to Wilanow.

Henry Seton Merriman

One evening, when clouds had been gathering all day and the twilight was shorter than usual, he was benighted in the low lands that lie parallel with the Saska Island. He knew his whereabouts, however, and soon struck that long and lonely river-side road, the Czerniakowska, which leads into the manufacturing districts where the sugar-refineries and the iron-foundries are. It was inches deep in dust, and he rode in silence on the silent way. Before him loomed the chimney of the large iron-works, which clang and rattle all day in the ears of the idlers in the Lazienki Park.

Before he reached the high wall that surrounds these works on the land side he got out of the saddle and carefully tried the four shoes of his horse. One of them was loose. He loosened it further, working at it patiently with the handle of his whip. Then he led the horse forward and found that it limped, which seemed to satisfy him. As he walked on, with the bridle over his arm, he consulted his watch. There was just light enough to show him that it was nearly six.

The iron-foundries were quiet now. They had been closed at five. From the distant streets the sound of the traffic came to his ears in a long, low roar, like the breaking of surf upon shingle far away.

Cartoner led his horse to the high double door that gave access to the iron-foundry. He turned the horse very exactly and carefully, so that the animal's shoulder pressed against that half of the door which opened first. Then he rang the bell, of which the chain swung gently in the wind. It gave a solitary clang inside the deserted works. After a few moments there was the sound of rusted bolts being slowly withdrawn, and at the right moment Cartoner touched the horse with his whip, so that it started forward against the door and thrust it open, despite the efforts of the gate-keeper, who staggered back into the dimly lighted yard.

Cartoner looked quickly round him. All was darkness except an open doorway, from which a shaft of light poured out, dimly illuminating cranes and carts and piles of iron girders. The gate-keeper was hurriedly bolting the gate. Cartoner led his horse towards the open door, but before he reached it a number of men ran out and fell on him like hounds upon a fox. He leaped back, abandoning his horse, and striking the first-comer full in the chest with his fist. He charged the next and knocked him over; but from the third he retreated, leaping quickly to one side.

"Bukaty!" he cried; "don't you know me?"

"You, Cartoner!" replied Martin. He spread out his arms, and the men behind him ran against them. He turned and said something to them in Polish, which Cartoner did not catch. "You here!" he said. And there was a ring in the gay, rather light voice, which the Englishman had never heard there before. But he had heard it in other voices, and knew the meaning of it. For his work had brought him into contact with refined men in moments when their refinement only serves to harden that grimmer side of human nature of which half humanity is in happy ignorance, which deals in battle and sudden death.

"It is too risky," said some one, almost in Martin's ear, in Polish, but Cartoner heard it. "We must kill him and be done with it."

There was an odd silence for a moment, only broken by the stealthy feet of the gate-keeper coming forward to join the group. Then Cartoner spoke, quietly and collectedly. His nerve was so steady that he had taken time to reflect as to which tongue to make use of. For all had disadvantages, but silence meant death.

"This near fore-shoe," he said in French, turning to his horse, "is nearly off. It has been loose all the way from Wilanow. This is a foundry, is it not? There must be a hammer and some nails about."

Martin gave a sort of gasp of relief. For a moment he had thought there was no loop-hole.

Cartoner looked towards the door, and the light fell full upon his patient, thoughtful face. The faces of the men standing in a half-circle in front of him were in the dark.

"Good! He's a brave man!" muttered the man who had spoken in Martin's ear. It was Kosmaroff. And he stepped back a pace.

"Yes," said Martin, hastily, "this is a foundry. I can get you a hammer."

His right hand was opening and shutting convulsively. Cartoner glanced at it, and Martin put it behind his back. He was rather breathless, and he was angrily wishing that he had the Englishman's nerve.

"You might tell these men," he said, in French, "of my mishap; perhaps one of them can put it right, and I can get along home. I am desperately hungry. The journey had been so slow from Wilanow."

He had already perceived that Kosmaroff understood both English and French, and that it was of him that Martin was afraid. He spoke slowly, so as to give Martin time to pull himself together. Kosmaroff stepped forward to the horse and examined the shoe indicated. It was nearly off.

Martin turned, and explained in Polish that the gentleman

had come for a hammer and some nails—that his horse had nearly lost a shoe. Cartoner had simply forced him to become his ally, and had even indicated the line of conduct he was to pursue.

"Get a hammer—one of you," said Kosmaroff, over his shoulder, and Martin bit his lip with a sudden desire to speak—to say more than was discreet. He took his cue in some way from Cartoner, without knowing that wise men cease persuading the moment they have gained consent. Never comment on your own victory.

Never had Cartoner's silent habit stood him in such good stead as during the following moments, while a skilled workman replaced the lost shoe. Never had he observed so skilled a silence, or left unsaid such dangerous words. For Kosmaroff watched him as a cat may watch a bird. Behind, were the barred gates, and in front, the semicircle of men, whose faces he could not see, while the full light glared through the open doorway upon his own countenance. Two miles from Warsaw—a dark autumn night, and eleven men to one. He counted them, in a mechanical way, as persons in face of death nearly always do count, with a cold deliberation, their chances of life. He played his miserable little cards with all the skill he possessed, and his knowledge of the racial characteristics of humanity served him. For he acted slowly, and gave his enemies leisure to see that it would be a mistake to kill him. They would see it in time; for they were not Frenchmen, nor of any other Celtic race, who would have killed him first and recognized their mistake afterwards. They were Slavs—of the most calculating race the world had produced—a little slow in their calculations. So he gave them time, just as Russia must have time; but she will reach the summit eventually, when her farsighted policy is fully evolved—long, long after reader and writer are dust.

Cartoner gave the workman half a rouble, which was accepted with a muttered word of thanks, and then he turned towards the great doors, which were barred. There was another pause, while the gate-keeper looked inquiringly at Kosmaroff.

"I am very much obliged to you," said Cartoner to Martin, who went towards the gate as if to draw back the bolt. But at a signal from Kosmaroff the gate-keeper sprang forward and opened the heavy doors.

Martin was nearest, and instinctively held the stirrup, while Cartoner climbed into the saddle.

"Saved your life!" he said, in a whisper.

"I know," answered Cartoner, turning in his saddle to lift his hat to the men grouped behind him. He looked over their heads into the open doorway, but could see nothing. Nevertheless, he knew where were concealed the arms brought out into the North Sea by Captain Cable in the *Minnie*.

"More than I bargained for," he muttered to himself, as he rode away from the iron-foundry by the river. He put his horse to a trot and presently to a canter along the deserted, dusty road. The animal was astonishingly fresh and went off at a good pace, so that the man sent by Kosmaroff to follow him was soon breathless and forced to give up the chase.

Approaching the town, Cartoner rode at a more leisurely pace. That his life had hung on a thread since sunset did not seem to affect him much, and he looked about him with quiet eyes, while the hand on the bridle was steady.

He was, it seemed, one of those fortunate wayfarers who see their road clearly before them, and for whom the barriers of duty and honor, which stand on either side of every man's path, present neither gap nor gate. He had courage and patience, and was content to exercise both, without weighing the changes of reward too carefully. That he read his duty in a different sense to that understood by other men was no doubt only that which this tolerant age calls a matter of temperament.

"That Cartoner," Deulin was in the habit of saying, "takes certain things so seriously, and other things—social things, to which I give most careful attention—he ignores. And yet we often reach the same end by different routes."

Which was quite true. But Deulin reached the end by a happy guess, and that easy exercise of intuition which is the special gift of the Gallic race, while Cartoner worked his way towards his goal with a steady perseverance and slow, sure steps.

"In a moment of danger give me Cartoner," Deulin had once said.

On more than one occasion Cartoner had shown quite clearly, without words, that he understood and appreciated that odd mixture of heroism and frivolity which will always puzzle the world and draw its wondering attention to France. The two men never compared notes, never helped each other, never exchanged the minutest confidence.

Joseph P. Mangles was different. He spoke quite openly of his work.

"Got a job in Russia," he had stolidly told any one who asked him. "Cold, unhealthy place." He seemed to enter upon his duties with the casual interest of the amateur, and, in a way, exactly embodied the attitude of his country towards Europe, of which the many wheels within wheels may spin and whir or halt and grind without in any degree affecting the great republic. America can afford to content herself with the knowledge of what has happened or is happening. Countries nearer to the field of action must know what is going to happen.

Cartoner rode placidly to the stable where he had hired his horse, and delivered the beast to its owner. He had no one in Warsaw to go to and relate his adventures. He was alone, as he had been all his life—alone with his failures and his small successes—content, it would seem, to be a good servant in a great service.

He went to the restaurant of the Hotel de France, which is a quiet place of refreshment close to the Jasna, which has no political importance, like the restaurant of the Europe, and there dined. The square was deserted as he stumbled over the vile pavement towards his rooms. The concierge was sitting at the door of the quiet house where he had taken an apartment. All along the street the dvornik of every house thus takes his station at the half-closed door at nightfall. And it is so all through the town. It is a Russian custom, imported among others into the free kingdom of Poland, when the great empire of the north cast the shadow of its protecting wing over the land that is watered by the Vistula. So, no man may come or go in Warsaw without having his movements carefully noted by one who is directly responsible to the authorities for the good name of the house under his care.

"The poet is in. There is a letter up-stairs," said the door-keeper to Cartoner, as he passed in. Cartoner's servant was out, and the lamps were turned low when he entered his sitting-room. He knew that the letter must be the reply to his application for a recall. He turned up the lamp, and, taking the letter from the table where it lay in a prominent position, sat down in a deep chair to read it at leisure.

It bore no address, and prattled of the crops. Some of it seemed to be nonsense. Cartoner read it slowly and carefully. It was an order, in brief and almost brutal language, to stay where he was and do the work intrusted to him. For a man who writes in a code must perforce avoid verbosity.

XV

A TALE HALF TOLD

The heart soon accustoms itself to that existence which is called living upon a volcano. Prince Bukaty had indeed known no other life, and to such as had daily intercourse with him he was quite a peaceful and jovial gentleman. He had brought up his children in the same atmosphere of strife and peril, and it is to be presumed that the fit had survived, while the unfit princess, his wife, had turned her face to the wall quite soon, not daring to meet the years in which there could be no hope of alleviation.

The prince's friends were not in Warsaw; many were at the mines. Some lived in Paris; others were exiled to distant parts of Russia. His generation was slowly passing away, and its history is one of the grimmest stories untold. Yet he sat in that bare drawing-room of a poor man and read his *Figaro* quite placidly, like any bourgeois in the safety of the suburb, only glancing at the clock from time to time.

"He is late," he said once, as he folded the paper, and that was all.

It was nearly eleven o'clock, and Martin had been expected to return to dinner at half-past six. Wanda was working, and she, too, glanced towards the clock at intervals. She was always uneasy about Martin, whose daring was rather of the reckless type, whose genius lay more in leadership than in strategy. As to her father, he had come through the sixties, and had survived the persecution and the dangers of Wielopolski's day—he could reasonably be expected to take care of himself. With regard to herself, she had no fear. Hers was the woman's lot of watching others in a danger which she could not share.

It was nearly half-past eleven when Martin came in. He was in riding-costume and was covered with dirt. His eyes, rimmed with dust, looked out of a face that was pale beneath the sunburn. He threw himself into a chair with an exclamation of fatigue.

"Had any dinner?" asked his father.

Wanda looked at her brother's face, and changed color herself. There was a suggestion of the wild rose in Wanda's face, with its delicate, fleeting shades of pink and white, while the slim strength of her limbs and carriage rather added to a characteristic which is essentially English or Polish. For American girls suggest a fuller flower on a firmer stem.

"Something has happened," said Wanda, quietly.

"Yes," replied Martin, stretching out his slight legs.

The prince laid aside his newspaper, and looked up quickly. When his attention was thus roused suddenly his eyes and his whole face were momentarily fierce. Some one had once said that the history of Poland was written on those deep-lined features.

"Anything wrong?" he asked.

"Nothing that affects affairs," replied Martin. "Everything is safe."

Which seemed to be catch-words, for Kosmaroff had made use of almost the identical phrases.

"I am quite confident that there is no danger to affairs," continued Martin, speaking with the haste and vehemence of a man who is anxious to convince himself. "It was a mere mischance, but it gave us all a horrid fright, I can tell you—especially me, for I was doubly interested. Cartoner rode into our midst to-night."

"Cartoner?" repeated the prince.

"Yes. He rang the bell, and when the door was opened—we were expecting some one else—he led his horse into our midst, with a loose shoe."

"Who saw him?" asked the prince.

"Every one."

"Kosmaroff?"

"Yes. And if I had not been there it would have been all up with Cartoner. You know what Kosmaroff is. It was a very near thing."

"That would have been a mistake," said the prince, reflectively. "It was the mistake they made last time. It has never paid yet to take life in driblets."

"That is what I told Kosmaroff afterwards, when Cartoner

had gone. It was evident that it could only have been an accident. Cartoner could not have known. To do a thing like that, he must have known all—or nothing."

"He could not have known all," said the prince. "That is an impossibility."

"Then he must have known nothing," put in Wanda, with a laugh, which at one stroke robbed the matter of much of its importance.

"I do not know how much he perceived when he was in—as to his own danger, I mean—for he has an excellent nerve, and was steady; steadier than I was. But he knows that there was something wrong," said Martin, wiping the dust from his face with his pocket-handkerchief. His hand shook a little, as if he had ridden hard, or had been badly frightened. "We had a bad half-hour after he left, especially with Kosmaroff. The man is only half-tamed, that is the truth of it."

"That is more to his own danger than to any one else's," put in Wanda, again. She spoke lightly, and seemed quite determined to make as little of the incident as possible.

"Then how do matters stand?" inquired the prince.

"It comes to this," answered Martin, "that Poland is not big enough to hold both Kosmaroff and Cartoner. Cartoner must go. He must be told to go, or else—"

Wanda had taken up her work again. As she looked at it attentively, the color slowly faded from her face.

"Or else—what?" she inquired.

Martin shrugged his shoulders.

"Well, Kosmaroff is not a man to stick at trifles."

"You mean," said Wanda, who would have things plainly, "that he would assassinate him?"

Wanda glanced at her father. She knew that men hard pressed are no sticklers. She knew the story of the last insurrection, and of the wholesale assassination, abetted and encouraged by the anonymous national government of which the members remain to this day unknown. The prince made an indifferent gesture of the hand.

"We cannot go into those small matters. We are playing a bigger game that that. It has always been agreed that no individual life must be allowed to stand in the way of success."

"It is upon that principle that Kosmaroff argues," said Martin, uneasily.

"Precisely; and as I was not present when this happened—as it is, moreover, not my department—I cannot, personally, act in the matter."

"Kosmaroff will obey nobody else."

"Then warn Cartoner," the prince said, in a final voice. His had always been the final word. He would say to one, go; and to another, come.

"I cannot do it," said Martin, looking at Wanda. "You know my position—how I am watched."

"There is only one person in Warsaw who can do it," said Wanda—"Paul Deulin."

"Deulin could do it," said the prince, thoughtfully. "But I never talk to Deulin of these matters. Politics are a forbidden subject between us."

"Then I will go and see Monsieur Deulin the first thing to-morrow morning," said Wanda, quietly.

"You?" asked her father. And Martin looked at her in silent surprise. The old prince's eyes flashed suddenly.

"Remember," he said, "that you run the risk of making people talk of you. They may talk of us—of Martin and me —the world has talked of the Bukatys for some centuries— but never of their women."

"They will not talk of me," returned Wanda, composedly. "I will see to that. A word to Mr. Cartoner will be enough. I understood him to say that he was not going to stay long in Warsaw."

The prince had acquired the habit of leaving many things to Wanda. He knew that she was wiser than Martin, and in some ways more capable.

"Well," he said, rising. "I take no hand in it. It is very late. Let us go to bed."

He paused half-way towards the door.

"There is one thing," he said, "which we should be wise to recollect—that whatever Cartoner may know or may not know will go no farther. He is a diplomatist. It is his business to know everything and to say nothing."

"Then, by Heaven, he knows his business!" cried Martin, with his reckless laugh.

There are three entrances to the Hotel de l'Europe, two beneath the great archway on the Faubourg, where the carriages pass through into the court-yard—where Hermani was assassinated—where the people carried in the bodies of those historic five, whose mutilated corpses were photographed and hawked all through eastern Europe. The third is a side door, used more generally by habitues of the restaurant. It was to this third door that Wanda drove the next morning. She knew the porter there. He was in those days a man with a history and Wanda was not ignorant of it.

"Miss Cahere—the American lady?" she said. And the porter gave her the number of Netty's room. He was too busy a man to offer to escort her thither.

Wanda mounted the stairs along the huge corridor. She passed Netty's room, and ascended to the second story. All fell out as she had wished. At the head of the second staircase there is a little glass-partitioned room, where the servants sit when they are unemployed. In this room, reading a French newspaper, she found Paul Deulin's servant, a well-trained person. And a well-trained French servant is the best servant in the world. He took it for granted that Wanda had come to see his master, and led the way to the spacious drawing-room occupied by Deulin, who always travelled *en prince*.

"I am given for my expenses more money than I can spend," he said, in defence of his extravagant habits, "and the only people to whom I want to give it are those who will not accept it."

Deulin was not in the room, but he came in almost as soon as Wanda had found a chair. She was looking at a book, and did not catch the flash of surprise in his eyes.

"Did Jean show you in?" he said.

"Yes."

"That is all right. He will keep everybody else out. And he will lie. It would not do, you know, for you to be talked about. We all have enemies, Wanda. Even plain people have enemies."

Wanda waited for him to ask her why she had come.

"Yes," he said, glancing at her and drawing a chair up to the table near which she was sitting. "Yes! What is the matter?"

"An unfortunate incident," answered Wanda, "that is all."

"Good. Life is an unfortunate incident if we come to that. I hope I predicted it. It is so consoling to have predicted misfortune when it comes. Your father?"

"No."

"Martin?"

"No."

"Cartoner," said Deulin, dropping his voice half a dozen tones, and leaning both elbows on the table in a final way, which dispensed with the necessity of reply.

"Allons. What has Cartoner been doing?"

"He has found out something."

"Oh, la! la!" exclaimed Deulin, in a whisper—giving voice to that exclamation which, as the cultured reader knows,

French people reserve for a really serious mishap. "I should have thought he knew better."

"And I cannot tell you what it is."

"And I cannot guess. I never find out things, and know nothing. An ignorant Frenchman, you know, ignores more than any other man."

"It came to Martin's knowledge," explained Wanda, looking at him across the table, with frank eyes. But Deulin did not meet her eyes. "Look a man in the eyes when you tell him a lie," Deulin had once said to Cartoner, "but not a woman."

"It came to Martin's knowledge by chance, and he says that—" Wanda paused, drew in her lips, and looked round the room in an odd, hurried way—"that it is not safe for Mr. Cartoner to remain any longer in Warsaw, or even in Poland. Mr. Cartoner was very kind to us in London. We all like him. Martin cannot, of course, say anything for him. My father won't—"

Deulin was playing a gay little air with his fingers on the table. His touch was staccato, and he appeared to be taking some pride in his execution.

"Years ago," he said, after a pause, "I once took it upon myself to advise Cartoner. He was quite a young man. He listened to my advice with exemplary patience, and then acted in direct contradiction to it—and never explained. He is shockingly bad at explanation. And he was right, and I was wrong."

He finished his gay little air with an imaginary chord, played with both hands.

"Voila!" he said. "I can do nothing, fair princess."

"But surely you will not stand idle and watch a man throw away his life," said Wanda, looking at him in surprise.

He raised his eyes to hers for a moment, and they were startlingly serious. They were dark eyes, beneath gray lashes. The whole man was neat and gray and—shallow, as some thought.

"My dear Wanda," he said, "for forty years and more I have watched men—and women—do worse than throw their lives away. And it has quite ceased to affect my appetite."

Wanda rose from her chair, and Deulin's face changed again. He shot a sidelong glance at her and bit his lip. His eyes were keen enough now.

"Listen!" he said, as he followed her to the door. "I will give him a little hint—the merest ghost of a hint—will that do?"

"Thank you," said Wanda, going more slowly towards the door.

"Though I do not know why we should, any of us, trouble about this Englishman."

Wanda quickened her pace a little, and made no answer.

"There are reasons why I should not accompany you," said Deulin, opening the door. "Try the right-hand staircase, and the other way round."

He closed the door behind her, and stood looking at the chair which Wanda had just vacated.

"Only the third woman who knows what she wants," he said, "and yet I have known thousands—thousands."

XVI

MUCH—OR NOTHING

If we contemplate our neighbour's life with that calm indifference to his good or ill which is the only true philosophy, it will become apparent that the gods amuse themselves with men as children amuse themselves with toys. Most lives are marked by a series of events, a long roll of monotonous years, and perhaps another series of events. In some the monotonous years come first, while others have a long breathing space of quiet remembrance before they go hence and are no more seen.

A child will take a fly and introduce him to the sugar-basin. He will then pull off his wings in order to see what he will do without them. The fly wanders round beneath the sugar-basin, his small mind absorbed in a somewhat justifiable surprise, and then the child loses all interest in him. Thus the gods—with men.

Cartoner was beginning to experience this numb surprise. His life, set down as a series of events, would have made what the world considers good reading nowadays. It would have illustrated to perfection; for it had been full of incidents, and Cartoner had acted in these incidents—as the hero of the serial sensational novel plays his monthly part—

Henry Seton Merriman

with a mechanical energy calling into activity only one-half of his being. He had always known what he wanted, and had usually accomplished his desires with the subtraction of that discount which is necessary to the accomplishment of all human wishes. The gods had not helped him; but they had left him alone, which is quite as good, and often better. And in human aid this applies as well, which that domestic goddess, the managing female of the family, would do well to remember.

The gods had hitherto not been interested in Cartoner, and, like the fly on the nursery window that has escaped notice, he had been allowed to crawl about and make his own small life, with the result that he had never found the sugar-basin and had retained his wings. But now, without apparent reason, that which is called fate had suddenly accorded him that gracious and inconsequent attention which has forever decided the sex of this arbiter of human story.

Cartoner still knew what he wanted, and avoided the common error of wanting too much. For the present he was content with the desire to avoid the Princess Wanda Bukaty. And this he was not allowed to do. Two days after the meeting at the Mokotow—the morning following the visit paid by Wanda to the Hotel de l'Europe—Cartoner was early astir. He drove to the railway station in time to catch the half-past eight train, and knowing the ways of the country, he took care to arrive at ten minutes past eight. He took his ticket amid a crowd of peasants—wild-looking men in long coats and high boots, rough women in gay shades of red, in short skirts and top-boots, like their husbands.

This was not a fashionable train, nor a through train to one of the capitals. A religious fete at a village some miles out of Warsaw attracted the devout from all parts, and the devout are usually the humble in Roman Catholic countries.

Railways are still conducted in some parts of Europe on the prison system, and Cartoner, glancing into the third-class waiting room, saw that it was thronged. The second-class room was a little emptier, and beyond it the sacred green-tinted shades of the first-class waiting-room promised solitude. He went in alone. There was one person in the bare room, who rose as he came in. It was Wanda. The gods were kind—or cruel.

"You are going away?" she said, in a voice so unguardedly glad that Cartoner looked at her in surprise. "You have seen Monsieur Deulin, and you are going away."

"No, I have not seen Deulin since the races. He came to my rooms yesterday, but I was out. My rooms are watched, and he did not come again."

"We are all watched," said Wanda, with a short and careless laugh. "But you are going away—that is all that matters."

"I am not going away. I am only going across the frontier, and shall be back this afternoon."

Wanda turned and looked towards the door. They were alone in the room, which was a vast one. If there were any other first-class passengers, they were waiting the arrival of the train from Lemberg in the restaurant, which is the more usual way of gaining access to the platform. She probably guessed that he was going across the frontier to post a letter.

"You must leave Warsaw," she said; "it is not safe for you to stay here. You have by accident acquired some knowledge which renders it imperative for you to go away. Your life, you understand, is in danger."

She kept her eyes on the door as she spoke. The ticket-collector on duty at the entrance of the two waiting-rooms was a long way off, and could not hear them even if he understood English, which was improbable. There were so many other languages at this meeting-place of East and West which it was essential for him to comprehend. The room was absolutely bare; not so much as a dog could be concealed in it. It these two had anything to say to each other this was assuredly the moment, and this bare railway station the place to say it in.

Cartoner did not laugh at the mention of danger, or shrug his shoulders. He was too familiar with it, perhaps, to accord it this conventional salutation.

"Martin would have warned you," she went on, "but he did not dare to. Besides, he thought that you knew something of the danger into which you had unwittingly run."

"Not unwittingly," said Cartoner, and Wanda turned to look at him. He said so little that his meaning needed careful search.

"I cannot tell you much—" she began, and he interrupted her at once.

"Stop," he said, "you must tell me nothing. It was not unwitting. I am here for a purpose. I am here to learn everything—but not from you."

"Martin hinted at that," said Wanda, slowly, "but I did not believe him."

And she looked at Cartoner with a sort of wonder in her eyes. It was as if there were more in him—more of him— than she had ever expected. And he returned her glance with a simplicity and directness which were baffling enough. He looked down at her. He was taller than she, which was as it should be. For half the trouble of this troubled world comes from the fact that, for one reason or another, women are not always able to look up to the men with whom they have dealings.

"It is true enough," he said, "fate has made us enemies, princess."

"You said that even the Czar could not do that. And he is stronger than fate—in Poland. Besides—"

"Yes."

"You, who say so little, were indiscreet enough to confide something in your enemy. You told me you had written for your recall."

And again her eyes brightened, with an anticipating gleam of relief.

"It has been refused."

"But you must go—you must go!" she said, quickly. She glanced at the great clock upon the wall. She had only ten minutes in which to make him understand. He was an eminently sensible person. There were gleams of gray in his closely cut hair.

"You must not think that we are alarmists. If there is any family in the world who knows what it is to live peaceably, happily—quite gayly—" she broke off with a light laugh, "on a volcano—it is the Bukatys. We have all been brought up to it. Martin and I looked out of our nursery window on April 8, 1861, and saw what was done on that day. My father was in the streets. And ever since we have been accustomed to unsettled times."

"I know," said Cartoner, "what it is to be a Bukaty." And he smiled slowly as she looked at him with gray, fearless eyes. Then suddenly her manner, in a flash, was different.

"Then you will go?" she pleaded, softly, persuasively. And when he turned away his eyes from hers, as if he did not care to meet them, she glanced again, hurriedly, at the clock. There is a cunning bred of hatred, and there is another cunning, much deeper. "Say you will go!"

And, sternly economical of words, he shook his head.

"I do not think you understand," she went on, changing her manner and her ground again. And to each attack he could only oppose his own stolid, dumb form of defence. "You do not understand what a danger to us your presence here is. It is needless to tell you all this," with a gesture she indicated the well-ordered railway station, the hundred marks of a high state of civilization, "is skin deep. That things in Poland are not at all what they seem. And, of course, we are implicated. We live from day to day in uncertainty. And my father is such an old man; he has had such a hopeless struggle all his life. You have only to look at his face—"

"I know," admitted Cartoner.

"It would be very hard if anything should happen to him now, after he has gone through so much. And Martin, who is so young in mind, and so happy and reckless! He would be such an easy prey for a political foe. That is why I ask you to go."

"Yes, I know," answered Cartoner, who, like many people reputed clever, was quite a simple person.

"Besides," said Wanda, with that logic which men, not having the wit to follow it, call no logic at all, "you can do no good here, if all your care and attention are required for the preservation of your life. Why have they refused your recall? It is so stupid."

"I must do the best I can," replied Cartoner.

Wanda shrugged her shoulders impatiently, and tapped her foot on the ground. Then suddenly her manner changed again.

"But we must not quarrel," she said, gently. "We must not misunderstand each other," she added, with a quick and uneasy laugh, "for we have only five minutes in all the world."

"Here and now," he corrected, with a glance at the clock, "we have only five minutes. But the world is large."

"For you," she said quickly, "but not for me. My world is Warsaw. You forget I am a Russian subject."

But he had not forgotten it, as she could see by the sudden hardening of his face.

"My presence in Warsaw," he said, as if the train of thought needed no elucidating, "is in reality no source of danger to you—to your father and brother, I mean. Indeed, I might be of some use. I or Deulin. Do not misunderstand my position. I am of no political importance. I am nobody—nothing but a sort of machine that has to report upon events that are past. It is not my business to prevent events or to make history. I merely record. If I choose to be prepared for that which may come to pass, that is merely my method of preparing my report. If nothing happens I report nothing. I have not to say what might have happened—life is too short to record that. So you see my being in Warsaw is really of no danger to your father and brother."

"Yes, I see—I see!" answered Wanda. She had only three minutes now. The door giving access to the platform had long been thrown open. The guard, in his fine military uniform and shining top-boots, was strutting the length of the train. "But it was not on account of that that we asked Monsieur Deulin to warn you. It does not matter about my father and Martin. It is required of them—a sort of family tradition. It is their business in life—almost their pleasure."

"It is my business in life—almost my pleasure," said Cartoner, with a smile.

"But is there no one at home—in England—that you ought to think of?" in an odd, sharp voice.

"Nobody," he replied, in one word, for he was chary with information respecting himself.

Wanda had walked towards the platform. Immediately opposite to her stood a carriage with the door thrown open. In those days there were no corridor carriages. Two minutes now.

"We must not be seen together on the platform," she said. "I am only going to the next station. We have a small farm there, and some old servants whom I go to see."

She stood within the open doorway, and seemed to wait for him to speak.

"Thank you," he said, "for warning me."

And that was all.

"You must go," he added, after a moment's pause.

Still she lingered.

"There is so much to say," she said, half to herself. "There is so much to say."

The train was moving when Cartoner stepped into a carriage at the back. He was alone, and he leaned back with a look of thoughtful wonder in his eyes, as if he were questioning whether she were right—whether there was much to say—or nothing.

XVII

IN THE SENATORSKA

"It is," said Miss Julie Mangles, "in the Franciszkanska that one lays one's hand on the true heart of the people."

"That's as may be, Jooly," replied her brother, "but I take it that the hearts of the women go to the Senatorska."

For Miss Mangles, on the advice of a polyglot concierge, had walked down the length of that silent street, the Franciszkanska, where the Jews ply their mysterious trades and where every shutter is painted with bright images of the wares sold within the house. The street is a picture-gallery of the human requirements. The chosen people hurry to and fro with curved backs and patient, suffering faces that bear the mark of eighteen hundred years of persecution. No Christian would assuredly be a Jew; and no Jew would be a Polish Jew if he could possibly help it. For a Polish Jew must not leave the country, may not even quit his native town, unless it suits a paternal government that he should go elsewhere. He has no personal liberty, and may not exercise a choice as to the clothes that he shall wear.

"I shall," said Miss Mangles, "write a paper on the Jewish question in this country."

And Joseph changed the position of his cigar from the left-hand to the right-hand corner of his mouth, very dexterously from within, with his tongue. He saw no reason why Jooly should not write a paper on the Semitic question in Russia, and read it to a greedy multitude in a town-hall, provided that the town-hall was sufficiently far West.

"Seen the Senatorska, Netty?" he inquired. But Netty had not seen the Senatorska, and did not know how to find it.

"Go out into the Faubourg," her uncle explained, "and just turn to the left and follow all the other women. It is the street where the shops are."

Two days later, when Miss Julie Mangles was writing her paper, Netty set out to find the Senatorska. Miss Mangles was just putting down—as the paper itself recorded—the hot impressions of the moment, gathered after a walk down the Street of the Accursed. For they like their impressions served hot out West, and this is a generation that prefers vividness to accuracy.

Netty found the street quite easily. It was a sunny morning, and many shoppers were abroad. In a degree she followed her uncle's instructions, and instinct did the rest. For the Senatorska is not an easy street to find. The entrance to it is narrow and unpromising, like either end of Bond Street.

The Senatorska does not approach Bond Street or the Rue de la Paix, and Netty, who knew those thoroughfares, seemed to find little to interest her in the street where Stanislaus Augustus Poniatowski—that weak dreamer—built his great opera-house and cultivated the ballet. The shops are, indeed, not worthy of a close attention, and Netty was passing them indifferently enough when suddenly she became absorbed in the wares of a silver-worker. Then she turned, with a little cry of surprise, to find a gentleman standing hatless beside her. It was the Prince Martin Bukaty.

"I was afraid you did not remember me," said Martin. "You looked straight at me, and did not seem to recognize me."

"Did I? I am so short-sighted, you know. I had not forgotten you. Why should I?"

And Netty glanced at Martin in her little, gentle, appealing way, and then looked elsewhere rather hastily.

"Oh, you travellers must see so many people you cannot be expected to remember every one who is introduced to you at a race-meeting."

"Of course," said Netty, looking into the silversmith's shop. "One meets a great number of people, but not many that one likes. Do you not find it so?"

"I am glad," answered Martin, "that you do not meet many people that you like."

"Oh, but you must not think that I dislike people," urged Netty, in some concern; "I should be very ungrateful if I did. Everybody is so kind. Do you not find it so? I hate people to be cynical. There is much more kindness in the world than anybody suspects. Do you not think so?"

"I do not know. It has not come my way, perhaps. It naturally would come in yours."

And Martin looked down at her beneath the pink shade of her parasol with that kindness in his eyes of which Netty had had so large a share.

"Oh no!" she protested, with a little movement of the shoulders descriptive of a shrinking humility. "Why should I? I have done nothing to deserve it. And yet, perhaps you are right. Everybody is so kind—my uncle and aunt—everybody. I am very fortunate, I am sure. I wonder why it is?"

And she looked up inquiringly into Martin's face as if he could tell her, and, indeed, he looked remarkably as if he could—if he dared. He had never met anybody quite like Netty—so spontaneous and innocent and easy to get on with. Conversation with her was so interesting and yet so little trouble. She asked a hundred questions which were quite easy to answer; and were not stupid little questions about the weather, but had a human interest in them, especially when she looked up like that from under her parasol, and there was a pink glow on her face, and her eyes were dark, almost as violets.

"Ought I to be here?" she asked. "Going about the streets alone, I mean?"

"You are not alone," answered Martin, with a laugh.

"No, but—perhaps I ought to be."

And Martin, looking down, saw nothing but the top of the pink parasol.

"In America, you know," said the voice from under the parasol, "girls are allowed to do so much more than in Europe. And it is always best to be careful, is it not?—to follow the customs of the country, I mean. In France and Germany people are so particular. I wanted to ask you what is the custom in Warsaw."

Martin stepped to one side in order to avoid the parasol.

"In Warsaw you can do as you like. We are not French, and Heaven forbid that we should resemble the Germans in anything. Here every one goes about the streets as they do in England or America."

As if to confirm this, he walked on slowly, and she walked by his side.

"I can show you the best shops," he said, "such as they are. This is Ulrich's, the flower shop. Those violets are Russian. The only good thing I ever heard of that came from Russia. Do you like violets?"

"I love them," answered Netty, and she walked on rather hurriedly to the next shop.

"You would naturally."

"Why?" asked Netty, looking with a curious interest at the packets of tea in the Russian shop next to Ulrich's.

"Is it not the correct thing to select the flower that matches the eyes?"

"It is very kind of you to say that," said Netty, in a voice half-afraid, half-reproachful.

"It is very kind of Heaven to give you such eyes," answered Martin, gayly. He was more and more surprised to find how easy it was to get on with Netty, whom he seemed to have known all his life. Like many lively persons, he rather liked a companion to possess a vein of gravity, and this Netty seemed to have. He was sure that she was religious and very good.

"You know," said Netty, hastily, and ignoring his remark, "I am much interested in Poland. It is such a romantic country. People have done such great things, have they not, in Poland? I mean the nobles—and the poor peasants, too in their small way, I suppose?"

"The nobles have come to great grief in Poland—that is all," replied Martin, with a short laugh.

"And it is so sad," said Netty, with a shake of the head; "but I am sure it will all come right some day. Do you think so? I am sure you are interested in Poland—you and your sister and your father."

"We are supposed to be," admitted Martin. "But no one cares for Poland now, I am afraid. The rest of the world has other things to think of, and, in England and America, Poland is forgotten now—and her history, which is the saddest history of any nation in the world."

"But I am sure you are wrong there," said Netty, earnestly. "I know a great number of people who are sorry for the Poles and interested in them."

"Are you?" asked Martin, looking down at her.

"Yes," she replied, with downcast eyes. "Come," she said, after a pause, with a sort of effort, "we must not stand in front of this shop any longer."

"Especially," he said, with a laugh, as he followed her, "as it is a Russian shop. Wherever you see tea and articles of religion mixed up in a window, that is a Russian shop, and if you sympathize with Poland you will not go into it. There are, on the other hand, plenty of shops in Warsaw where they will not serve Russians. It is to those shops that you must go."

Netty looked at him doubtfully.

"I am quite serious," he said. "We must fight with what weapons we have."

"Yes," she answered, indicating the shops, "these people, but not you. You are a prince, and they cannot touch you. They would not dare to take anything from you."

"Because there is nothing to take," laughed Martin, gayly; "we were ruined long ago. They took everything there was to take in 1830, when my father was a boy. He could not work for his living, and I may not either; so I am a prince without a halfpenny to call his own."

"I am so sorry!" she said, in a soft voice, and, indeed, she looked it.

Then she caught sight of Paul Deulin a long way off, despite her short sight, which was perhaps spasmodic, as short sight often is. She stopped, and half turned, as if to dismiss Martin. When Deulin perceived them he was standing in the middle of the pavement, as if they had just met. He came up with a bow to Netty and his hand stretched out to Martin—his left hand, which conveyed the fact that he was an old and familiar friend.

"I suppose you are on your way back to the Europe to lunch?" he said to Netty. "I am in luck. I have come just in time to walk back with you, if you will permit it."

And he did not wait for permission, but walked on beside Netty, while Martin took off his hat and went in the opposite direction. It was not the way he wanted to go but something had made him think that Netty desired him to go, and he departed with a pleasant sensation as of a secret possessed in common with her. He walked back quickly to the flower-shop kept by Ulrich, in the Senatorska.

A rare thing happened to Paul Deulin at this moment. He fell into a train of thought, and walked some distance by the side of Netty without speaking. It was against his principles altogether. "Never be silent with a woman," he often said. "She will only misconstrue it."

"It was odd that I should meet you at that moment," he said, at length, for Netty had not attempted to break the silence. She never took the initiative with Paul Deulin, but followed quite humbly and submissively the conversational lead which he might choose to give. He broke off and laughed. "I was going to say that it was odd that I should have met you at a moment that I was thinking of you; but it would be odder still if I could manage to meet you at a moment when I was not thinking of you, would it not?"

"It was very kind of you," said Netty, "to think of me at the race-meeting the other day, and to introduce me to the Bukatys. I am so interested in the princess. She is so pretty, is she not? Such lovely hair, and I think her face is so interesting—a face with a history, is it not?"

"Yes," answered Deulin, rather shortly, "Wanda is a nice girl." He did not seem to find the subject pleasing, and Netty changed her ground.

"And the prince," she said, "the old one, I mean—for this one, Prince Martin, is quite a boy, is he not?"

"Oh yes—quite a boy," replied Deulin, absently, as he looked back over his shoulder and saw Martin hurry into the flower-shop where he had first perceived Netty and the young prince talking together.

"It is so sad that they are ruined—if they are really ruined."

"There is no doubt whatever about that," answered Deulin.

"But," said Netty, who was practical, "could nothing induce him—the young prince, I mean—to abandon all these vague political dreams and accept the situation as it is, and settle down to develop his estates and recover his position?"

"You mean," said Deulin, "the domestic felicities. Your fine and sympathetic heart would naturally think of that. You go about the world like an unemployed and wandering angel, seeking to make the lives of others happier. Those are dreams, and in Poland dreams are forbidden—by the Czar. But they are the privilege of youth, and I like to catch an occasional glimpse of your gentle dreams, my dear young lady."

Netty smiled a little pathetically, and glanced up at him beneath her lashes, which were dark as lashes should be that veil violet eyes.

"Now you are laughing at me, because I am not clever," she said.

"Heaven forbid! But I am laughing at your dream for Martin Bukaty. He will never come to what you suggest as the cure for his unsatisfactory life. He has too much history behind him, which is a state of things never quite understood in your country, mademoiselle. Moreover, he has not got it in him. He is not stable enough for the domestic felicities, and Siberia—his certain destination—is not a good mise-en-scene for your dream. No, you must not hope to do good to your fellow-beings here, though it is natural that you should seek the ever-evasive remedy—another privilege of youth."

"You talk as if you were so very old," said Netty, reproachfully.

"I am very, very old," he replied, with a laugh. "And there is no remedy for that. Even your kind heart can supply no cure for old age."

"I reserve my charity and my cures for really deserving cases," answered Netty, lightly. "I think you are quite capable of taking care of yourself."

"And of evolving my own dreams?" he inquired. But she made no answer, and did not appear to notice the glance of his tired, dark eyes.

"I know so little," she said, after a pause, "so very little of Poland or Polish history. I suppose you know everything— you and Mr. Cartoner?"

"Oh, Cartoner! Yes, he knows a great deal. He is a regular magazine of knowledge, while I—I am only a little stall in Vanity Fair, with everything displayed to the best advantage in the sunshine. Now, there is a life for you to exercise your charity upon. He is brilliantly successful, and yet there is something wanting in his life. Can you not prescribe for him?"

Netty smiled gravely.

"I hardly know him sufficiently well," she said. "Besides, he requires no sympathy if it is true that he is the heir to a baronetcy and a fortune."

Deulin's eyebrows went up into his hat, and he made, for his own satisfaction, a little grimace of surprise.

"Ah! is that so?" he inquired. "Who told you that?"

But Netty could not remember where she had heard what she was ready to believe was a mere piece of gossip. Neither did she appear to be very interested in the matter.

XVIII

JOSEPH'S STORY

Mr. Mangles gave a dinner-party the same evening. "It is well," he had said, "to show the nations that the great powers are in perfect harmony." He made this remark to Deulin and Cartoner, whom he met at the Cukiernia Lourse—a large confectioner's shop and tea-house in the Cracow Faubourg—which is the principal cafe in Warsaw. And he then and there had arranged that they should dine with him.

"I always accept the good Mangles' invitations. Firstly, I am in love with Miss Cahere. Secondly, Julie P. Mangles amuses me consumedly. In her presence I am dumb. My breath is taken away. I have nothing to say. But afterwards, in the night, I wake up and laugh into my pillow. It takes years off one's life," said Deulin, confidentially, to Cartoner, as they sipped their tea when Mr. Joseph P. Mangles had departed.

As Deulin was staying under the same roof he had only to descend from the second to the first floor, when the clock struck seven. By some chance he was dressed in good time, and being an idle person, with a Gallic love of street-life, he drew back his curtain, and stood at the window waiting for the clock to strike.

"I shall perhaps see the heir to the baronetcy arrive," he said to himself, "and we can make our entry together."

It happened that he did see Cartoner; for the square below the windows was well lighted. He saw Cartoner turn out of the Cracow Faubourg into the square, where innumerable droskies stand. He saw, moreover, a man arrive at the corner immediately afterwards, as if he had been following Cartoner, and, standing there, watch him pass into the side door of the hotel.

Deulin reflected for a moment. Then he went into his bedroom, and took his coat and hat and stick. He hurried down-stairs with them, and gave them into the care of the porter at the side door, whose business it is to take charge of the effects of the numerous diners in the restaurant. When he entered the Mangles' drawing-room a few minutes later he found the party assembled there. Netty was dressed in white, with some violets at her waistband. She was listening to her aunt and Cartoner, who were talking together, and Deulin found himself relegated to the society of the hospitable Joseph at the other end of the room.

"You're looking at Cartoner as if he owed you money," said Mr. Mangles, bluntly.

"I was looking at him with suspicion," admitted Deulin, "but not on that account. No one owes me money. It is the other way round, and it is not I who need to be anxious, but the other party, you understand. No, I was looking at our friend because I thought he was lively. Did he strike you as lively when he came in?"

"Not what I should call a vivacious man," said Mangles, looking dismally across the room. "There was a sort of ripple on his serene calm as he came in perhaps."

"Yes," said Deulin, in a low voice. "That is bad. There is usually something wrong when Cartoner is lively. He is making an effort, you know."

They went towards the others, Deulin leading the way.

"What beautiful violets," said he to Netty. "Surely Warsaw did not produce those?"

"Yes, they are pretty," answered Netty, making a little movement to show the flowers to greater advantage to Deulin and to Cartoner also. Her waist was very round and slender. "They came from that shop in the Senatorska or the Wirzbowa, I forget, quite, which street. Ulrich, I think, was the name."

And she apparently desired to let the subject drop there.

"Yes," said Deulin, slowly. "Ulrich is the name. And you are fond of violets?"

"I love them."

Deulin was making a silent, mental note of the harmless taste, when dinner was announced.

"It was I who recommended Netty to investigate the Senatorska," said Mr. Mangles, when they were seated. But Netty did not wish to be made the subject of the conversation any longer. She was telling Cartoner, who sat next to her, a gay little story, connected with some piece of steamer gossip known only to himself and her. Is it not an accepted theory that quiet men like best those girls who are lively?

Miss Mangles dispensed her brother's hospitality with that rather labored ease of manner to which superior women are liable at such times as they are pleased to desire their inferiors to feel comfortable, and to enjoy themselves according to their lights.

Deulin perceived the situation at once, and sought information respecting Poland, which was most graciously accorded him.

"And you have actually walked through the Jewish quarter?" he said, noting, with the tail of his eye, that Cartoner was absent-minded.

"I entered the Franciszkanska near the old church of St. John, and traversed the whole length of the street."

"And you formed an opinion upon the Semitic question in this country?" asked the Frenchman, earnestly.

"I have."

And Deulin turned to his salmon, while Miss Mangles swept away in a few chosen phrases the difficulties that have puzzled statesmen for fifteen hundred years.

"I shall read a paper upon it at one of our historical Women's Congress meetings—and I may publish," she said.

"It would be in the interests of humanity," murmured Deulin, politely. "It would add to the... wisdom of the nations."

Across the table Netty was doing her best to make her uncle's guest happy, seeking to please him in a thousand ways, which need not be described.

"I know," she was saying at that moment, in not too loud a voice, "that you dislike political women." Heaven knows how she knew it. "But I am afraid I must confess to taking a great interest in Poland. Not the sort of interest you would dislike, I hope. But a personal interest in the people. I think I have never met people with quite the same qualities."

"Their chief quality is gameness," said Cartoner, thoughtfully.

"Yes, and that is just what appeals to English and Americans. I think the princess is delightful—do you not think so?"

"Yes," answered Cartoner, looking straight in front of him.

"There must be a great many stories," went on Netty, "connected with the story of the nation, which it would be so interesting to know—of people's lives, I mean—of all they have attempted and have failed to do."

Joseph was listening at his end of the table, with a kindly smile on his lined face. He had, perhaps, a soft place in that cynical and dry heart for his niece, and liked to hear her simple talk. Cartoner was listening, with a greater attention than the words deserved. He was weighing them with a greater nicety than experienced social experts are in the habit of exercising over dinner-table talk. And Deulin was talking hard, as usual, and listening at the same time; which is not by any means an easy thing to do.

"I always think," continued Netty, "that the princess has a story. There must, I mean, be some one at the mines or in Siberia, or somewhere terrible like that, of whom she is always thinking."

And Netty's eyes were quite soft with a tender sympathy, as she glanced at Cartoner.

"Perhaps," put in Deulin, hastily, between two of Julie's solemn utterances. "Perhaps she is thinking of her brother—Prince Martin. He is always getting into scrapes—ce jeune homme."

But Netty shook her head. She did not mean that sort of thought at all.

"It is your romantic heart," said Deulin, "that makes you see so much that perhaps does not exist."

"If you want a story," put in Joseph Mangles, suddenly, in his deep voice, "I can tell you one."

And because Joseph rarely spoke, he was accorded a silence.

"Waiter's a Finn, and says he doesn't understand English?" began Mangles, looking interrogatively at Deulin, beneath his great eyebrows.

"Which I believe to be the truth," assented the Frenchman.

"Cartoner and Deulin probably know the story," continued Joseph, "but they won't admit that they do. There was once a nobleman in this city who was like Netty; he had a romantic heart. Dreamed that this country could be made a great country again, as it was in the past—dreamed that the peasants could be educated, could be civilized, could be turned into human beings. Dreamed that when Russia undertook that Poland should be an independent kingdom with a Polish governor, and a Polish Parliament, she would keep her word. Dreamed that when the powers, headed by France and England, promised to see that Russia kept to the terms of the treaty, they would do it. Dreamed that somebody out of all that crew, would keep his word. Comes from having a romantic heart."

And he looked at Netty with his fierce smile, as if to warn her against this danger.

"My country," he went on, "didn't take a hand in that deal. Bit out of breath and dizzy, as a young man would be that had had to fight his own father and whip him."

And he bobbed his head apologetically towards Cartoner, as representing the other side in that great misunderstanding.

"Ever heard the Polish hymn?" he asked, abruptly. He was not a good story-teller perhaps. And while slowly cutting his beef across and across, in a forlorn hope that it might, perchance, not give him dyspepsia this time, he recited in a sing-song monotone:

"'O Lord, who, for so many centuries, didst surround Poland with the magnificence of power and glory; who didst cover her with the shield of Thy protection when our armies overcame the enemy; at Thy altar we raise our prayer: deign to restore us, O Lord, our free country!'"

He paused, and looked slowly round the table.

"Jooly—pass the mustard," he said.

Then, having helped himself, he lapsed into the monotone again, with a sort of earnest unction that had surely crossed the seas with those Pilgrim Fathers who set sail in quest of liberty.

"'Give back to our Poland her ancient splendor! Look upon fields soaked with blood! When shall peace and happiness blossom among us? God of wrath, cease to punish us! At Thy altar we raise our prayer: deign to restore us, O Lord, our free country!'"

And there was an odd silence, while Joseph P. Mangles ate sparingly of the beef.

"That is the first verse, and the last," he said at length. "And all Poland was shouting them when this man dreamed his dreams. They are forbidden now, and if that waiter's a liar, I'll end my days in Siberia. They sang it in the churches, and the secret police put a chalk mark on the backs of those that sang the loudest, and they were arrested when they came out—women and children, old men and maidens."

Miss Julie P. Mangles made a little movement, as if she had something to say, as if to catch, as it were, the eye of an imaginary chairman, but for once this great speaker was relegated to silence by universal acclaim. For no one seemed to want to hear her. She glanced rather impatiently at her brother, who was always surprising her by knowing more than she had given him credit for, and by interesting her, despite herself.

"The dreamer was arrested," he continued, pushing away his plate, "on some trivial excuse. He was not dangerous, but he might be. There was no warrant and no trial. The Czar had been graciously pleased to give his own personal attention to this matter which dispensed with all formalities and futilities... of justice. Siberia! Wife with great difficulty obtained permission to follow. They were young—last of the family. Better that they should be the last—thought the paternal government of Russia. But she had influential relatives—so she went. She found him working in the mines. She had taken the precaution of bringing doctor's certificates. Work in the mines would inevitably kill him. Could he not obtain in-door work? He petitioned to be made the body-servant of the governor of his district—man who had risen from the ranks—and was refused. So he went to the mines again—and died. The wife had in her turn been arrested for attempting to aid a prisoner to escape. Then the worst happened—she had a son, in prison, and all the care and forethought of the paternal government went for nothing. The pestilential race was not extinct, after all. The ancestors of that prison brat had been kings of Poland. But the paternal government was not beaten yet. They took the child from his mother, and she fretted and died. He had nobody now to care for him, or even to know who he was, but his foster-father— that great and parental government."

Joseph paused, and looked round the table with a humorous twinkle in his eyes.

"Nice story," he said, "isn't it? So the brat was mixed up with other brats so effectually that no one knew which was which. He grew up in Siberia, and was drafted into a Cossack regiment. And at last the race was extinct; for no one knew. No one, except the recording angel, who is a bit of a genealogist, I guess. Sins of the fathers, you know. Some-body must keep account of 'em."

The dessert was on the table now; for the story had taken longer in the telling than the reading of it would require.

"Cartoner, help Netty to some grapes," said the host, "and take some yourself. Story cannot interest you—must be ancient history. Well—after all, it was with the recording angel that the Russian government slipped up. For the recording angel gave the prison brat a face that was historical. And if I get to Heaven, I hope to have a word with that humorist. For an angel, he's uncommon playful. And the brat met another private in the Cossack regiment who recognized the face, and told him who he was. And the best of it is that the government has weeded out the dangerous growth so carefully that there are not half a dozen people in Poland, and none in Russia, who would recognize that face if they saw it now."

Joseph poured out a glass of wine, which he drank with outstretched chin and dogged eyes.

"Man's loose in Poland now," he added.

And that was the end of the story.

XIX

THE HIGH-WATER MARK

Netty did not smoke. She confessed to being rather an old-fashioned person. Which is usually accounted to her for righteousness by men, who, so far as women are concerned, are intensely conservative—such men, at all events, whose opinion it is worth a woman's while to value.

Miss Mangles, on the other hand, made a point of smoking a cigarette from time to time in public. There were two reasons. The ostensible reason, which she gave freely when asked for it, and even without the asking—namely, that she was not going to allow men to claim the monopoly of tobacco. There was the other reason, which prompts so many actions in these blatant times—the unconscious reason that, in going counter to ancient prejudices respecting her sex, she showed contempt for men, and meted out a bitter punishment to the entire race for having consistently and steadily displayed a complete indifference to herself.

Miss Mangles announced her intention of smoking a cigarette this evening, upon which Netty rose and said that if they were not long over their tobacco they would find her in the drawing-room.

Henry Seton Merriman

The Mangles' salon was separated from the dining-room by Joseph's apartment—a simple apartment in no way made beautiful by his Spartan articles of dress and toilet. The drawing-room was at the end of the passage, and there was a gas-jet at each corner of the corridor. Netty went to the drawing-room, but stopped short on the threshold. Contrary to custom, the room was dark. The old-fashioned chandelier in the centre of the large, bare apartment glittered in the light of the gas-jet in the passage. Netty knew that there were matches on the square china stove opposite to the door, which stood open. She crossed the room, and as she did so the door behind her, which was on graduated hinges, swung to. She was in the dark, but she knew where the stove was.

Suddenly her heart leaped to her throat. There was some one in the room. The soft and surreptitious footstep of a person making his way cautiously to the door was unmistakable. Netty tried to speak—to ask who was there. But her voice failed. She had read of such a failure in books, but it had never been her lot to try to speak and to find herself dumb until now.

Instinctively she turned and faced the mysterious and terrifying sound. Then her courage came quite suddenly to her again. Like many diminutive persons, she was naturally brave. She moved towards the door, her small slippers and soft dress making no sound. As the fugitive touched the door-handle she stretched out her hand and grasped a rough sleeve. Instantly there was a struggle, and Netty fought in the dark with some one infinitely stronger and heavier than herself. That it was a man she knew by the scent of tobacco and of rough working-clothes. She had one hand on the handle, and in a moment turned it and threw open the door. The light from without flooded the room, and the man leaped back.

It was Kosmaroff. His eyes were wild; he was breathless. For a moment he was not a civilized man at all. Then he made an effort, clinched his hands, and bit his lips. His whole demeanor changed.

"You, mademoiselle!" he said, in broken English. "Then Heaven is kind—Heaven is kind!"

In a moment he was at her feet, holding her two hands, and pressing first one and then the other to his lips. He was wildly agitated, and Netty was conscious that his agitation in some way reached her. In all her life she had never known what it was to be really carried away until that moment. She had never felt anything like it—had never seen a man like this—at her feet. She dragged at her hands, but could not free them.

"I came," he said—and all the while he had one eye on the passage to see that no one approached—"to see you, because I could not stay away! You think I am a poor man. That is as may be. But a poor man can love as well as a rich man—and perhaps better!"

"You must go! you must go!" said Netty. And yet she would have been sorry if he had gone. The worst of reaching the high-water mark is that the ebb must necessarily be dreary. In a flash of thought she recollected Joseph Mangles' story. This was the sequel. Strange if he had heard his own story through the door of communication between Mangles' bedroom and the dining-room. For the other door, from the salon to the bedroom, stood wide open.

"You think I have only seen you once," said Kosmaroff. "I have not. I have seen you often. But the first time I saw you—at the races—was enough. I loved you then. I shall love you all my life!"

"You must go—you must go!" whispered Netty, dragging at her hands.

"I won't unless you promise to come to the Saski Gardens now—for five minutes. I only ask five minutes. It is quite safe. There are many passing in and out of the large door. No one will notice you. The streets are full. I made an excuse to come in. A man I know was coming to these rooms with a parcel for you. I took the parcel. See, there is the tradesman's box. I brought it. It will take me out safely. But I won't go till you promise. Promise, mademoiselle!"

"Yes!" whispered Netty, hurriedly. "I will come!"

Firstly, she was frightened. The others might come at any moment. Secondly—it is to be feared—she wanted to go. It was the high-water mark. This man carried her there and swept her off her feet—this working-man, in his rough clothes, whose ancestor had been a king.

"Go and get a cloak," he said. "I will meet you by the great fountain."

And Netty ran along the corridor to her room, her eyes alight, her heart beating as it had never beaten before.

Kosmaroff watched her for a moment with that strange smile that twisted his mouth to one side. Then he struck a match and turned to the chandelier. The globe was still warm. He had turned out the gas when Netty's hand was actually on the handle.

"It was a near thing," he said to himself in Russian, which language he had learned before any other, so that he still thought in it. "And I found the only way out of that hideous danger."

As he thus reflected he was putting together hastily the contents of Joseph Mangles's writing-case, which were spread all over the table in confusion. Then he hurried into the bedroom, closed one or two drawers which he had left open, put the despatch-case where he had found it, and, with a few deft touches, set the apartment in order. A moment later he lounged out at the great doorway, dangling the tradesman's box on his arm.

It was a fine moonlight night, and the gardens were peopled by shadows moving hither and thither beneath the trees. The shadows were mostly in couples. Others had come on the same errand as Kosmaroff—for a better motive, perhaps, or a worse. It was the very end of St. Martin's brief summer, and when winter lays its quiet mantle on these northern plains lovers must needs seek their opportunities in-doors.

Kosmaroff arrived first, and sat down thoughtfully on a bench. He was one of the few who were not muffled in great-coats and wraps against the autumn chill. He had known a greater cold than Poland ever felt.

"I suppose she will come," he said in his mind, watching the gate through which Netty must enter the gardens. "It matters little if she does not. For I do not know what I shall say when she does come. Must leave that to the inspiration of the moment—and the moonlight. She is pretty enough to make it easy."

In a few moments Netty passed through the gate and came towards him—not hurriedly or furtively, as some maiden in a book to her first clandestine meeting—but with her head thrown back, and with an air of having business to transact, which was infinitely safer and less likely to attract the attention of the idle. It was she who spoke first.

"I am going back at once," she said. "It was very wrong to come. But you frightened me so. Was it very wrong? Do you think it was wrong of me to come, and despise me for it?"

"You promised," he whispered, eagerly; "you promised me five minutes. Out of a whole lifetime, what is it? For I am going away from Warsaw soon, and I shall never see you again perhaps, and shall have only the memory of these five minutes to last me all my life—these five minutes and that minute—that one minute in the hotel."

And he took her hand, which was quite near to him, somehow, on the stone bench, and raised it to his lips.

"We are going away, too," she said. She was thinking also of that one minute in the doorway of the salon, when she had touched high-water mark. "We are on our way to St. Petersburg, and are only waiting here till my uncle has finished some business affairs on which he is engaged."

"But he is not a business man," said Kosmaroff, suddenly interested. "What is he doing here?"

"I do not know. He never talks to me of his affairs. I never know whether he is travelling for pleasure, or on account of his business in America, or for political purposes. He never explains. I only know that we are going on to St. Petersburg."

"And I shall not see you again. What am I to do all my life without seeing you? And the others—Monsieur Deulin and that Englishman, Cartoner—are they going to St. Petersburg, too?"

"I do not know," answered Netty, hastily withdrawing her hand, because a solitary promenader was passing close by them. "They never tell me either. But…"

"But what! Tell me all you know, because it will enable me, perhaps, to see you again in the distance. Ah! if you knew! If you could only see into my heart!"

And he took her hand again in the masterful way that thrilled her, and waited for her to answer.

"Mr. Cartoner will not go away from Warsaw if he can help it."

"Ah!" said Kosmaroff. "Why—tell me why?"

But Netty shook her head. They were getting into a side issue assuredly, and she had not come here to stray into side issues. With that skill which came no doubt with the inspiration of the moment in which Kosmaroff trusted he got back into the straight path again at one bound—the sloping, pleasant path in which any fool may wander and any wise man lose himself.

"It is for you that he stays here," he said. "What a fool I was not to see that! How could he know you, and be near you, and not love you?"

"I think he has found it quite easy to do it," answered Netty, with an odd laugh. "No, it is not I who keep him in Warsaw, but somebody who is clever and beautiful."

"There is no one more beautiful than you in Warsaw."

And for a moment Netty was silenced by she knew not what.

"You say that to please me," she said at last. And her voice was quite different—it was low and uneven.

Henry Seton Merriman

"I say it because it is the truth. There is no one more beautiful than you in all the world. Heaven knows it."

And he looked up with flashing black eyes to that heaven in which he had no faith.

"But who is there in Warsaw," he asked, "whom any one could dream of comparing with you?"

"I have no doubt there are hundreds. But there is one whom Mr. Cartoner compares with me—and even you must know that she is prettier than I am."

"I do not know it," protested Kosmaroff, again taking her hand. "There is no one in all the world."

"There is the Princess Wanda Bukaty," said Netty, curtly.

"Ah! Does Cartoner admire her? Do they know each other? Yes, I remember I saw them together at the races."

"They knew each other in London," said Netty. "They knew each other when I first saw them together at Lady Orlay's there. And they have often met here since."

Kosmaroff seemed to be hardly listening. He was staring in front of him, his eyes narrow with thought and suspicion. He seemed to have forgotten Netty and his love for her as suddenly as he had remembered it in the salon a few minutes earlier.

"Is it that he has fallen in love—or is it that he desires information which she alone can give him?" he asked at length. Which was, after all, the most natural thought that could come to him at that moment and in that place. For every man must see the world through his own eyes.

Before she could answer him the town clocks struck ten. Netty rose hastily and drew her cloak round her.

"I must go," she said; "I have been here much more than five minutes. Why did you let me stay? Oh—why did you make me come?"

And she hurried towards the gate, Kosmaroff walking by her side.

"You will come again," he said. "Now that you have come once—you cannot be so cruel. Now that you know. I am nearly always at the river, at the foot of the Bednarska. You might walk past, and say a word in passing. You might even come in my boat. Bring that woman with the black hair, your aunt, if necessary. If would be safer, perhaps. Do you speak French?"

"Yes—and she does not."

"Good—then we can talk. I must not go beyond the gate. Good-bye—and remember that I love you—always, always!"

He stood at the gate and watched her hurry across the square towards the side door of the hotel, where the concierge was so busy that he could scarcely keep a note of all who passed in and out.

"It is all fair—all fair," said Kosmaroff to himself, seeking to convince himself. "Besides—has the world been fair to me?"

Which argument has made the worst men that walk the earth.

XX

A LIGHT TOUCH

Soon after ten o'clock Miss Mangles received a message that Netty, having a headache, had gone to her room. Miss Cahere had never given way to that weakness, which is, or was, euphoniously called the emotions. She was not old-fashioned in that respect.

But to-night, on regaining her room, she was conscious, for the first time in her life, of a sort of moral shakiness. She felt as if she might do or say something imprudent. And she had never felt like that before. No one in the world could say that she had ever been imprudent. That which the lenient may call a school-girl escapade—a mere flight to the garden for a few minutes—was scarcely sufficient to account for this feeling. She must be unwell, she thought. And she decided, with some wisdom, not to submit herself to the scrutiny of Paul Deulin again.

Mr. Mangles had not finished his excellent cigar; and although Miss Mangles did not feel disposed for another of those long, innocent-looking Russian cigarettes offered by Deulin, she had still some views of value to be pressed upon the notice of the inferior sex.

Deulin had been glancing at the clock for some time, and, suspiciously soon after learning that they were not to see Netty again, he announced with regret that he had letters to write, and must take his leave. Cartoner made no excuse, but departed at the same time.

"I will come down to the door with you," said Deulin, in the passage. He was always idle, and always had leisure to follow his sociable instincts.

At the side door, while Cartoner was putting on his coat, he stepped rather suddenly out into the street, and before Cartoner had found his hat was back again.

"It is a moonlight night," he said. "I will walk with you part of the way."

He turned, as he spoke, towards his coat and hat and stick, which were hanging near to where Cartoner had found his own. He did not seem to think it necessary to ask the usual formal permission. They knew each other too well for that. Cartoner helped the Frenchman on with his thin, light overcoat, and reaching out his hand took the stick from the rack, weighing and turning it thoughtfully in his hand.

"That is the Madrid Stick," said the Frenchman. "You were with me when I bought it."

"And when you used it," added Cartoner, in his quietest tone, as he led the way to the door. "Generally keep your coat in the hall?" he inquired, casually, as they descended the steps.

"Sometimes," replied Deulin, glancing at the questioner sideways beneath the brim of his hat.

It was, as he had said, a beautiful night. The moon was

almost full and almost overhead, so that the streets were in most instances without shadow at all; for they nearly all run north and south, as does the river.

"Yes," said Deulin, taking Cartoner's arm, and leading him to the right instead of the left; for Cartoner was going towards the Cracow Faubourg, which was the simplest but not the shortest way to the Jasna. "Yes—let us go by the quiet streets, eh? We have walked the pavement of some queer towns in our day, you and I. The typical Englishman, so dense, so silent, so unobservant—who sees nothing and knows nothing and never laughs, but is himself the laughing-stock of all the Latin races and the piece de resistance of their comic papers. And I, at your service, the typical Frenchman; all shrugs and gesticulations and mustache—of politeness that is so insincere—of a heart that is so unstable. Ah! these national characteristics of comic journalism—how the stupid world trips over them on to its vulgar face!"

As he spoke he was hurrying Cartoner along, ever quicker and quicker, with a haste that must have been unconscious, as it certainly was unnatural to one who found a thousand trifles to interest him in the streets whenever he walked there.

Cartoner made no answer, and his companion expected none. They were in a narrow street now—between the backs of high houses—and had left the life and traffic of frequented thoroughfares behind them. Deulin turned once and looked over his shoulder. They were alone in the street. He released Cartoner's arm, through which he had slipped his left hand in an effusive French way. He was fingering his stick with his right hand in an odd manner, and walked with his head half turned, as if listening for footsteps behind him. Suddenly he swung round on his heels, facing the direction from which they had just come.

Two men were racing up the street, making but little noise on the pavement.

"Any coming from the other side?" asked Deulin.

"No."

"In the doorway," whispered the Frenchman. He was very quick and quite steady. And there is nothing more dangerous on earth than a steady Frenchman, who fights with his brain as well as his arm. Deulin was pushing his companion back with his left hand into a shallow doorway that had the air of being little used. The long blade of his sword-stick, no thicker at the hilt than the blade of a sailor's sheath-knife, and narrowing to nothing at the point, glittered in the moonlight.

"Here," he said, and thrust the empty stick into Cartoner's hand. "But you need not use it. There are only two. Ah! Ah!"

With a sharp little cry of delight he stepped out into the moonlight, and so quick were his movements in the next moments that the eye could scarcely follow them. Those who have seen a panther in liberty know there is nothing so graceful, so quick, so lithe and noiseless in animal life. And Deulin was like a panther at that moment. He leaped across the pavement to give one man a stinging switch across the cheek with the flat of the blade, and was back on guard in front of Cartoner like a flash. He ran right round the two men, who stood bewildered together, and did not know where to look for him. Once he lifted his foot and planted a kick in the small of his adversary's back, sending him staggering against the wall. He laughed, and gave little, sharp cries of "Ah!" and "La!" breathlessly. He did a hundred tricks of the fencing-floor—performed a dozen turns and sleights of hand. It was a marvel of agility and quickness. He struck both men on shoulder, arm, hand, head, and leg; forward, back-handed, from above and below. He never awaited their attack—but attacked them. Was it not Napoleon who said that the surest way to defend is to attack?

The wonder was that, wielding so keen a point, he never hurt the men. The sword might have been a lady's riding-whip, for its bloodlessness, from the stinging cuts he inflicted. But the whistle of it through the air was not the whistle of leather. It was the high, clear, terrifying note of steel.

The two men, in confusion, backed across the road, and finally ran to the opposite pavement, where they were half hidden by a deep shadow. Without turning, Deulin backed towards Cartoner, who stood still in the doorway.

"Even if they are armed," said Deulin, "they won't fire. They don't want the police any more than we do. Can tell you, Cartoner, it would not suit my book at all to get into trouble in Warsaw now."

While he spoke he watched the shadows across the road.

"Both have knives," he said, "but they cannot get near me. Stay where you are."

"All right," said Cartoner. "Haven't had a chance yet."

And he gave a low laugh, which Deulin had only heard once or twice before in all the years that they had known each other.

"That's the best," he said, half to himself, "of dealing with a man who keeps his head. Here they come, Cartoner—here they come."

And he went out to meet them.

But only one came forward. They knew that unless they kept together, Deulin could not hold them both in check. The very fact of their returning to the attack—thus, with a cold-blooded courage—showed that they were Poles. In an instant Deulin divined their intention. He ran forward, his blade held out in front of him. Even at this moment he could not lay aside the little flourish—the quick, stiff pose—of the fencer.

His sword made a dozen turns in the air, and the point of it came down lightly, like a butterfly, on the man's shoulder. He lowered it further, as if seeking a particular spot, and then, deliberately, he pushed it in as if into a cheese.

"Voila, mon ami," he said, with a sort of condescension as if he had made him a present. As, indeed, he had. He had given him his life.

The man leaped back with a little yelp of pain, and his knife clattered on the stones. He stood in the moonlight, looking with horror-struck eyes at his own hand, of which the fingers, like tendrils, were slowly curling up, and he had no control over them.

"And now," said Deulin, in Polish, "for you."

He turned to the other, who had been moving surreptitiously round towards Cartoner, who had, indeed, come out to meet him; but the man turned and ran, followed closely by his companion.

Deulin picked up the knife, which lay gleaming on the cobble-stones, and came towards Cartoner with it. Then he turned aside, and carefully dropped it between the bars of the street gutter, where it fell with a muddy splash.

Henry Seton Merriman

"He will never use that hand again," he said. "Poor devil! I only hope he was well paid for it."

"Doubt it."

Deulin was feeling in the pocket of his top-coat.

"Have you an old envelope?" he inquired.

Cartoner handed him what he asked for. It happened to be the envelope of the letter he had received a few days earlier, denying him his recall. And Deulin carefully wiped the blade of the sword-stick with it. He tore it into pieces and sent it after the knife. Then he polished the bright steel with his pocket-handkerchief, from the evil point to the hilt, where the government mark and the word "Toledo" were deeply engraved.

"Unless I keep it clean it sticks," he explained. "And if you want it at all, you want it in a hurry—like a woman's heart, eh?"

He was looking up and down the street as he spoke, and shot the blade back into its sheath. He turned and examined the ground to make sure that nothing was left there.

"The light was good," he said, appreciatively, "and the ground favorable for—for the autumn manoeuvres."

And he broke into a gay laugh.

"Come," he said. "Let us go back into the more frequented streets. This back way was not a success—only proves that it never does to turn tail."

"How did you know," asked Cartoner, "that this was coming off?"

"Quite simple, my friend. I was at the window when you arrived at the Europe. You were followed. Or, at all events, I thought you were followed. So I made up my mind to walk back with you and see. Veni, vidi, vici—you understand?"

And again his clear laugh broke the silence of that back street, while he made a pass at an imaginary foe with his stick.

"I thought we might escape by the quieter streets," he went on. "For it is our business to seek peace and ensure it. But it was not to be. Neither could I warn you, because we have never interfered in each other's business, you and I. That is why we have continued, through many chances and changes, to be friends."

They walked on in silence for a few moments. Then Cartoner spoke, saying that which he was bound to say in his half-audible voice.

"It was like you, to come like that and take the risk," he said, "and say nothing."

But Deulin stopped him with a quick touch on his arm.

"As to that," he said, "silence, my friend. Wait. Thank me, if you will, five years hence—ten years hence—when the time comes. I will tell you then why I did it."

"There can only be one reason why you did it," muttered the Englishman.

"Can there? Ah! my good Cartoner, you are a fool—the very best sort of fool—and yet, in the matter of intellect, you are as superior to me as I am superior to you... in swordsmanship."

And he made another pass into thin air with his stick.

"I should like to fight some one to-night," he said. "Some one of the very first order. I feel in the vein. I could do great things to-night—and the angels in heaven are talking of me."

In his light-hearted way he bared his head and looked up to the sky. But there was a deeper ring in his voice. It almost seemed as if he were sincere.

As he stood there, bareheaded, with his coat open and his shirt gleaming in the moonlight, a carriage rattled past, and stopped immediately behind them. The door was opened from within, and the only occupant, alighting quickly, came towards them.

"There is only one man in Warsaw who would apostrophize the gods like that," he said. The speaker was Prince Martin Bukaty.

He recognized Cartoner at this moment.

"You!" he said, and there was a sharp note in his voice. "You, Cartoner! What are you doing in the streets at this time of night?"

"We have been dining with Mangles," explained Deulin.

"And we do not quite know what we are doing, or where we are going," added Cartoner. "But we think we are going home."

"You seem to be on the spree," said Martin, with a laugh in his voice, and none in his eyes.

"We are," answered Deulin.

"Come," said Martin, turning to send away the carriage. "Come—your shortest way is through our place now. My father and Wanda are out at a ball, or something, so I am afraid you will not see them."

"Do it," whispered Deulin's voice from behind.

And Cartoner followed Martin up the narrow passage that led to the garden of the Bukaty Palace.

XXI

A CLEAR UNDERSTANDING

Martin led the way without speaking. He opened the door with a key, and passed through first. The garden was dark; for the trees in it had grown to a great height, and, protected as they were from the wild winds that sweep across the central plain of Europe, they had not shed their leaves.

A few lights twinkled through the branches from the direction of the house, and the shape of the large conservatory was dimly outlined, as though there were blinds within, partially covering the glass.

"Yes," said Martin, carefully closing the door behind him. "You find me in sole possession. My father and sister have gone to a reception—a semi-political affair at which they are compelled to put in an appearance. It only began at half-past nine. They will not be home till midnight. Mind those branches, Cartoner! You will come in, of course."

And he hurried on again to open the next door.

"Thank you, for a few minutes," answered Deulin, and seeing a movement of dissent on Cartoner's part, he laid his hand on his arm.

"It is better," he said, in an undertone. "It will put them completely off the scent. There are sure to be more than two in it."

So, reluctantly, Cartoner followed Martin into the Bukaty Palace for the first time.

"Come," said the young prince, "into the drawing-room. I see they have left the lights on there."

He pushed open the door of the long, bare room, and stood aside to allow his guests to pass.

"Holloa!" he exclaimed, an instant later, following them into the room.

At the far end of it, where two large folding-doors opened to the conservatory, half turning to see who came, stood Wanda. She had some flowers in her hand, which she had just taken from her dress.

"Back again already?" asked Martin, in surprise.

"Yes," answered Wanda. "There were some people there he did not want to meet, so we came away again at once."

"But I thought they could not possibly be there."

"They got there," answered Wanda, "by some ill chance, from Petersburg, just in time."

And as she spoke she shook hands with Cartoner.

"It is not such an ill chance, after all," said Deulin, "since it gives us the opportunity of seeing you. Where is your father?"

"He is in his study."

"I rather want to see him," said Deulin, looking at Martin.

"Come along, then," was the answer. "He will be glad to see you. It will cheer him up."

And Wanda and Cartoner were left alone. It had all come about quickly and simply—so much quicker and simpler than human plans are the plans of Heaven.

Wanda, still standing in the doorway of the conservatory, of which the warm, scented air swept out past her into the great room, watched her brother and Deulin go and close the door behind them. She turned to Cartoner with a smile as if about to speak; but she saw his face, and she said nothing, and her own slowly grew grave.

He came towards her, upright and still and thoughtful. She did not look at him, but past him towards the closed door. He only looked at her with quiet, remembering eyes. Then he went straight to the point, as was his habit.

"I was wrong," he said, "when I said that fate could be hampered by action. Nothing can hamper it. For fate has brought me here again."

He stood before her, and the attitude in some way conveyed that by the word "here" he only thought and meant near to her. There was a strange look in her eyes of suspense and fear, and something else which needs no telling to such as have seen it, and cannot be conveyed in words to those who have not.

"A clear understanding," he said abruptly, recalling her own words. "That is your creed."

She gave a little nod, and still looked past him towards the door with deep, submissive eyes. One would have thought that she had done something wrong which was being brought home to her. Explain the thought, who can!

"I made another mistake," he said. "Have been acting on it for years. I thought that a career was everything. I dreamed, I suppose, of an embassy—of a viceroyalty, perhaps—when I was quite young, and thought the world was easy to conquer. All that... vanished when I saw you. If it comes, well and good. I should like it. Not for my own sake."

She made a little movement, and her eyelids flickered. Ah! that clear understanding, which poor humanity cannot put into words!

"If it doesn't come"—he paused, and snapped the finger and thumb that hung quiescent at his side—"well and good. I shall have lived. I shall have known what life is meant to be. I shall have been the happiest man in the world."

He spoke slowly in his gently abrupt way. Practice in a difficult profession had taught him to weigh every word he uttered. He had never been known to say more than he meant.

"There never has been anybody else," he continued. "All that side of life was quite blank. The world was empty until you came and filled it, at Lady Orlay's that afternoon. I had come half round the world—you had come across Europe. And fate had fixed that I should meet you there. At first I did not believe. I thought it was a mistake—that we should drift apart again. Then came my orders to leave for Warsaw. I knew then that you would inevitably return. Still I tried to get out of it—fought against it—tried to avoid you. And you knew what it all came to."

She nodded again, and still did not meet his eyes. She had not spoken to him since he entered the room.

"There never can be anybody else," he said. "How could there be?"

And the abrupt laugh that followed the question made her catch her breath. She had, then, the knowledge given to so few, that so far as this one fellow-creature was concerned she was the whole earth—that he was thrusting upon her the greatest responsibility that the soul can carry. For to love is as difficult as it is rare, but to be worthy of love is infinitely harder.

"I knew from the first," he continued, "that there is no hope. Whichever way we turn there is no hope. I can spare you the task of telling me that."

She turned her eyes to his at last.

"You knew?" she asked, speaking for the first time.

"I know the history of Poland," he said, quietly. "The country must have your father—your father needs you. I could not ask you to give up Poland—you know that."

They stood in silence for a few moments. They had had so little time together that they must needs have learned to understand each other in absence. The friendship that grows in absence and the love that comes to life between two people who are apart, are the love and friendship which raise men to such heights as human nature is permitted to attain.

"If you asked me," said Wanda, at length, with an illegible smile—"I should do it."

"And if I asked you I should not love you. If you loved me, you would one day cease to do so; for you would remember what I had asked you. There would be a sort of flaw, and you would discover it—and that would be the end."

"Is it so delicate as that?" she asked.

"It is the frailest thing in the world—and the strongest," he answered, with his thoughtful smile. "It is a very delicate sort of—thought, which is given to two people to take care of. And they never seem to succeed in keeping it even passably intact—and not one couple in a million carry it through life unhurt. And the injuries never come from the outer world, but from themselves."

"Where did you learn all that?" she asked, looking at him with her shrewd, smiling eyes.

"You taught me."

"But you have a terribly high ideal."

"Yes."

"Are you sure you do not expect the impossible?"

"Quite."

She shook her head doubtfully.

"Are you sure you will never have to compromise? All the world compromises."

"With its conscience," said Cartoner. "And look at the result."

"Then you are good," she returned, looking at him with a speculative gravity, "as well as concise—and rather masterful."

"It is clear," he said, "that a man who persuades a woman to marry against her inclination, or her conviction, or her conscience, is seeking her unhappiness and his own."

"Ah!" she cried. "But you ask for a great deal."

"I ask for love."

"And," she said, going past that question, "no obstacles."

"No obstacles that both could not conscientiously face and set aside."

"And if one such object—quite a small one—should be found?"

"Then they must be content with love alone."

Wanda turned from him, and fell into thought for some moments. They seemed to be feeling their way forward on that difficult road where so many hasten and such numbers fall.

"You have a way," she said, "of putting into words—so few words—what others only half think, and do not half attempt to act up to. If they did—there would, perhaps, be no marriages."

"There would be no unhappy ones," said Cartoner.

"And it is better to be content with love alone?"

"Content," was his sole answer.

Again she thought in silence for quite a long time, although their moments were so few. A clock on the mantel-piece struck half-past ten. Cartoner had bidden Joseph P. Mangles good-night only half an hour earlier, and his life had been in peril—he had been down to the depths and up to the heights since then. When the gods arrive they act quickly.

"So that is your creed," she said at length. "And there is no compromise?"

"None," he answered.

And she smiled suddenly at the monosyllable reply. She had had to deal with men of no compromise more than the majority of villa-dwelling women have the opportunity of doing, and she knew, perhaps, that such are the backbone of human nature.

"Ah!" she said, with a quick sigh, as she turned and looked down the length of the long, lamp-lit room. "You are strong—you are strong for two."

He shook his head in negation, for he knew that hers was that fine, steely strength of women which endures a strain all through a lifetime of which the world knows nothing. Then, acting up to her own creed of seeking always the clear understanding, she returned to the point they had left untouched.

"And if two people had between them," she suggested, wonderingly, "that with which you say they might be content, if they had it, and were sure they had it, and had with it a perfect trust in each other, but knew that they could never have more, could they be happy?"

"They could be happier than nearly everybody else in the world," he answered.

"And if they had to go on all their lives—and if one lived in London and the other in Warsaw—Warsaw?"

"They could still be happy."

"If she—alone at one end of Europe—" asked Wanda, with her worldly-wise searching into detail—"if she saw slowly vanishing those small attractions which belong to youth, for which he might care, perhaps?"

"She could still be happy."

"And he? If he experienced a check in his career, or had some misfortune, and felt lonely and disappointed—and there was no one near to—to take care of him?"

"He could still be happy—if—"

"If—?"

"If he knew that she loved him," replied Cartoner, slowly.

Wanda turned and looked at him with an odd little laugh, and there were tears in her eyes.

"Oh! you may know that," she said, suddenly descending from the uncertain heights of generality. "You may be quite sure of that. If that is what you want."

"That is what I want."

As he spoke he took her hand and slowly raised it to his lips. She looked at his bent head, and when her eyes rested on the gray hairs at his temples, they lighted suddenly with a gleam which was strangely protecting and dimly maternal.

"I want you to go away from Warsaw," she said. "I would rather you went even if you say—that you are afraid to stay."

"I cannot say that."

"Besides," she added, with her head held high, "they would not believe you if you did."

"I promise you," he answered, "not to run any risks, to take every care. But we must not see each other. I may have to go away without seeing you."

She gave a little nod of comprehension, and held her lips between her teeth. She was looking towards the door; for she had heard voices in that direction.

"I should like," she said, "to make you a promise in return. It would give me great satisfaction. Some day you may, perhaps, be glad to remember it."

The voices were approaching. It was Deulin's voice, and he seemed to be speaking unnecessarily loud.

"I promise you," said Wanda, with unfathomable eyes, "never to marry anybody else."

And the door opened, giving admittance to Deulin, who was laughing and talking. He came forward looking, not at Wanda and Cartoner, but at the clock.

"To your tents, O Israel!" he said.

Cartoner said good-night at once, and went to the door. For a moment Deulin was left alone with Wanda. He went to a side-table, where he had laid his sword-stick. He took it up, and slowly turned it in his hand.

"Wanda," he said, "remember me in your prayers to-night!"

XXII

THE WHITE FEATHER

It is to be presumed that the majority of people are willing enough to seek the happiness of others; which desire leads the individual to interfere in her neighbor's affairs, while it burdens society with a thousand associations for the welfare of mankind or the raising of the masses.

Looking at the question from the strictly commonsense point of view, it would appear to the observer that those who do the most good or the least harm are the uncharitable. Better than the eager, verbose man is he who stands on the shore cynically watching a landsman in a boat without proffering advice as to how the vessel should be navigated, who only holds out a cold and steady hand after the catastrophe has happened, or, if no catastrophe supervenes, is content to walk away in that silent wonder which the care of Providence for the improvident must ever evoke.

Paul Deulin was considered by his friends to be a cynic; and a French cynic is not without cruelty. He once told Wanda that he had seen men and women do much worse than throw their lives away, which was probably the unvarnished truth. But there must have been a weak spot in his cynicism. There always is a weak spot in the vice of the most vicious. For he

Henry Seton Merriman

sat alone in his room at the Hotel de l'Europe, at Warsaw, long into the night, smoking cigarette after cigarette, and thinking thoughts which he would at any other juncture have been the first to condemn. He was thinking of the affairs of others, and into his thoughts there came, moreover, the affairs, not of individuals, but of nations. A fellow-countryman once gave it as his opinion that so long as the trains ran punctually and meals were served at regular intervals he could perceive no difference between one form of government and another. And in the majority of instances the fate of nations rarely affects the lives of individuals.

Deulin, however, was suddenly made aware of his own ignorance of affairs that were progressing in his immediate vicinity, and which were affecting the lives of those around him. More than any other do Frenchmen herd together in exile, and Deulin knew all his fellow-countrymen and women in Warsaw, in whatsoever station of life they happened to move. He had a friend behind the counter of the small feather-cleaning shop in the Jerozolimska. This lady was a French Jewess, who had by some undercurrent of Judaism drifted from Paris to Warsaw again and found herself once more among her own people. The western world is ignorant of the strength of Jewry in Poland.

Deulin made a transparent excuse for his visit to the cleaner's shop. He took with him two or three pairs of those lavender gloves which Englishmen have happily ceased to wear by day.

"One likes," he said to the stout Jewess, "to talk one's own tongue in a foreign land."

And he sat down quite affably on the hither side of the counter. Conversation ran smoothly enough between these two, and an hour slipped past before Deulin quitted the little shop. It was still early in the day, and he hurried to Cartoner's rooms in the Jasna. He bought a flower at the corner of the Jerozolimska as he went along, and placed it in his buttonhole. He wore his soft felt hat at a gay angle, and walked the pavement at a pace and with an air belonging to a younger generation.

"Ah!" he cried, at the sight of Cartoner, pipe in mouth, at his writing-table. "Ah! if you were only idle, as I am"—he paused, with a sharp, little sigh—"if you only could be idle, how much happier you would be!"

"A Frenchman," replied Cartoner, without looking up, "thinks that noise means happiness."

"Then you are happy—you pretend to happiness?" inquired Deulin, sitting down without being invited to do so, and drawing towards him a cigarette-case that lay upon the table.

"Yes, thank you," replied Cartoner, lightly. He seemed, too, to be gay this morning.

"Don't thank me—thank the gods," replied Deulin, with a sudden gravity.

"Well," said Cartoner presently, without ceasing to write, "what do you want?"

Deulin glanced at his friend with a gleam of suspicion.

"What do I want?" he inquired, innocently.

"Yes. You want something. I always know when you want something. When you are most idle you are most occupied."

"Ah!"

Cartoner wrote on while Deulin lighted a cigarette and smoked half of it with a leisurely enjoyment of its bouquet.

"There is a certain smell in the Rue Royale, left-hand side looking towards the Column—the shady side, after the street has been watered—that my soul desires," said the Frenchman, at length.

"When are you going?" asked Cartoner, softly.

"I am not going; I wish I were. I thought I was last night. I thought I had done my work here, and that it would be unnecessary to wait on indefinitely for—"

"For what?"

"For the upheaval," explained Deulin, with an airy wave of his cigarette.

"This morning—" he began. And then he waited for Cartoner to lay aside his pen and lean back in his chair with the air of thoughtful attention which he seemed to wear towards that world in which he moved and had his being. Cartoner did exactly what was expected of him.

"This morning I picked up a scrap of information." He drew towards him a newspaper, and with a pencil made a little drawing on the margin. The design was made in three strokes. It was not unlike a Greek cross, Deulin threw the paper across the table.

"You know that man?"

"I do not know his name," replied Cartoner.

"No; no one knows that," replied Deulin. "It is one of the

very few mysteries of the nineteenth century. All the others are cleared up."

Cartoner made no answer. He sat looking at the design, thinking, perhaps, with wonder of the man who in this notoriety-loving age was still content to be known only by a mark.

"Up to the present I have not attached much importance to those rumors which, happily, have never reached the newspaper," said Deulin, after a pause. "One has supposed that, as usual, Poland is ready for an upheaval. But the upheaval does not come. That has been the status quo for many years here. Suppose—suppose, my friend, that they manufacture their own opportunity, or agree with some other body of malcontents as to the creating of an opportunity."

"Anarchy?" inquired Cartoner.

"The ladies of the party call it Nihilism," replied the Frenchman, with an inimitable gesture, conveying the fact that he was not the man to gainsay a lady.

"Bukaty would not stoop to that. Remember they are a patient people. They waited thirty years."

"And struck too hastily, after all," commented Deulin. "Bukaty would not link himself with these others, who talk so much and do so little. But there are others besides Bukaty, who are younger, and can afford to wait longer, and are therefore less patient—men of a more modern stamp, without his educational advantages, who are nevertheless sincere enough in their way. It may not be a gentlemanly way—"

"The man who goes by the name of Kosmaroff is a gentleman, according to his lights," interrupted Cartoner.

"Ah! since you say so," returned Deulin, with a significant gesture, "yes."

"Bon sang," said Cartoner, and did not trouble to complete the saying. "He is too much of a gentleman to herd with the extremists."

But Deulin did not seem to be listening. He was following his own train of thought.

"So you know of Kosmaroff?" he said, studying his companion's face. "You know that, too. What a lot you know behind that dull physiognomy. Where is Kosmaroff? Perhaps you know that."

"In Warsaw," guessed Cartoner.

"Wrong. He has gone towards Berlin—towards London, by the same token."

Deulin leaned across the table and tapped the symbol that he had drawn on the margin of the newspaper, daintily, with his finger-nail.

"That parishioner is in London, too," he said, in his own tongue—and the word means more in French.

Cartoner slowly tore the margin from the newspaper and reduced the drawing to small pieces. Then he glanced at the clock.

"Trying to get me out of Warsaw," he said. "Giving me a graceful chance of showing the white feather."

Deulin smiled. He had seen the glance, and he was quicker than most at guessing that which might be passing in another man's mind. The force of habit is so strong that few even think of a train without noting the time of day at the same moment. If Cartoner was thinking of a train at that instant, it could only be the train to Berlin on the heels of Kosmaroff, and Deulin desired to get Cartoner away from Warsaw.

"The white feather," he said, "is an emblem that neither you nor I need trouble our minds about. Don't get narrow-minded, Cartoner. It is a national fault, remember. For an Englishman, you used to be singularly independent of the opinion of the man in the street or the woman at the tea-table. Afraid! What does it matter who thinks we are afraid?"

And he gave a sudden staccato laugh which had a subtle ring in it of envy, or of that heaviness which is of a life that is waxing old.

"Look here," he said, after a pause, and he made a little diagram on the table, "here is a bonfire, all dry and crack-ling—here, in Warsaw. Here—in Berlin or in London—is the man with the match that will set it alight. You and I have happened on a great event, and stand in the shadow that it casts before it, for the second—no, for the third time in our lives. We work together again, I suppose. We have always done so when it was possible. One must watch the dry wood, the other must know the movements of the man with the kindling. Take your choice, since your humor is so odd. You stay or you go—but remember that it is in the interests of others that you go."

"Of others?"

"Yes—of the Bukatys. Your presence here is a danger to them. Now go or stay, as you like."

Cartoner glanced at his companion with watchful eyes. He

Henry Seton Merriman

was not deliberating; for he had made up his mind long ago, and was now weighing that decision.

"I will go," he said, at length. And Deulin leaned back in his chair with a half-suppressed yawn of indifference. It was, as Cartoner had observed, when he was most idle that this gentleman had important business in hand. He had a gay, light, easy touch on life, and, it is to be supposed, never set much store upon the gain of an object. It seemed that he must have played the game in earnest at one time, must have thrown down his stake and lost it, or won it perhaps, and then had no use for his gain, which is a bitterer end than loss can ever be.

"I dare say you are right," he said. "And, at all events, you will see the last of this sad city."

Then he changed the subject easily, and began to talk of some trivial matter. From one question to another he passed, with that air of superficiality which northern men can never hope to understand, and here and there he touched upon those grave events which wise men foresaw at this period in European history.

"I smell," he said, "something in the atmosphere. Strangers passing in the street look at one with a questioning air, as if there were a secret which one might perhaps be party to. And I, who have no secrets."

He spread out his hands, with a gay laugh.

"Because," he added, with a sudden gravity, "there is nothing in life worth making a secret of—except one's income. There are many reasons why mine remains unconfessed. But, my friend, if anything should happen—anything—anywhere—we keep each other advised. Is it not so?"

"Usual cipher," answered Cartoner.

"My salutations to Lady Orlay," said Deulin, with a reflective nod. "That woman who can keep a secret."

"I thought you had none."

"She knows the secret—of my income," answered the Frenchman. "Tell her—no! Do not tell her anything. But go and see her. When will you leave?"

"To-night."

"And until then? Come and lunch with me at the Russian Club. No! Well, do as you like. I will say good-bye now. Heavens! how many times have we met and said good-bye again in hotels and railway stations and hired rooms! We have no abiding city and no friends. We are sons of Ishmael, and have none to care when we furl our tents and steal away."

He paused, and looked round the bare room, in which there was nothing but the hired furniture.

"The police will be in here five minutes after you are out," he said, curtly. "You have no message—" He paused to pick up from the floor a petal of his flower that had fallen. Then he walked to the window and looked out. Standing there, with his back to Cartoner, he went on: "No message to any one in Warsaw?"

"No," answered Cartoner.

"No—you wouldn't have one. You are not that sort of man. Gad! You are hard, Cartoner—hard as nails."

Cartoner did not answer. He was already putting together his possessions—already furling his solitary tent. It was only natural that he was loath to go; for he was turning his back on danger, and few men worthy of the name do that with alacrity, whatever their nationality may be; for gameness is not solely a British virtue, as is supposed in English public schools.

Suddenly Deulin turned round and shook hands.

"Don't know when we shall next meet. Take care of yourself. Good-bye."

And he went towards the door. But he paused on the threshold.

"The matter of the 'white feather' you may leave to me. You may leave others to me, too, so far as that goes. The sons of Ishmael must stand together."

And, with an airy wave of the hand and his rather hollow laugh, he was gone.

XXIII

COEUR VOLANT

In that great plain which is known to geographers as the Central European Depression the changes of the weather are very deliberate. If rain is coming, the cautious receive full warning of its approach. The clouds gather slowly, and disperse without haste when their work is done. For some days it had been looking like rain. The leaves on the trees of the Saski Gardens were hanging limp and lifeless. The whole world was dusty and expectant. Cartoner left Warsaw in a deluge of rain. It had come at last.

In the afternoon Deulin went to call at the Bukaty Palace. He was ushered into the great drawing-room, and there left to his own devices. He did an unusual thing. He fell into a train of thought so absorbing that he did not hear the door open or the soft sound of Wanda's dress as she entered the room. Her gay laugh brought him down to the present with a sort of shock.

"You were dreaming," she said.

"Heaven forbid!" he answered, fervently. "Dreams and white hairs—No, I was listening to the rain."

He turned and looked at her with a sudden defiance in his eyes, as if daring her to doubt him.

"I was listening to the rain. The summer is gone, Wanda—it is gone."

He drew forward a chair for her, and glanced over his shoulder towards the large folding-doors, through which the conservatory was visible in the fading light. The rain drummed on the glass roof with a hopeless, slow persistency.

"Can you not shut that door?" he said. "Bon Dieu! what a suicidal note that strikes—that hopeless rain—a northern autumn evening! There was a chill in the air as I drove down the Faubourg. If I were a woman I should have tea, or a cry. Being a man, I curse the weather and drive in a hired carriage to the pleasantest place in Warsaw."

Without waiting for further permission, he went and closed the large doors, shutting out the sound of the rain and the sight of the streaming glass, with sodden leaves stuck here and there upon it. Wanda watched him with a tolerant smile. Her daily life was lived among men; and she knew that it is not only women who have unaccountable humors, a sudden anger, or a quick and passing access of tenderness. There was a shadow of uneasiness in her eyes. He had come to tell her something. She knew that. She remembered that when this diplomatist looked most idle he was in reality about his business.

"There," he said, throwing himself back in an easy-chair and looking at her with smiling lips and eyes deeply, tragically intelligent. "That is more comfortable. Can you tell me nothing that will amuse me? Do you not see that my sins sit heavily on me this evening?"

"I do not know if it will amuse you," answered Wanda, in her energetic way, as if taking him at his word and seeking to rouse him, "but Mr. Mangles and Miss Cahere are coming to tea this evening."

Deulin made a grimace at the clock. If he had anything to say, he seemed to be thinking, he must say it quickly. Wanda was, perhaps, thinking the same.

"Separately they are amusing enough," he said, slowly, "but they do not mingle. I have an immense respect for Joseph P. Mangles."

"So has my father," put in Wanda, rather significantly.

"Ah! that is why you asked them. Your father knows that in a young country events move by jerks—that the man who is nobody to-day may be somebody to-morrow. The mammon of unrighteousness, Wanda."

"Yes."

"And you are above that sort of thing."

"I am not above anything that they deem necessary for the good of Poland," she answered, gravely. "They give every-thing. I have not much to give, you see."

"I suppose you have what every woman has—to sacrifice upon some altar or another—your happiness!"

Wanda shrugged her shoulders and said nothing. She glanced across at him. He knew something. But he had learned nothing from Cartoner. Of that, at least, she was sure.

"Happiness, or a hope of happiness," he went on, reflectively.

"Perhaps one is as valuable as the other. Perhaps they are the same thing. If you gain a happiness you lose a hope, remember that. It is not always remembered by women, and very seldom by men."

"Is it so precious? It is common enough, at all events."

"What is common enough?" he asked, absent-mindedly.

"Hope."

"Hope! connais pas!" he exclaimed, with a sudden laugh. "You must ask some one who knows more about it. I am a man of sorrow, Wanda; that is why I am so gay."

And his laugh was indeed light-hearted enough.

"The rain makes one feel lonely, that is all," he went on, as if seeking to explain his own humor. "Rain and cold and half a dozen drawbacks to existence lose their terrors if one has an in-door life to turn to and a fire to sit by. That is why I am here."

And he drew his chair nearer to the burning logs. Wanda now knew that he had something to tell her—that he had come for no other purpose. And, that he should be delicate and careful in his approach, told her that it was of Cartoner he had come to speak. While the delicacy and care showed her that he had guessed something, it also opened up a new side to his character. For the susceptibilities of men and women who have passed middle age are usually dull, and often quite dead, to the sensitiveness of younger hearts. It almost seemed that he divined that Wanda's heart was sensitive and sore, like an exposed nerve, though she showed the world a quiet face, such as the Bukatys had always shown through as long and grim a family history as the world has known.

"Do you not feel lonely in this great room?" he asked, looking round at the bare walls, which still showed the dim marks left by the portraits that had gone to grace an imperial gallery.

"No, I think not," answered Wanda. She followed his glance round the room, wondering, perhaps, if the rest of her life was to be weighed down by the sense of loneliness which had come over her that day for the first time.

Deulin, like the majority of Frenchmen, had certain mental gifts, usually considered to be the special privilege of women. He had a feminine way of skirting a subject—of walking round, as it were, and contemplating it from various side issues, as if to find out the best approach to it.

"The worst of Warsaw," he said, "is its dulness. The theatres are deplorable. You must admit that. And of society, there is, of course, none. I have even tried a travelling circus out by the Mokotow. One must amuse one's self."

He looked at her furtively, as if he were ashamed of having to amuse himself, and remembered too late how much the confession might mean.

"It was sordid," he continued. "One wondered how the performers could be content to risk their lives for the benefit of such a small and such an undistinguished audience. There was a trapeze troupe, however, who interested me. There was a girl with a stereotyped smile—like cracking nuts. There was a young man whose conceit took one's breath away. It was so hard to reconcile such preposterous vanity with the courage that he must have had. And there was a large, modest man who interested me. It was really he who did all the work. It was he who caught the others when they swung across the tent in mid-air. He was very steady and he was usually the wrong way up, hanging by his heels on a swinging trapeze. He had the lives of the others in his hands at every moment. But it was the others who received the applause—the nut-cracker girl who pirouetted, and the vain man who tapped his chest and smiled condescendingly. But the big man stood in the background, scarcely bowing at all, and quite forgetting to smile. One could see from the expression of his patient face that he knew it did not matter what he did for no one was looking at him—which was only the truth. Then, when the applause was over, he turned and walked away, heavy-shouldered and rather tired—his day's work done. And, I don't know why, I thought—of Cartoner."

She expected the name. Perhaps she wished for it, though she never would have spoken it herself. She had yet to learn to do that.

"Yes," said Deulin, after a pause, pursuing, it would appear, his own thoughts, "the world would get on very well without its talkers. No great man has ever been a great talker. Have you noticed that in history?"

Wanda made no answer. She was still waiting for the news that he had to tell her. The logs on the fire fell about with a crackle, and Deulin rose to put them in order. While thus engaged he continued his monologue.

"I suppose that is why I feel lonely this afternoon. In a sense, I am alone. Cartoner has gone, you know. He has left Warsaw."

Deulin glanced at the mirror over the mantel-piece, and if he had had any doubts they were now laid aside, for there was only gladness in Wanda's face. It was good news, then. And

Deulin was clever enough to know the meaning of that.

"Gone!" she said. "I am very glad."

"Yes," answered Deulin, gravely, as he returned to his chair. "It is a good thing. I left him this morning, placidly preparing to depart at half an hour's warning. He was packing, with that repose of manner which you have perhaps noticed. Better than Vespers, better than absolution, is Cartoner's repose of manner—for me, bien entendu. But, then, I am not a devout man."

"Then you have done what I asked you to do," said Wanda, "some time ago, and I am very grateful."

"Some time ago? It was only yesterday."

"Was it? It seems more than that," said Wanda. And Deulin nodded his head slowly.

"I was able to give him some information which made him change his plans quite suddenly," he explained. "So he packed up and went. He had not much to pack. We travel light—he and I. We have no despatch-boxes or note-books or diaries. What we remember and forget we remember and forget in our own heads. Though I doubt whether Cartoner forgets anything."

"And you?" asked Wanda, turning upon him quickly.

"I? Oh! I do my best," he said, lightly. "But if you desire to forget anything you should begin early. It is not a habit acquired in later life."

He rose as he spoke and looked at the clock. He had a habit of peering and contracting his round brown eyes which made many people think that he was short-sighted.

"I do not think I will wait for the Mangles," he said. "Especially Julie. I do not feel in the humor for Julie. By-the-way—" He paused, and contemplated the fire thoughtfully. "You never talk politics, I know. With the Mangles you may go further, and not even talk of politicians. It is no affair of theirs that Cartoner may have quitted Warsaw—you understand?"

"I should have thought Mr. Joseph Mangles the incarnation of discretion," said Wanda.

"Ah! You have found out Mangles, have you? I wonder if you have found us all out. Yes, Mangles is discreet, but Netty is not. I call her Netty—well, because I regard her with a secret and consuming passion."

"And have an equally secret and complete contempt for her discretion."

"Ah!" he exclaimed, and turned to look at her again. "Have I concealed my admiration so successfully as that? Perhaps I have overdone the concealment."

"Perhaps you have overdone the contempt," suggested Wanda. "She is probably more discreet than you think, but I shall not put her to the test."

"You see," said Deulin, in an explanatory way, "Cartoner may have had reasons of his own for leaving without drum or trumpet. You and I are the only persons in Warsaw who know of his departure, except the people in the passport-office—and the others, whose business it is to watch us all. You have a certain right to know; because in a sense you brought it all about, and it concerns the safety of your father and Martin. So I took it upon myself to tell you. I was not instructed to do so by Cartoner. I have no message of politeness to give to any one in Warsaw. Cartoner merely saw that it was his duty to go, and to go at once; so he went at once. And with a characteristic simplicity of purpose, he ignored the little social trammels which the majority of mankind know much better than they know their Bible, and follow much more closely. He was too discreet to call and say good-bye—knowing the ways of servants in this country. He will be much too discreet to send a conge card by post, knowing, as he does, the Warsaw post-office."

He took up his hat as he sat, and broke suddenly into his light and pleasant laugh.

"You are wondering," he said, "why I am taking this unusual course. It is not often, I know, that one speaks well of one's friend behind his back. It is six for Cartoner and half a dozen for myself. To begin with, Cartoner is my friend. I should not like him to be misunderstood. Also, I may do the same at any moment myself. We are here to-day and gone to-morrow. Sometimes we remember our friends and sometimes we forget them."

"At all events," said Wanda, shaking hands, "you are cautious. You make no promises."

"And therefore we break none," he answered, as he crossed the threshold.

He had hardly gone before Netty entered the room, followed closely by Mr. Mangles. She was prettily dressed. She appeared to be nervous and rather shy. The two girls shook hands in silence. Joseph Mangles, standing well in the middle of the room, waited till the first greeting was over, and then, with that solemn air of addressing an individual as if he or she were an assembly, he spoke.

"Princess," he said, "my sister begs to be excused. She is unable to take tea this afternoon. Last night she considered herself called upon to make a demonstration in the cause that she has at heart. She smoked two cigarettes towards the emancipation of your sex, princess. Just to show her independence—to show, I surmise, that she didn't care a— that she did not care. She cares this afternoon. She had a headache."

And he bowed with a courtesy with which some old-fashioned men still attempt to oppose the progress of women.

XXIV

IN THE WEST INDIA DOCK ROAD

It is not only in name that this great thoroughfare has the sound of the sea, the suggestion of a tarry atmosphere, and that mystery which hangs about the lives of simple sailor men. To thousands and thousands of foreigners the word London means the West India Dock Road, and nothing more. There are sailors sailing on every sea who cherish the delusion that they have seen life and London when they have passed the portals of one of the large public-houses of the West India Dock Road.

There are others who are not sailors, speaking one of the half-dozen tongues of eastern Europe, of which the average educated Briton does not even know the name, whose lives are bounded on the west by Aldgate Pump, on the east by the Dock Gates, on the north by Houndsditch, and on the south by St. Katherine's Dock and Tower Hill. A man who would wish to knock at any door in this district, and speak to him who opened it in his native tongue, would have to pass five years of his life between the Baltic and the Black Sea, the Carpathians and the Caucasus. Galician, Ruthenian, Polish, Magyar would be required as a linguistic basis, while variations of the same added to Russian and German for those who have served in one army or another, would

Henry Seton Merriman

probably be useful.

There are many odd trades in the West India Dock Road, and none of them, it would seem, so profitable as the fleecing of sailors. But by a queer coincidence the callings mostly savor of the same painful process. They run to leather for the most part, and the manufacture of those *articles de luxe* which are chiefly composed of colored morocco and gum. There is also a trade in furs. Half-way down the West India Dock Road, where the shops are most sordid, and the bird-fanciers congregate, there is quite a large fur store, of which the window, clad in faded red, is adorned by a white rabbit-skin, laid flat upon a fly-blown newspaper, and a stuffed sea-gull with a singularly knowing squint.

There was once a name above the shop, but the owner of it, for reasons of his own, or so soon, perhaps, as he realized that he was in a country where no one wants to know your name, or cares about your business, had carelessly painted it out with a pot of black paint and a defective brush, which had last been used for red.

On each side of the shop-window is a door, one leading to the warehouse and workshop at the back. Through this door there passes quite a respectable commerce. The skin of the domestic cat, drawn hither on coster carts from the remoter suburbs, passes in to this door to emerge from it later in neat wooden cases addressed to enterprising merchants in Trondhjem, Bergen, Berlin, and other northern cities from which tourists are in the habit of carrying home mementoes in the shape of the fur and feather of the country. There is also a small importation of American fur to be dressed and treated and re-despatched to the Siberian fur dealers from whom the American globe-trotter prefers to buy. A number of unhealthy work-people—men, women, and ancient children—also use this door, entering by it in the morning, and only coming into the air again after dark. They have yellow faces and dusty clothes. A long companionship with fur has made them hirsute; for the men are unshaven, and the women's heads are burdened with heavy coils of black hair.

The other door, which is little used, seems to be the entrance to the dwelling-house of the nameless foreigner. On the left-hand door-post is nailed a small tin tablet, whereon are inscribed in the Russian character three words, which, being translated, read: "The Brothers of Liberty." As no one of importance in the West India Dock Road reads the Russian characters, there is no harm done, or else some disappointment would necessarily be experienced by the passer-by to think that any one so nearly related to liberty should choose to live in that spot. Neither would the Trafalgar Square agitator be pleased were he called upon to suppose that the siren whom he pursues with such ardor on rainy Sunday afternoons could ever take refuge behind the dingy Turkey-red curtain that hides the inner parts of the furrier's store from vulgar gaze.

"That's their lingo," said Captain Cable to himself, with considerable emphasis, one dull winter afternoon when, after much study of the numbers over the shop doors, he finally came to a stand opposite the furrier's shop.

He stepped back into the road to look up at the house, thereby imperilling his life amid the traffic. A costermonger taking cabbages from the Borough Market to Limehouse gave the captain a little piece of his mind in the choicest terms then current in his daily intercourse with man, and received in turn winged words of such a forcible and original nature as to send him thoughtfully eastward behind his cart.

"That's their lingo, right enough," said the captain, examining the tin tablet a second time. "That's Polish, or I'm a Dutchman."

He was, as a matter of fact, wrong, for it was Russian, but this was, nevertheless, the house he sought. He looked at the dingy building critically, shrugged his shoulders, and, tilting forward his high-crowned hat, he scratched his head with a grimace indicative of disappointment. It was not to come to such a house as this that he had put on what he called his "suit"; a coat and trousers of solid pilot-cloth designed to be worn as best in all climates and at all times. It was not in order to impress such people as must undoubtedly live behind those faded red curtains that he had unpacked from the state-room locker his shore-going hat, high, and of fair, round shape, such as is only to be bought in the shadow of Limehouse steeple.

The house was uninviting. It had a furtive, dishonest look about it. Captain Cable saw this. He was a man who studied weather and the outward signs of a man. He rang the bell all the louder, and stood squarely on the threshold until the door was opened by a dirty man in a dirty apron, who looked at him in lugubrious silence.

"Name of Cable," said the captain, turning to expectorate on the pavement, after the manner of far-sighted sailors who are about to find themselves on carpet. The man made a slight grimace, and craned forwards with an interrogative ear held ready for a repetition.

"Name of Cable," repeated the captain. "Dirty!" he added, just by way of inviting his hearer's attention, and adding that personal note without which even the shortest conversation is apt to lose interest.

This direct address seemed to have the desired effect, for the man stood aside.

"Heave ahead!" he said, pointing to an open door. For the only English he knew was the English they speak in the Baltic. The captain cocked his bright blue eye at him, his attention caught by the familiar note. And he stumped along the passage into the dim room at the end. It was a small, square room, with a window opening upon some leads, where discarded bottles and blackened moss surrounded the remains of a sparrow. The room was full of men—six or seven foreign faces were turned towards the new-comer. Only one, however, of these faces was familiar to Captain Cable. It was the face of the man known on the Vistula as Kosmaroff.

The captain nodded to him. He had a large nodding acquaintance. It will be remembered that he claimed for his hands a cleanliness which their appearance seemed to define as purely moral. In his way he was a proud man, and stand-offish at that. He looked slowly round, and found no other face to recognize. But he looked a second time at a small, dark man with gentle eyes, whose individuality must have had something magnetic in it. Captain Cable was accustomed to judge from outward things. He picked out the ruling mind in that room, and looked again at its possessor as if measuring himself against him.

"Take a chair, captain," said Kosmaroff, who himself happened to be standing. He was leaning against the high, old-fashioned mantel-piece, which had seen better days— and company—and smoking a cigarette. He was clad in a cheap, ready-made suit; for his heart was in his business, and he scraped and saved every kopeck. But the cheap clothing could not hide that ease of movement which bespeaks a long descent, or conceal the slim strength of limb which is begotten of the fine, clean, hard bone of a fighting race.

The captain looked round, and sought his pocket-hand-kerchief, with which to dust the proffered seat, mindful of

Henry Seton Merriman

his "suit."

"Do you speak German, captain?" inquired Kosmaroff.

And Captain Cable snorted at the suggestion.

"Sailed with a crew of Germans," he answered; "I understand a bit, and I know a few words. I know the German for d—n your eyes, and handy words like that."

"Then," said Kosmaroff, addressing the gentle-eyed man, "we had better continue our talk in German. Captain Cable is a man who likes plain dealing."

He himself spoke in the language of the Fatherland, and Captain Cable stiffened at the sound of it, as all good Britons should.

"We have not much to say to Captain Cable," replied the man who seemed to be a leader of the Brothers of Liberty. He spoke in a thin tenor voice, and was what the French call *chetif* in appearance—a weak man, fighting against physical disabilities and an indifferent digestion.

"It is essential in the first place," he continued, "that we should understand each other; we the conquerors and you the conquered."

With a gesture he divided the party assembled into two groups, the smaller of which consisted only of Kosmaroff and another. And then he looked out of the window with his woman-like, reflective smile.

"We the Russians, and you the Poles. I fear I have not made myself quite clear. I understand, however, that we are to trust the last comer entirely, which I do with the more confidence that I perceive that he understands very little of what we are saying."

Captain Cable's solid, weather-beaten face remained rigid like a figure-head. He looked at the speaker with an ill-concealed pity for one who could not express himself in plain English and be done with it.

"Our circumstances are such that no correspondence is possible," continued the speaker. "Any agreement, therefore, must be verbal, and verbal agreements should be quite clear—the human memory is so liable to be affected by circumstances—and should be repeated several times in the hearing of several persons. I understand, therefore, that, after a period of nearly twenty years, Poland—is ready again."

There was a short silence in that dim and quiet room.

"Yes," said Kosmaroff, deliberately, at length.

"And is only awaiting her opportunity."

"Yes."

One of the Brothers of Liberty, possibly the secretary of that body, which owned its inability to put anything in writing, had provided a penny bottle of ink and a sticky-looking, red pen-holder. The speaker took up the pen suspiciously, and laid it down again. He rubbed his finger and thumb together. His suspicions had apparently been justifiable. It was a sticky one! Then he lapsed into thought. Perhaps he was thinking of the pen-holder, or perhaps of the history of the two nations represented in that room. He had a thoughtful face, and history is a fascinating study, especially for those who make it. And this quiet man had made a little in his day.

"An opportunity is not an easy thing to define," he said at length. "Any event may turn out to be one. But, so far as we can judge, Poland's opportunity must lie in two or three possible events at the most. One would be a war with England. That, I am afraid, I cannot bring about just yet."

He spoke quite seriously, and he had not the air of a man subject to the worst of blindness—the blindness of vanity.

"We have all waited long enough for that. We have done our best out on the frontier and in the English press, but cannot bring it about. It is useless to wait any longer. The English are fiery enough—in print—and ready enough to fight—in Fleet Street. In Russia we have too little journalism—in England they have too much."

Captain Cable yawned at this juncture with a maritime frankness.

"Another opportunity would be a social upheaval," said the Russian, drumming on the table with his slim fingers. "The time has not come for that yet. A third alternative is a mishap to a crowned head—and that we can offer to you."

Kosmaroff moved impatiently.

"Is that all?" he exclaimed. "I have heard that talk for the last ten years. Have you brought me across Europe to talk of that?"

The Russian looked at him calmly, stroking his thin, black mustache, and waited till he had finished speaking.

"Yes—that is all I have to propose to you—but this time it is more than talk. You may take my word for that. This time we shall all succeed. But, of course, we want money, as usual. Ah! what a different world this would be if the poor could only be rich for one hour. We want five thousand roubles. I understand you have control of ten times that amount. If Poland will advance us five thousand roubles she shall have her opportunity—and a good one—in a month from now."

He held up his hand to command silence, for Kosmaroff, with eyes that suddenly blazed in anger, had stepped forward to the table, and was about to interrupt. And Kosmaroff, who was not given to obedience, paused, he knew not why.

"Think," said the other, in his smooth, even voice—"one month from now, after waiting twenty years. In a month you yourself may be in a very different position to that you now occupy. You commit yourselves to nothing. You do not even give ground for the conclusion that the Polish party ever for a moment approved of our methods. Our methods are our own affair, as are the risks we are content to run. We have our reasons, and we seek the approval of no man."

There was a deadly coldness in the man's manner which seemed to vouch for the validity of those reasons which he did not submit to the judgment of any.

"Five thousand roubles," he concluded. "And in exchange I give you the date—so that Poland may be ready."

"Thank you," said Kosmaroff, who had regained his composure as suddenly as he had lost it. "I decline—for myself and for the whole of Poland. We play a cleaner game than that."

He turned and took up his hat, and his hand shook as he did it.

"If I did not know that you are a patriot according to your lights—if I did not know something of your story, and of those reasons that you do not give—I should take you by the throat and throw you out into the street for daring to make such a proposal to me," he said, in a low voice.

"To a deserter from a Cossack regiment," suggested the other.

"To me," repeated Kosmaroff, touching himself on the breast and standing at his full height. No one spoke, as if the silent spell of History were again for a moment laid upon their tongues.

"Captain Cable," said Kosmaroff, "you and I have met before, and I learned enough of you then to tell you now that this is no place for you, and these men no company for you. I am going—will you come?"

"I'm agreeable," said Captain Cable, dusting his hat.

When they were out in the street, he turned to Kosmaroff and looked up into his face with bright and searching eyes.

"Who's that man?" he asked, as if there had been only one in the room.

"I do not know his name," replied Kosmaroff.

They were standing on the doorstep. The dirty man had closed the door behind them, and, turning on his heel, Kosmaroff looked thoughtfully at the dusty woodwork of it. Half absent-mindedly he extended one finger and made a design on the door. It was not unlike a Greek cross.

"That is who he is," he said.

Captain Cable followed the motion of his companion's finger.

"I've heard of him," he said. "And I heard his voice—sort of soft-spoken—on Hamburg quay one night, many years ago. That is why I refused the job and came out with you."

XXV

THE CAPTAIN'S STORY

More especially in northern countries nature lays her veto upon the activity of men, and winter calls a truce even to human strife. Cartoner awaited orders in London, for all the world was dimly aware of something stirring in the north, and no one knew what to expect or where to look for the unexpected.

It was a cold winter that year, and the Baltic closed early. Captain Cable chartered the *Minnie* in the coasting trade, and after Christmas he put her into one of the cheaper dry-docks down the river towards Rotherhithe. His ship was, indeed, in dry-dock when the captain opened with the Brothers of Liberty those negotiations which came to such a sudden and untoward end.

Paul Deulin wrote one piteous letter to Cartoner, full of abuse of the cold and wet weather. "If the winter would only set in," he said, "and dry things up and freeze the river, which has overflowed its banks almost to the St. Petersburg Station, on the Praga side, life would perhaps be more endurable."

Then the silence of the northern winter closed over him too, and Cartoner wrote in vain, hoping to receive some small details of the Bukatys and perhaps a mention of Wanda's name. But his letters never reached Warsaw, or if they travelled to the banks of the Vistula they were absorbed into that playful post-office where little goes in and less comes out.

There were others besides Cartoner who were wintering in London who likewise laid aside their newspaper with a sigh half weariness, half relief, to find that their parts of the world were still quiet.

"History is assuredly at a stand-still," said an old traveller one evening at the club, as he paused at Cartoner's table. "The world must be quiet indeed with you here in London, all the winter, eating your head off."

"I am waiting," replied Cartoner.

"What for?"

"I do not know," he said, placidly, continuing his dinner.

Later on he returned to his rooms in Pall Mall. He was a great reader, and was forced to follow the daily events in a dozen different countries in a dozen different languages. He was surrounded by newspapers, in a deep arm-chair by the table, when that came for which he was waiting. It came in the form of Captain Cable in his shore-going clothes. The little sailor was ushered in by the well-trained servant of this bachelor household without surprise or comment.

Cartoner made him welcome with a cigar and an offer of refreshment, which was refused. Captain Cable knew that as you progress upward in the social scale the refusal of refreshment becomes an easier matter until at last you can really do as you like and not as etiquette dictates, while to decline the beggar's pint of beer is absolute rudeness.

"We've always dealt square by each other, you and I," said the captain, when he had lighted his cigar. Then he fell into a reminiscent humor, and presently broke into a chuckling laugh.

"If it hadn't been for you, them Dons would have had me up against the wall and shot me, sure as fate," he said, bringing his hand down on his knee with a keen sense of enjoyment. "That was ten years ago last November, when the *Minnie* had been out of the builder's yard a matter of six months."

"Yes," said Cartoner, putting the dates carefully together in his mind. It seemed that the building of the *Minnie* was not the epoch upon which he reckoned his periods.

"She's in Morrison's dry-dock now," said the captain, who in a certain way was like a young mother. For him all the topics were but a number of by-ways leading ultimately to the same centre. "You should go down and see her, Mr. Cartoner. It's a big dock. You can walk right round her in the mud at the bottom of the dock and see her finely."

Cartoner said he would. They even arranged a date on which to carry out this plan, and included in it an inspection of the *Minnie's* new boiler. Then Captain Cable remembered what he had come for, and the plan was never carried out after all.

"Yes," he said, "you've a reckoning against me, Mr. Cartoner. I have never done you a good turn that I know of, and you saved my life, I believe, that time—you and that Frenchman who talks so quick, Moonseer Deulin—that time, over yonder."

And he nodded his head towards the southwest with the accuracy of one who never loses his bearings. For there are some people who always know which is the north; and others who, if asked suddenly, do not know their left hand from their right; and others, again, who say—or shout—that all men are created equal.

"I've been done, Mr. Cartoner—that is what I've come to tell you. Me that has always been so smart and has dealt straight by other men. Done, hoodwinked, tricked—same as a Sunday-school teacher. And I can do you a good turn by telling you about it; and I can do the other man a bad turn, which is what I want to do. Besides, it's dirty work. Me, that has always kept my hands—"

He looked at his hands, and decided not to pursue the subject.

"You'll say that for me, Mr. Cartoner—you that has known me ten years and more."

"Yes, I'll say that for you," answered Cartoner, with a laugh.

"They did me!" cried the captain, leaning forward and banging his hand down on the table, "with the old trick of a bill of lading lost in the post and a man in a gold-laced hat that came aboard one night and said he was a government official from the Arsenal come for his government stuff. And it wasn't government stuff, and he wasn't a government official. It was—"

Captain Cable paused and looked carefully round the room. He even looked up to the ceiling, from a long habit of living beneath deck skylights.

"Bombs!" he concluded—"bombs!"

Henry Seton Merriman

Then he went further, and qualified the bombs in terms which need not be set down here.

"You know me and you know the *Minnie*, Mr. Cartoner!" continued the angry sailor. "She was specialty built with large hatches for machinery, and—well, guns. She was built to carry explosives, and there's not a man in London will insure her. Well, we got into the way of carrying war material. It was only natural, being built for it. But you'll bear me out, and there are others to bear me out, that we've only carried clean stuff up to now—plain, honest, fighting stuff for one side or the other. Always honest—revolutions and the like, and an open fight. But bombs—"

And here again the captain made use of nautical terms which have no place on a polite page.

"There's bombs about, and it's me that has been carrying them," he concluded. "That is what I have got to tell you."

"How do you know?" asked Cartoner, in his gentle and soothing way.

The captain settled himself in his chair, and crossed one leg over the other.

"Know the Johannis Bulwark, in Hamburg?"

Cartoner nodded.

"Know the Seemannshaus there?"

"Yes. The house that stands high up among the trees over-looking the docks."

"That's the place," said Captain Cable. "Well, one night I was up there, on the terrace in front of the house where the sailors sit and spit all day waiting to be taken on. Got into Hamburg short-handed. I was picking up a crew. Not the right time to do it, you'll say, after dark, as times go and forecastle hands pan out in these days. Well, I had my reasons. You can pick up good men in Hamburg if you go about it the right way. A man comes up to me. Remembered me, he said; had sailed with me on a voyage when we had machinery from the Tyne that was too big for us, and we couldn't get the hatches on. We sailed after nightfall, I recollect, with hatches off, and had the seas slopping in before the morning. He remembered it, he said. And he asked me if it was true that I was goin'—well, to the port I was bound for. And I said it was God's truth. Then he told me a long yarn of two cases outshipped that was lying down at the wharf. Transshipment goods on a through bill of lading. And the bill of lading gone a missing in the post. A long story, all lies, as I ought to have known at the time. He had a man with him—forwarding agent, he called him. This chap couldn't speak English, but he spoke German, and the other man translated as we went along. I couldn't rightly see the other man's face. Little, dark man—with a queer, soft voice, like a woman wheedlin'! Too d—d innocent, and I ought to have known it. Don't you ever be wheedled by a woman, Mr. Cartoner. Got a match?"

For the captain's cigar had gone out. But he felt quite at home, as he always did—this unvarnished gentleman from the sea—and asked for what he wanted.

"Well, to make a long yarn short, I took the cases. Two of them, size of an orange-box. We were full, so I had them in the state-room alongside of the locker where I lie down and get a bit of sleep when I feel I want it. And they paid me well. It was government stuff, the soft-spoken man said, and the freight would come out of the taxes and never be missed. We went into heavy weather, and, as luck would have it, one of the cases broke adrift and got smashed. I mended it myself, and had to open it. Then I saw that it was explosives. Lie number one! It was packed in wadding so as to save a jar. It was too small for shells. Besides, no government sends loaded shells about, 'cepting in war time. At the moment I did not think much about it. It was heavy weather, and I had a new crew. There were other things to think about. And, I tell you, when I got to port, a chap with gold lace on him came aboard and took the stuff away."

Cartoner's attention was aroused now. There was something in this story, after all. There might be everything in it when the captain told what had brought these past events back to his recollection.

"I'm not going to tell you the port of discharge," said Captain Cable, "because in doing that I should run foul of other people who acted square by me, and I'll act square by them. I'll tell you one thing, though, I sighted the Scaw light on that voyage. You can have that bit of information—you, that's half a sailor. You can put that in your pipe and smoke it."

And he glanced at Cartoner's cigarette with the satisfaction of a conversationalist who has pulled off a good simile.

"'Safternoon," he continued, "I went to see some people about a little job for the *Minnie*. She'll be out of dock in a fortnight. You will not forget to come down and see her?"

"I should like to see her," said Cartoner. "Go on with your story."

"Well, this afternoon I went to see some parties that had a charter to offer me. Foreigners—every man Jack of them. Spoke in German, out of politeness to me. The Lord knows what they would have spoken if I hadn't been there. It was bad enough as it was. But it wasn't the lingo that got me; it was the voice. 'Where have I heard that voice?' thinks I. And then I remembered. It was at the Seemannshaus, at Hamburg, one dark night. 'You're a pretty government official,' I says to myself, sitting quiet all the time, like a cat in the engine-room. I wouldn't have taken the job at any rate, owing to that voice, which I have never forgotten, and yet never thought to hear again. But while the parley voo was still going on, up jumps a man—the only man I knew there—name beginning with a K—don't quite remember it. At any rate, up he jumps, and says that that room was no place for me nor yet for him. Dare say you know the man, if I could remember his name. Sort of thin, dark man, with a way of carrying his head—quarter-deck fashion—as if he was a king or a Hooghly pilot. Well, we gets up and walks out, proudlike, as if we had been insulted. But blessed if I knew what it was all about. 'Who's that man!' I asks when we were in the street. And the other chap turns and makes a mark upon the door, which he rubs out afterwards as if it was a hanging matter. 'That's who that is,' he says."

Cartoner turned, and with one finger made an imaginary design on the soft pile of the table-cloth. Captain Cable looked at it critically, and after a moment's reflection admitted in an absent voice that his hopes for eternity were exceedingly small.

"You are too much for me," he said, after a pause. "You that deal in politics and the like."

"And the other man's name is Kosmaroff," said Cartoner.

"That's it—a Russian," answered Captain Cable, rising, and looking at the clock. His movements were energetic and very quick for his years. He carried with him the brisk atmosphere of the sea and the hardness of a life which tightens men's muscles and teaches them to observe the outward signs of man and nature.

"It beats me," he said. "But I've told you all I can—all, perhaps, that you want to hear. For it seems that you are putting two and two together already. I think I've done right. At any rate, I'll stand by it. It makes me uneasy to think of that stuff having been below the *Minnie's* hatches."

"It makes me uneasy, too," said Cartoner. "Wait a minute till I put on another coat. I am going out. We may as well go down together."

He came back a moment later, having changed his coat. He was attaching the small insignia of a foreign order to the lapel.

"Going to a swarree?" asked Cable, as between men of the world.

"I am going to look for a man I want to see to-night, and I think I shall find him, as you say, at a soiree," answered Cartoner, gravely.

Out in the street he paused for a moment. A cab was already waiting, having dashed up from the club stand.

"By-the-way," he said, "I shall not be able to come down and see the *Minnie* this time. I shall be off by the eight o'clock train to-morrow morning."

"Going foreign?" asked the captain.

"Yes, I am going abroad again," answered Cartoner, and there was a sudden ring of exultation in his voice. For this was after all, a man of action who had strayed into a profession of which the strength is to sit still.

XXVI

IN THE SPRING

The Mangles passed the winter at Warsaw, and there learned the usual lesson of the traveller: that countries reputed hot or cold are neither so hot nor so cold as they are represented. The winter was a hard one, and Warsaw, of all European cities, was, perhaps, the last that any lady would select to pass the cold months in.

"I have my orders," said Mangles, rather grimly, "and I must stay here till I am moved on. But the orders say nothing about you or Netty. Go to Nice if you like."

And Julie seemed half inclined to go southward. But for one reason or another—reasons, it may be, put forward by Netty in private conversation with her aunt—the ladies lingered on.

"The place is dull for you," said Mangles, "now that Cartoner seems to have left us for good. His gay and sparkling conversation would enliven any circle."

And beneath his shaggy brows he glanced at Netty, whose smooth cheek did not change color, while her eyes met his with an affectionate smile.

Henry Seton Merriman

"You seemed to have plenty to say to each other coming across the Atlantic," she said. "I always found you with your heads close together whenever I came on deck."

"Don't think we sparkled much," said Joseph, with his under lip well forward.

"It is very kind of Uncle Joseph," said Netty, afterwards, to Miss Mangles, "to suggest that we should go south, and, of course, it would be lovely to feel the sunshine again, but we could not leave him, could we? You must not think of me, auntie; I am quite happy here, and should not enjoy the Riviera at all if we left uncle all alone here."

Julie had a strict sense of duty, which, perhaps, Netty was cognizant of; and the subject was never really brought under discussion. During a particularly bad spell of weather Mr. Mangles again and again suggested that he should be left at Warsaw, but on each occasion Netty came forward with that complete unselfishness and sweet forethought for others which all who knew her learned to look for in her every action.

Warsaw, she admitted, was dull, and the surrounding country simply impossible. But the winter could not last forever, she urged, with a little shiver. And it really was quite easy to keep warm if one went for a brisk walk in the morning. To prove this she put on the new furs which Joseph had bought her, and which were very becoming to her delicate coloring, and set out full of energy. She usually went to the Saski Gardens, the avenues of which were daily swept and kept clear of snow; and as often as not, she accidentally met Prince Martin Bukaty there. Sometimes she crossed the bridge to Praga, and occasionally turned her steps down the Bednarska to the side of the river which was blocked by ice now, wintry and desolate. The sand-workers were still laboring, though navigation was, of course, at a stand-still.

Netty never saw Kosmaroff, however, who had gone as suddenly as he came—had gone out of her life as abruptly as he burst into it, leaving only the memory of that high-water mark of emotion to which he had raised her. Leaving also that blankest of all blanks in the feminine heart, an unsatisfied curiosity. She could not understand Kosmaroff, any more than she could understand Cartoner. And it was natural that she should, in consequence, give much thought to them both. There was, she felt, something in both alike which she had not got at, and she naturally wanted to get at it. It might be a sorrow, and her kind heart drew her attention to any hidden thought that might be a sorrow. She might be able to alleviate it. At any rate, being a woman, she, no doubt, wanted to stir it up, as it were, and see what the result would be.

Prince Martin was quite different. He was comparatively easy to understand. She knew the symptoms well. She was so unfortunate. So many people had fallen in love with her, through no fault of her own. Indeed, no one could regret it more than she did. She did not, of course, say these things to her aunt, Julie, or to that dear old blind stupid, her uncle, who never saw or understood anything, and was entirely absorbed in his cigars and his newspapers. She said them to herself—and, no doubt, found herself quite easy to convince—as other people do.

Prince Martin was very gay and light-hearted, too. If he was in love, he was gayly, frankly, openly in love, and she hoped that it would be all right—whatever that might mean. In the mean time, of course, she could not help it if she was always meeting him when she went for her walk in the Saski Gardens. There was nowhere else to walk, and it was to be supposed that he was passing that way by accident. Or if he had found out her hours and came there on purpose she really could not help it.

Deulin came and went during the winter. He seemed to have business now at Cracow, now at St. Petersburg. He was a bad correspondent, and talked much about himself, without ever saying much; which is quite a different thing. He had the happy gift of imparting a wealth of useless information. When in Warsaw he busied himself on behalf of the ladies, and went so far as to take Miss Mangles for a drive in his sleigh. To Netty he showed a hundred attentions.

"I cannot understand," she said, "why everybody is so kind to me."

"It is because you are so kind to everybody," he answered, with that air of appearing to mean more than he said, which he seemed to reserve for Netty.

"I do not understand Mr. Deulin," said Netty to her uncle one day. "Why does he stay here? What is he doing here?"

And Joseph P. Mangles merely stuck his chin forward, and said in his deepest tones:

"You had better ask him!"

"But he would not tell me."

"No."

"And Mr. Cartoner," continued Netty, "I understood he was coming back, but he does not seem to come. No one seems to know. It is so difficult to get information about the merest trifles. Not that I care, of course, who comes and who goes."

"Course not," said Mangles.

After a pause, Netty looked up again from her work.

"Uncle," she said, "I was wondering if there was anything wrong in Warsaw."

"What made you wonder that?"

"I do not know. It feels, sometimes, as if there were something wrong. Mr. Cartoner went away so suddenly. The people in the streets are so odd and quiet. And down stairs in the restaurant, at dinner, I see them exchange glances when the Russian officers come into the room. I distrust the quietness of the people, and—uncle—Mr. Deulin's gayety—I distrust that, too. And then, you; you so often ask us to go away and leave you here alone."

Mangles laughed, curtly, and folded his newspaper.

"Because it is a dull hole," he said, "that is why I want you to go away. It has got on your nerves. It is because you have not lived in a conquered country before. All conquered countries are like that."

Which was a very long explanation for Joseph Mangles to make. And he never again proposed that Netty and her aunt should go to Nice. But Netty's curiosity was not satisfied, and she knew that Deulin would answer no question seriously. Why did not Kosmaroff come back? Why did Cartoner stay away? As soon as etiquette allowed, she called at the Bukaty Palace. She made an excuse in some illustrated English and American magazines which might interest the Princess Wanda. But there was no one at home. She understood from the servant, who spoke a little German, that they had gone to their country house, a few miles from Warsaw.

The next morning Netty went for a walk in the Saski Gardens. The weather had changed suddenly. It was quite mild and springlike. At last the grip of winter seemed to be slackening. There were others in the gardens who held their faces up to the sky, and breathed in the softer air with a sort of expectancy; who seemed to wonder if the winter had really broken, or if this should only be a false hope. It was one of the first days in March—a month wherein all nature slowly stirs after her long sleep, and men pull themselves together to new endeavor. The majority of great events in the world's history have taken place in the spring months. Is not the Ides of March written large in the story of this planet?

Netty had not been many minutes in the gardens when Prince Martin came to her. He had laid aside his fur coat for a lighter cloak of English make, which made him look thinner. His face, too, was thin and spare, like the face of a man who is working hard at work or sport. But he was gay and light-hearted as ever. Neither did he make any disguise of his admiration for Netty.

"It is three days," he said, "since I have seen you. And it seems like three years."

Which is the sort of remark that can only be ignored by the discreet. Besides, Prince Martin did not go so far as to state why the three days had been so tedious. It might be for some other reason altogether.

"My uncle has been pressing us to go away," said Netty, "to the south of France, to Nice, but—"

"But what?"

"Well," answered Netty, after a pause, "you see for yourself—we have not gone."

"It is a very selfish hope—but I hope you will stay," said Prince Martin. He looked down at her, and the thought of her possible departure caught him like a vise. He was a person of impulse, and (which is not usual) his impulse was as often towards good as towards evil. She looked, besides looking pretty, rather small and frail, and dependent at that moment, and all the chivalry of his nature was aroused. It was only natural that he should think that she had all the qualities he knew Wanda to possess, and, of course, in an infinitely higher degree. Which is the difference between one's own sister and another person's. She was good, and frank, and open. The idea of concealment between himself and her was to be treated with scorn.

"I will tell you," he said, "if at any time there is any reason why you cannot stay."

"But why should there be any reason—" she began, and a quick movement that he made to look round and see who was in sight, who might be within hearing, made her stop.

"Oh! I do not want you to tell me anything. I do not want to know," she said hurriedly. Which was the absolute truth; for politics bored her horribly.

He looked at her with a laugh, and only loved her all the more, for persisting in her ignorance of those matters which are always better left to men.

"I almost missed," he said gayly, "an excellent opportunity of holding my tongue."

"Only—" began Netty, as if in continuation of her protest against being told anything.

"Only what?"

"Only—be careful," she said, with downcast eyes. And, of course, that brought him, figuratively, to her feet. He vowed he would be careful, if it was for her sake. If she would only say that it was for her sake. And at the moment he really meant it. He was as honest as the day. But he did not know, perhaps, that the best sort of men are those who persistently and repeatedly break their word in one respect. For they will vow to a woman never to run into danger, to be careful, to be cowards. And when the danger is there, and the woman is not—their vow is writ in water.

Netty tried to stop him. She was very much distressed. She almost had tears in her eyes, but not quite. She put her gloved hands over her ears to stop them, but did not quite succeed in shutting out his voice. The gloves were backed with a dark, fine fur, which made her cheeks look delicate and soft as a peach.

"I will not hear you," she said. "I will not. I will not."

Then he seemed to recollect something, and he stopped short.

"No," he said; "you are quite right. I have no business to ask you to hear me. I have nothing to offer you. I am poor. At any moment I may be an outlaw. But at any moment I may have more to offer you. Things may go well, and then I should be in a very different position."

Netty looked away from him, and seemed to be trying to think. Or, perhaps, she was only putting together recollections which had all been thought out before. She could be a princess. She remembered that. She had only been in Europe six months, and here was a prince at her feet. But there were terrible drawbacks. Warsaw was one of them, and poverty, that greatest of all drawbacks, was the other.

"I can tell you nothing now," he said. "But soon, before the summer, there may be great changes in Poland."

Then his own natural instinct told him that position, or poverty, wealth or success, had nothing to do with the cause he was pleading. He did not even know whether Netty was rich or poor, and he certainly did not care.

"What did you mean," he asked, "when you said 'Be careful'? What did you mean—tell me?"

His gay, blue eyes were serious enough now. They were alight with an honest and good love. Never of a cold and calculating habit, he was reckless of observation. He did not care who saw. He would have taken her hands and forced her to face him had she not held them behind her back. She was singularly calm and self-possessed. People who appear nervous often rise to the occasion.

"I do not know what I meant," she said; "I do not know. You must not ask me. It slipped out when I was not thinking. Oh! please be generous, and do not ask me."

By some instinct she had leaped to the right mark. She had asked a Bukaty to be generous.

"Some day," he said, "I will ask you."

And he walked with her to the gate of the gardens in silence.

XXVII

A SACRIFICE

Though the fine weather did not last, it was a promise of better things, like the letter that precedes a welcome friend. After it the air seemed warmer, though snow fell again, and the thermometer went below zero.

Wanda and her father did not return to Warsaw as they had intended.

So long as the frost holds, the country is endurable; nay, it is better than the towns on those great plains of eastern Europe; but when the thaw comes, and each small depression is a puddle, every low-lying field a pond, and whole plains become lakes, few remain in the villages who can set their feet upon the pavement. The early spring, so closely associated in most minds with the song of birds and the budding of green things, is in Poland and Russia a period of waiting for the water to drain off the flat land; a time to look to one's thickest top-boots in these countries, where men and women are booted to the knee, and every third house displays the shoemaker's sign upon its door-post.

The Bukatys' country-house, like all else that the past had left them, was insignificant. In olden days it had been a farm, one of the smallest, used once or twice during the winter as a shooting-lodge; for it stood in the midst of vast forests. It was not really ancient, for it had been built in the days of Sobieski, when that rough warrior and parvenu king built himself the house in the valley of the Vistula, where he saw all his greatness vanish, and ended his days in that grim solitude which is the inheritance of master-minds. The hand of the French architect is to be detected even in this farm; for Poland, more frankly and consciously than the rest of the world, drew all her inspiration and her art from France. Did not France once send her a king? Was not Sobieski's wife a Frenchwoman, who, moreover, ruled that great fighter with her little finger, stronger than any rod of iron? If ever a Frenchman was artificially made from other racial materials, he was the last king of Poland, Stanislas Augustus Poniatowski.

Built on raised ground, the farm-house was of stone. It had been a plain, square building; but in the days of Poniatowski some attempt had been made at ornamentation in the French style. A pavilion had been built in the garden amid the pine-trees. A sun-dial had been placed on the lawn, which was now no longer a lawn, but had lapsed again into a meadow. The cows had polished the sun-dial with their rough sides, while the passage of cold winters and wet springs had left the plaster ornamentation mossy and broken.

Here, amid a simple people, the Bukatys spent a portion of the year. They usually came in the winter, because it was in the winter they were needed. The feudal spirit, which was strong in the old prince and weaker in his children, has two sides to it; but its enemies have only remembered one. The prince took it as a matter of course that it was his duty to care for his peasants, and relieve as far as lay in his power the distress which came upon them annually with the regularity of the recurring seasons. With a long winter and a wet spring, with a heavy taxation, and a standing bill at the village shop kept by a Jew, and the village inn kept by another, these peasants never had any money. And so far as human foresight can perceive, there seems to be no reason why they ever should.

By some chain of reasoning, which assuredly had a flaw in it, the prince seemed to have arrived at the conclusion that he was put into the world to help his peasants, and those who were now no longer his serfs. And, though he spoke to them as if they were of a different creation and not his equals—as the French Revolution set about to prove, but only succeeded in proving the contrary—he cared for their bodies as he would have cared for a troop of sheep. He only saw that they were hungry, and he fed them. Wanda only saw that there were among them sick who could not pay for a doctor, and could not have gone to the expense of obeying his orders had they called one in. She only saw that there were mothers who had to work in the fields, while their children died of infantine and comparatively simple complaints at home, because their rightful nurse could not spare the time to nurse them. It was no wonder that the roof of the farm-house leaked, and that the cows were invited to feed upon the front lawn.

Clad in a sheepskin coat, with great jack-boots flapping above his knees, the prince spent all his days on horseback, riding from house to house, giving a little money and a good deal of sound and practical advice, listening to the old, old stories of undrained land and poor crops, of bad seed and broken tools; and cheering the tellers with his great laugh and some small witticism. For they are a gay people, these Poles, through it all. "Ils sont legers, actifs, insouciants," said Napoleon, that keenest searcher of the human heart, who knew them a hundred years ago when their troubles were comparatively fresh. And it is an odd thing that adversity rarely breaks a man's spirit, but often strengthens it.

Wanda sometimes rode, but usually went on foot, and had more than enough work to fill the days now growing longer and lighter. She, like her father, was brisk and cheerful in her well-being—like him, she was intolerant of anything that savored of laziness or lack of spirit. They liked the simple life and the freedom from the restraint that hung round their daily existence in Warsaw. But the old man watched the weather, and longed to be about larger business, which alone could satisfy the restless spirit of activity handed down to him by the forefathers who had stirred all Europe, and spoken fearlessly to kings.

Wanda was not sorry when the thaw gave way to renewed frost. The snow lay thickly on the ground, and weighed down the branches of the pines. In the stillness which brooded over the land during day and night alike the only sound they ever heard was the sharp crack of a branch breaking beneath its burden. They had lived in this still world of snow and forest for some weeks, and had seen and heard nothing of men.

"This frost cannot last," said the prince. "The spring must come soon, and then we shall have to go back to the world and its business."

But the world and its business thereof did not wait until the brief frost was over. It came to them that same night. For Kosmaroff was essentially of the active world, and carried with him wherever he went the spirit of unrest.

He arrived on foot soon after nine o'clock. He was going on to Warsaw on foot the same night, he announced, before the greetings were over.

"And you have had nothing to eat," said Wanda, glancing at his spare, weather-beaten face. He was the impersonation of hardness and activity; a man in excellent physical training, inured to cold and every hardship. He had simply opened the front door and walked in, throwing his rough sheepskin coat aside in the outer hall. The snow was on his boots nearly to the knee. The ice hung from his mustache and glistened on his eyebrows. He held his coarse blue handkerchief in his hand, and wiped his face from time to time as the ice melted.

"No," he answered, "I have had nothing to eat. But the servants do not know I am here. I saw the lights in their windows at the other end of the house. I would rather go hungry than let them know that I am here."

"You will not go hungry from this house," said the prince, with his rather fierce laugh.

"I will get you what you want," said Wanda, lighting a candle. "There are no servants, however, so you need not think of that. There are only the farmer and his wife—and my maid, who is English, and silent."

So, before telling his news, Kosmaroff sat down and ate, while Wanda waited on him, and Prince Bukaty poured out wine for this rough man in the homespun clothing and heavy boots of the Vistula raftsman, who yet had the manner of a gentleman and that quiet air of self-possession in all societies which is not to be learned in schools nor yet acquired at any academy.

"When you have finished," said Wanda, "you can talk of your affairs. I shall leave you to yourselves."

"Oh, there is not much to say," answered Kosmaroff. "I have done no good on my journey. Things make no progress."

"You expect too much," said the prince. He had helped himself to a glass of wine, and fingered the glass reflectively as he spoke. "You expect the world to move more quickly than it can. It is old and heavy, remember that. I have a fellow-feeling for it, with my two sticks. You would never make a diplomatist. I have heard of negotiations going forward for five years, and then falling through, after all."

Kosmaroff smiled, his odd, one-sided smile, and cut himself a piece of bread. There was a faint suggestion of the riverside in his manner at table. This was a man into whose life the ceremony of sit-down meals had never entered largely. He ate because he was hungry—not, as many do, to pass the time.

"One thing I came to tell you I can tell you now," he said. "In fact, it is better that the princess should hear it; for in a way it concerns her also. But, please, do not stand," he added, turning to her. "I have all I want. It is kind of you to wait on me as if I were a king—or a beggar."

His laugh had rather a cruel ring in it as he continued his meal.

"It is," he said, after a pause, "about that Englishman, Cartoner."

Wanda turned slowly, and resumed the chair she had quitted on Kosmaroff's sudden appearance at the door.

"Yes," she said, in a steady voice.

"He knows more than it is safe to know—safe for us—or for himself. One evening I could have put him out of the way, and it is a pity, perhaps, that it was not done. In a cause like ours, which affects the lives and happiness of millions, we

266   Henry Seton Merriman

should not pause to think of the life of one. This does not come into my sphere, and I have no immediate concern in it—" He stopped, and looked at the prince.

"But I have also no power," he added, "over those whose affair it is—you understand that. This comes under the hand of those who study the attitude of the European powers, our—well, I suppose I may say—our foreign office. It is their affair to know what powers are friendly to us—they were all friendly to us thirty years ago, in words—and who are our enemies. It is also their affair to find out how much the foreign powers know. It seems they must know something. It seems that Cartoner—knows everything. So it is reported in Cracow."

The prince shrugged his shoulders, and gave a short laugh.

"In Cracow," he said, "they are all words."

"There are certain men, it appears," continued Kosmaroff, "in the service of the governments—in one service it is called 'foreign affairs,' in another the 'secret service'—whose mission it is to find themselves where things are stirring, to be at the seat of war. They are, in jest, called the Vultures. It is a French jest, as you would conclude. And the Vultures have been congregating at Warsaw. Therefore, the powers know something. At Cracow, it is said—I ask your pardon for repeating it—that they know, and that Cartoner knows what he knows—through the Bukatys."

The prince's lips moved beneath his mustache, but he did not speak. Wanda, who was seated near the fire, had turned in her chair, and was looking at Kosmaroff over her shoulder with steady eyes. She was not taken by surprise. It was Cartoner himself who had foreseen this, and had warned her. There was deep down in her heart, even at this moment, a thrill of pride in the thought that her lover was a cleverer man than any she had had to do with. And, oddly enough, the next words Kosmaroff spoke made her his friend for the rest of her life.

"I have nothing against him. I know nothing of him, except that he is a brave man. It happens that I know that," he said. "He knows as well as I do that his life is unsafe in this country, and yet, before I left London I heard—for we have friends everywhere—that he had got his passport for Russia again. It is to be presumed that he is coming back, so you must be prepared. In case anything should happen to confirm these suspicions that come to us from Cracow, you know that I have no control over certain members of the party. If it was thought that you or Martin had betrayed anything—"

"I or Martin would be assassinated," said the prince with his loud laugh. "I know that. I have long known that we are going back to the methods of the sixties—suspicion and assassination. It has always been the ruin of Poland—that method."

"But you have no feelings with regard to this man?" asked Kosmaroff, sharply, looking from father to daughter, with a keen sidelong glance, as if the suspicion that had come from Cracow had not left him untouched.

"None whatever," answered the prince. "He is a mere passing acquaintance. He must be allowed to pass. We will drop him—you can tell your friends—it will not be much of a sacrifice compared to some that have been made for Poland."

Wanda glanced at her father. Did he mean anything?

"You know what they are," broke in Kosmaroff's eager voice. "They see a mountain in every molehill. Martin was seen at Alexandrowo with Cartoner. Wanda was seen speaking to him at the Mokotow. He is known to have called on you at your hotel in London."

"It is a question of dropping his acquaintance, my friend," said the prince, "and I tell you, he shall be dropped."

"It is more than that," answered Kosmaroff, half sullenly.

"You mean," said the prince, suddenly roused to anger, "that Martin and I are put upon our good behavior—that our lives are safe only so long as we are not seen speaking to Cartoner, or are not suspected of having any communication with him."

And Kosmaroff was silent.

He had ceased eating, and had laid aside his knife and fork. It was clear that his whole mind and body were given to one thought and one hope. He looked indifferently at the simple dishes set before him, and had satisfied his hunger on that nearest to him, because it came first.

"I tell you this," he said, after a silence, "because no one else dared to tell you. Because I know, perhaps better than any other, all that you have done—all that you are ready to do."

"Yes—yes. Everything must be done for Poland," said the prince, suddenly pacified by the recollection, perhaps, of what the speaker's life had been. Wanda had risen as if to go. The clock had just struck ten.

"And the princess says the same?" said Kosmaroff, rising also, and raising her hand to his lips to bid her good-night, after the Polish fashion.

"Yes," she answered, "I say the same."

XXVIII

IN THE PINE-WOODS

The prince was early astir the next morning. He was a hardy old man, and covered great distances on his powerful horse. Neither cold nor rain prevented him from undertaking journeys to some distant village which had once owned his ancestor as lord and master—in those days when a noble had to pay no more for killing a peasant than a farmer may claim for an injured sheep to-day.

The prince never discussed with Wanda those affairs in which, as a noble, he felt compelled to take an active interest. He had seen, perhaps, enough in the great revolution of his younger days to teach him that women—and even Polish women—should take no part in politics. He believed in a wise and studied ignorance of those things which it is better not to know. He made no reference to Kosmaroff at breakfast the next morning, and Wanda asked no questions. She had not slept until nearly morning, and had heard her father bolt the doors after the departure of the ex-Cossack. She had heard Kosmaroff's light and quick step on the frozen snow as he started on his seven-mile walk to Warsaw.

Cartoner's name, then, was not mentioned during the morning meal, which the prince ate with the deliberation of his years. The morning was bright and sunny, with a crisp air and sufficient frost to keep the snow from melting. The prince had recovered from his anger of the previous evening, and was gay. Wanda, too, seemed light-hearted enough. She was young and strong. In her veins there flowed the blood of a race that had always been "game," that had always faced the world with unflinching eyes, and had never craved its pity. Her father had lost everything, had lived a life of hardship, almost to privation for one of his rank; and witnessed the ruin or the downfall of all his friends; and yet he could laugh with the merry, while with the mourner it was his habit to purse up his lips beneath the grizzled mustache and mutter a few curt words, not of condolence, but of stimulation to endure.

He liked to see cheerful faces around him. They helped him, no doubt, to carry on to the end of his days that high-handed and dignified fight against ill-fortune which he had always waged.

"If you have a grievance," he always said to those who brought their tales of woe to his ears, "air it as much as you like, but speak up, and do not whine."

He had to listen to a great number of such tales, and to the majority of grievances could suggest no cure; for they were the grievances of Poland, and in these later times of Finland also, to which it appears there is no cure.

"I shall make a long round to-day," he said to Wanda, when he was in the saddle, with his short, old-fashioned stirrup, his great boots covering his knee and thigh from the wind, and his weather-beaten old face looking out from the fur collar of his riding-coat. "It may be the last time this winter. The spring must come soon."

And he went away at an easy canter.

Wanda, left alone for the whole day in the stillness of this forest farm, had her round to do also. She set out on foot soon after her father's departure, bound to a distant cottage in the depths of the pine-woods. The trees were quiet this morning; for it is only at the time of thaw, when the snow, gathering moisture from the atmosphere, gains in weight and breaks down the branches, that the woods crack as beneath the tread of some stealthy giant. But a frost seems to brace the trees which in the colder weather stand grim and silent, bearing their burden without complaint.

The sky was cloudless and the air quite still. There is no silence like that of a northern pine-wood in winter; for the creatures living in the twilight there have been given by God silent feet and a stealthy habit—the smaller ones going in fear of the larger, and the beasts of prey ever alert for their natural enemy—man. The birds kept for the most part to the outer fringes of the forest, nearer to the crops and the few, far cottages.

Wanda had grown from childhood amid the pines, and the gloomy forest-paths were so familiar as to have lost all power to impress her. In the nursery she had heard tales of wolves and bears, but had never seen them. They might be near or far; they might be watching through the avenues of straight and motionless stems. In their childhood it had been the delight of Martin and herself to trace in the snow the footprints of the wolves—near the house, in the garden, right up to the nursery window. They had gradually acquired the indifference of the peasants who work in the fields, or the woodmen at their labors amid the trees, who are aware that the silent, stealthy eyes are watching them, and work on without fear. The prince had taught the children fearlessness, or, perhaps, it was in their blood, and needed no education.

He had taught them to look upon the beasts of the forests not as enemies, but as quiet, watching friends.

Wanda went alone whithersoever she listed, without so much as turning her head to look over her shoulder. The pine-woods were hers; the peasants were her serfs in spirit, if not in deed. Here, at all events, the Bukatys were free to come and go. In cities they were watched, their footsteps dogged by human wolves.

There are few paths through the great forests of Poland, of Posen, and of Silesia, and what there are, are usually cut straight and at right angles to each other. There was a path just wide enough to give passage to the narrow timber carts from the farm direct to the woodman's cottage, and so flat is the face of the earth that the distant trees are like the masts of ships half-hidden by the curve of the world. It seems as if one could walk on and on forever, or drop from hunger and fatigue and lie unheeded for years in some forgotten corner. In the better-kept forests the paths are staked and numbered, or else it would be impossible to know the way amid such millions of trees—all alike, all of the same height. But the prince was too poor to vie with the wealthy land-owners of Silesia, and his forests were ill-kept.

In places the trees had fallen across the original path, and the few passers-by had made a new path to one side or the other. Sometimes a tree had grown outward towards the light and air, almost bridging the open space.

Wanda could not, therefore, see very far in front or behind, and was taken by surprise by the thud of a horse's feet on the beaten snow behind her. She turned, thinking it was her father, who for some reason had returned home, and, learning whither she had gone, had followed her. But it was not the prince. It was Cartoner. Before she had quite realized that it was he, he was on his feet leading his horse towards her.

She paused and looked at him, half startled; then, with a curt, inarticulate cry of joy she hurried towards him. Thus were given to them a few of those brief moments of complete happiness which are sometimes vouchsafed to human beings. Which must assuredly be moments stolen from heaven; for angels are so chary with them, giving them to a few favored ones only once or twice in a whole lifetime, and, to the large majority of mankind, never at all.

"Why have you come?" asked Wanda.

"To see you," replied this man of few words.

And the sound of his voice, the sight of his strong face, swept away all her troubles and anxieties; as if, with his greater physical strength, he had taken a burden which she could hardly lift, and carried it easily. For he always seemed to know how to meet every emergency and face every trouble. A minute ago she had been reflecting with relief that he was not in Poland, and now it seemed as if her heart must break had he been anywhere else. She forgot for the moment all the dangers that surrounded them; the hopelessness of their love, the thousand reasons why they should not meet. She forgot that a whole nation stood between them. But it was only for a moment—a moment borrowed from eternity.

"Is that the only reason?" she asked, remembering with a sort of shock that this world of glittering snow and still pine-trees was not their real world at all.

"Yes," he answered.

"But you cannot stay in Poland! You must go away again at

once! You do not know—" And she stopped short, for their respective positions were such that they always arrived at a point where only silence was left to them.

"Oh, yes," he answered with a short laugh. "I know. I am going away to-night—to St. Petersburg."

He did not explain that his immediate departure was not due to the fears that she had half expressed.

"I am so glad." She broke off, and looked at him with a little smile. "I am so glad you are going away."

She turned away from him with a sharp sigh. For she had now a new anxiety, which, however, like Aaron's rod, had swallowed all the rest.

"I would rather know that you were safe in England," she said, "even if I were never to see you again. But," and she looked up at him with a sort of pride in her eyes—that long-drawn pride of race which is strong to endure—"but you must never be hampered by a thought of me. I want you to be what you have always been. Ah! you need not shake your head. All men say the same of you—they are afraid of you."

She looked at him slowly, up and down.

"And I am not," she added, with a sudden laugh. For her happiness was real enough. The best sort of happiness is rarely visible to the multitude. It lies hidden in odd corners and quiet places; and the eager world which, presumably, is seeking it, hurries past and never recognizes it, but continues to mistake for it prosperity and riches, noise and laughter, even fame and mere cheap notoriety.

They walked slowly back towards the farm, and again the

gods were kind to them; for they forgot how short their time was, how quickly such moments fly. Much that they had to say to each other may not be expressed on paper, neither can any compositor set it up in type.

They were practical enough, however, and as they walked beneath the snow-clad pines they drew up a scheme of life which was astonishingly unlike the dreams and aspirations of most lovers. For it was devoid of selfishness, and they looked for happiness—not in an immediate gratification of all their desires and an instant fulfilment of their hopes, but in a mutual faith that should survive all separation and bridge the longest span of years. Loyalty was to be their watchword. Loyalty to self, to duty, and to each other.

Wanda did not, like the heroine of a novel, look for a passion that should stride over every obstacle to its object, that should ignore duty, which is only another word for honor, and throw down the spectres, Foresight, Common-sense, Respect, which must arise in the pathway of that madness, a brief passion. She was content, it seemed, that her lover should be wise, should be careful for the future, should take her life into his hands with a sort of quiet mastery as if he had a right to do so—a right, not to ruin and debase, such as is usually considered the privilege of that which is called a great passion and admired as such—but a right to shape, guard, and keep.

Cartoner had not much to say about his own feelings, which, perhaps, made him rather different from most lovers. He went so far as to consider the feelings of others and to place them before his own, which, of course, is quite unusual. And yet the scheme of life which was his reading of Love, and which Wanda extracted from him that sunny March morning and pieced together bit by bit in her own decided and conclusive way, seemed to content her. She seemed to gather from it that he loved her precisely as she wished to be loved, and that, come what might, she had already enough to make her life happier than the lives of most women.

And, of course, they hoped. For they were young, and human, and the spring was in the air. But their hope was one of those things of which they could not speak; for it involved knowledge of which Wanda had become possessed at the hand of the prince and Martin and Kosmaroff. It touched those things which Cartoner had come to Poland to learn, but not from Wanda.

The smell of the wood-smoke from the chimneys of the farm told them that they were nearing the edge of the forest, and Wanda stopped short.

"You must not go any nearer," she said. "You are sure no one saw you when you came?"

"No one," answered Cartoner, whom fortune had favored as he came. For he had approached the farm through the wood, and he had seen Wanda's footsteps in the snow. He had often ridden over the same ground on the very horse which he was now riding, and knew every inch of the way to Warsaw. He could get there without being seen, might even quit the city again unobserved.

For he knew—indeed, Wanda had told him—the dangers that surrounded him. He knew also that these dangers were infinitely greater for Martin and the prince.

"It is only what you foresaw," she said, "when—when we first understood."

"No, it is worse than I foresaw," he answered.

So they parted, with the knowledge that they must not meet again in Poland when their meeting must mean such imminent risk to others. They could not even write to each other while Wanda should be within the circle of the Russian postal service. There was but the one link between them— Paul Deulin; and to him neither would impart a confidence. Deulin had brought about this meeting to-day. Warned by telegram, he had met Cartoner at Warsaw Station, and had counselled him not to go out into the streets. Since he was only waiting a few hours in Warsaw for the St. Petersburg train, he must either sit in the station or take a horse and go for a ride into the country. The Bukatys, by-the-way, were not in town, but at their country house.

"Go and see them," he added. "A man living on a volcano may surely play with firearms if he wants to. And you are all on the volcano together. Pah! I know the smell of it. The very streets, my friend, reek of catastrophe."

Wanda was gay and light-hearted to the end. There was French blood in her veins—that gay, good blood which stained the streets of Paris a hundred years ago, and raised a standard of courage against adversity for all the world to imitate so long as history shall exist.

Cartoner turned once in his saddle and saw her standing in the sunlight waving him a farewell, with her eyes smiling and her lips hard pressed. Then he rode on, with that small, small hope to help him through his solitary wanderings which he knew to be identical with the hope of Poland, for which the time was not yet ripe. He was the watcher who sees most of the game, and knew that the time might never ripen till years after Wanda and he had gone hence and were no more seen.

XXIX

IN A BY-WAY

There are few roads in Poland. Sooner or later, Cartoner must needs join the great highway that enters Warsaw from the west, passing by the gates of the cemetery.

Deulin, no doubt, knew this, for Cartoner found him, riding leisurely away from the city, just beyond the cemetery. The Frenchman sat his horse with a straight leg and arm which made Cartoner think of those days ten years earlier, to which Deulin seldom referred, when this white-haired dandy was a cavalry soldier, engaged in the painful business of killing Germans.

Deulin did not think it necessary to refer to the object of Cartoner's ride. Neither did he mention the fact that he knew that this was not the direct way to St. Petersburg.

"I hired a horse and rode out to meet you," he said, gayly— he was singularly gay this morning, and there was a light in his eye—"to intercept you. Kosmaroff is back in Warsaw. I saw him in the streets—and he saw me. I think that man is the god in the machine. He is not a nonentity. I wonder who he is. There is blood there, my friend."

He turned his horse as he spoke, and rode back towards the city with Cartoner.

"In the mean time," he said, "I have the hunger of a beggar's dog. What are we to do? It is one o'clock—and I have the inside of a Frenchman. We are a great people. We tear down monarchies, and build up a new republic which is to last forever, and doesn't. We make history so quickly that the world stands breathless—but we always breakfast before mid-day."

He took out his watch, and showed its face to Cartoner, with a gesture which could not have been more tragic had it marked the hour of the last trump.

"And we dare not show our faces in the streets. At least, I dare not show mine in the neighborhood of yours in Warsaw. For they have got accustomed to me there. They think I am a harmless old man—a dentist, perhaps."

"My train goes from the St. Petersburg Station at three," said Cartoner. "I will have some lunch at the other station, and drive across in a close cab with the blinds down."

And he gave his low, gentle laugh. Deulin glanced at him as if there were matter for surprise in the sound of it.

"Like a monstrosity going to a fair," he said. "And I shall go with you. I will even lunch with you at the station—a station steak and a beery table. There is only one room at the station for those who eat and those who await their trains. So that the eaters eat before a famished audience like Louis XVI., and the travellers sit among the crumbs. I am with you. But let us be quick—and get it over. Did you see Bukaty?" he asked, finally, and, leaning forward, he sought an imaginary fly on the lower parts of his horse; for, after all, he was only a man, and lacked the higher skill or the thicker skin of the gentler sex in dealing with certain delicate matters.

"No, I only saw the princess," replied Cartoner. And they rode on in silence.

"You know," said Deulin, at length, gravely, "if that happens which you expect and I expect, and everybody here is hoping for—I shall seek out Wanda at once, and look after her. I do not know whether it is my duty or not. But it is my inclination; and I am much too old to put my duty before my inclination. So, if anything happens, and there follows that confusion which you and I have seen once or twice before, where things are stirring and dynasties are crumbling in the streets—when friends and foes are seeking each other in vain—you need not seek me or think about our friends in Warsaw. You need only think of yourself, remember that. I shall have eloped—with Wanda."

And he finished with an odd laugh, that had a tender ring in it.

"Bukaty and I," he went on, after a pause, "do not talk of these things together. But we have come to an understanding on that point. And when the first flurry is over and we come to the top for a breath of air, you have only to wire to my address in Paris to tell me where you are—and I will tell you where—we are. We are old birds at this sport—you and I—and we know how to take care of ourselves."

They were now in the outskirts of the town, among the wide and ill-paved streets where tall houses are springing up on the site of the huts once occupied by the Jews who are now quartered in the neighborhood of the Nowiniarska market-place. For the chosen people must needs live near a market-place, and within hearing of the chink of small coin. In the cities of eastern Europe that have a Jews' quarter there is a barrier erected between the daily lives of the two races, though no more than a narrow street may in reality divide them. Different interests, different hopes, aspirations, and desires are to be found within a few yards, and neighbors are as far apart as if a frontier line or the curse of Babel stood between them.

Cartoner and Deulin, riding through the Jewish quarter, were as safe from recognition as if they were in a country lane at Wilanow; for the men hurrying along the pavements were wrapped each in his own keen thought of gain, and if they glanced up at the horsemen at all, merely looked in order to appraise the value of their clothes and saddles—as if there were nothing beyond. For them, it would seem there is no beyond; nothing but the dumb waiting for the removal of that curse which has lasted nineteen hundred years, and instead of wearing itself out, seems to gain in strength as the world grows older.

"We will go by the back ways," said Cartoner, "and need never see any of our world in Warsaw at all."

The streets were crowded by men, for the women live an indoor life in an atmosphere that seems to bleach and fatten. The roads were little used for wheel traffic; for the commerce by which these people live is of so retail a nature that it seems to pass from hand to hand in mysterious cloth bundles and black stuff bags. The two horsemen were obliged to go slowly through the groups, who never raised their heads, or seemed to speak above a whisper.

"What do they talk of—what do they think—all day?" said Cartoner. And, indeed, the quiet of the streets had a suggestion of surreptitiousness. Even the children are sad, and stand about in melancholy solitude.

"I would sooner be a dog," answered Deulin, with a shake of the shoulders, as if Care had climbed into the saddle behind him. "Sooner a dog."

By these ways they reached the station, and there found a messenger to take the horses to their stable. All through the streets they had passed men in one uniform or another, who looked stout and well-fed, who strode in the middle of the pavement, while the Poles, whose clothes were poor and threadbare, shuffled aside in their patched and shambling boots to make way for the conqueror. Sometimes they would turn and look back at some sword-bearer who was more offensive than usual, with reflective eyes as if marking him in order to know him at a future time. As is always the case, it was the smaller officials who were the most offensive—the little Jacks-in-office from the postal administration, the common officers, the hundred obscure civil servants who wear a sword and uniform unworthily in any one of the three European empires. On the other hand, the men in real authority, and notably the officers of the better regiments, sought to conciliate by politeness and a careful retention of themselves in the background. But these well-intentioned efforts were of small avail; for racial things are stronger than human endeavor or the careful foresight of statesmen. Here in Warsaw the Muscovite, the Pole, the Jew—herding together in the same streets, under the same roof, obedient to one law, acknowledging one sovereign—were watching each other, hating each other.

At the street corners the smart, quiet police took note of each foot-passenger, every carriage, every stranger passing in a hired droschki. Cartoner and Deulin could see from the passing glance beneath the flat, green cap that they were seen and recognized at every turn. On the steps of the station they were watched with a polite pretense of looking the other way by two of the higher officials of the Russian-speaking police.

"I do not mind them," said Deulin, passing through the doorway to the booking-office. "It is not of them that we need be afraid. We are doing no harm, and they cannot send us out of the country while our passports hold out. They have satisfied themselves as to that. For they have been through my belongings twice, in my rooms at the Europe—I know when my things have been touched—they or some one else. Perhaps Kosmaroff; who knows?"

Thus he talked on in characteristic fashion, saying a hundred nothings as only Frenchmen and women can, touching life lightly like a skilled musician, running nimble fingers over the keys, and striking a chord half by accident here and there which was sonorous and had a deeper meaning. He ordered the luncheon, argued with the waiter, and rallied him on the criminal paucity of his menu.

"Yes," he said, "let it be beef. I know your mutton. It tastes like the smell of goat. So give us beef—your railway beef, which has travelled so far, but not by train. It has come on foot, to be killed and cut up by a locomotive, to be served by a waiter who has assuredly failed as a stoker."

He sat down as he spoke, and rearranged the small table, covered by a doubtful cloth, through which could be felt the chill of the marble underneath. Deulin always took the lead in these small matters, and Cartoner accepted his decision without comment. The Frenchman knew him so well, it seemed, that he knew his tastes, or suspected his indifference. While he thus rattled on he glanced sharply from time to time at his companion, and when the waiter was finally sent away with a hundred minute instructions, he turned suddenly to Cartoner.

"You are absorbed. What are you thinking about?" he said.

"I was thinking how well you speak Polish. And yet you have only been here once before," answered the Englishman, bluntly.

"When I was a young man there were opportunities of learning Polish in Paris," said Deulin. "Yes—I learned Polish when I was young—"

He had arranged the table to his satisfaction, had picked up several objects to examine them and replace them with care on the exact spot from whence he had taken them, and was now looking round the room with large, deep-lined eyes which were always tired and never at rest.

"When one is young, one learns so much in a short time, especially if that time is ill-spent," he said, airily. "That is why the virtuous are such poor company; they have no backbone to their past. With the others—'nous autres'—it is the evil deeds that form a sort of spinal column to our lives, rigid and strong, upon which to lean in old age when virtue is almost a necessity."

Finally he came round in his tour of inspection to the face opposite to him.

"Do you know," he said, sharply, "you are devilish absent-minded. It is a bad habit. It makes the world think that you have something on your mind. And having nothing on its own mind—or no mind to have anything on—it hates you for your airs of superiority."

He took up the bottle of wine which the waiter had set upon the table in front of him, inspected the label, and filled two glasses. He tasted the vintage, and made a wry face. Then he raised his shoulders with an air or reconciliation to the inevitable.

"When I was a young—a very young diplomatist—an old scoundrel in gold spectacles told me that one of the first rules of the game was to appear content with that which you cannot alter. We must apply that rule to this wine. It is our old friend, Chateau la Pompe. It will not hurt you. It will not loosen your tongue, my friend, you need not fear that."

He spoke so significantly that Cartoner looked across the table at him.

"What do you mean?"

Deulin laughed and made no answer.

"Do you think that my tongue requires loosening?"

And the Frenchman stroked his mustache as he looked thoughtfully into the steady, meditating eyes.

"It is not," he said, "that you assume a reserve which one might think unfair. It is merely that there are so many things which you do not think worth saying, or wise to speak of, or necessary to communicate, that—well—there is nothing left but silence. And silence is sometimes dangerous. Not as dangerous as speech, I allow—but dangerous, nevertheless."

Cartoner looked at him and waited. Across the little table the two schools went out to meet each other—the old school of diplomacy, all words; the new, all silence.

"Listen," said the Frenchman. "I once knew a man into whose care was given the happiness of a fellow-being. There is a greater responsibility, by-the-way, than the well-being of a whole nation, even of one of the two greatest nations in the world. And that is a care which you and I have had upon our shoulders for a brief hour here and there. It was the old story;

for it was the happiness of a woman. God knows the man meant well! But he bungled it. Bon Dieu—how he bungled it! He said too little. Ever since he has talked too much. She was a Polish woman, by-the-way, and that has left a tenderness, nay, a raw place, in my heart, which smarts at the sound of a Polish word. For I was the man."

"Well," asked Cartoner, "what do you want to know?"

"Nothing," answered the other, quick as thought. "I only tell you the story as a warning. To you especially, who take so much for said that has not been said. You are strong, and a man. Remember that a woman—even the strongest—may not be able to bear such a strain as you can bear."

Cartoner was listening attentively enough. He always listened with attention to his friend on such rare occasions as he chose to be serious.

"You know," went on Deulin, after a pause, during which the waiter had set before him a battered silver dish from which he removed the cover with a flourish full of promise—"you know that I would give into your care unreservedly anything that I possessed, such as a fortune, or—well—a daughter. I would trust you entirely. But any man may make a mistake. And if you make a mistake now, I shall never forgive you—never."

And his eyes flashed with a sudden fierceness as he looked at his companion.

"Is there anything I can do for you, my friend?" he asked, curtly.

"You have already promised to do the only thing I would ask you to do in Warsaw," replied Cartoner.

Deulin held up one hand in a gesture commanding silence.

"Not another word—they cost you so much, a few words—I understand perfectly."

Then with a rapid relapse into his gayer mood he turned to the dish before him.

"And now let us consider the railway beef. It promises little. But it cannot be so tough and indigestible as the memory of a mistake—I tell you that."

XXX

THE QUIET CITY

The most liberal-minded man in Russia at this time was the Czar. He had chosen his ministers from among the nobles who were at least tolerant of advance, if they did not actually advocate it. Much as he hated to make a change, he had in one or two instances parted with old and trusted servants—friends of his boyhood—rather than forgo one item of his policy. In other cases he had appealed to the memory of their long friendship in order to bring his nobles not to his own way of thinking, for he could not do that, but to his own plan of action.

"I do not agree with you, but I will serve you," had answered one of these, and the Czar, who did not know where to turn to find the man he needed, accepted such service.

For a throne stands in isolation, and no man may judge another by looking down upon him, but must needs descend into the crowd, and, mingling there on a lower level, pick out for himself the honest man or the clever man—or that rare being, the man who is both.

Kings and emperors may not do this, however. Despots dare not. Alexander II. acted as any ordinary man acts when he finds himself in a position to confer favors, to make appointments, to get together, as it were, a ministry, even if this takes no more dignified a form than a board of directors. He suspected that the world contained precisely the men he wanted, if he could only let down a net into it and draw them up. How, otherwise, could he select them? So he did the usual thing. He looked round among his relations, and, failing them, the friends of his youth. For an emperor, popularly supposed to have the whole world to choose from, has no larger a choice than any bourgeois looking round his own small world for a satisfactory executor.

Coming to the throne, as he did, in the midst of a losing fight, his first task was to conclude a humiliating peace. He must needs bow down to the upstart adventurer of France, who had tricked England into a useless war in order to steady his own tottering throne.

Alexander II., moreover, came to power with the avowed intention of liberating the serfs, which intention he carried out, and paid for with his own life in due time. Russia had been the only country to stand aloof on the slave question, thus branding herself in two worlds as still uncivilized. The young Czar knew that such a position was untenable. "Without the serf the Russian Empire must crumble away," his advisers told him. "With the serf she cannot endure," he answered And twenty-two millions of men were set free. In this act he stood almost alone; for hardly a single minister was with him heart and soul, though many obeyed him loyally enough against their own convictions. Many honestly thought that this must be the end of the Russian Empire.

It is hard to go against the advice of those near at hand; for their point of view must always appear to be the same as one's own, while counsel from afar comes as the word of one who is looking at things from another stand-point, and may thus be more easily mistaken.

Alexander II., called suddenly to reign over one-tenth part of the human race, men of different breed and color, of the three great contending religions and a hundred minor churches, was himself a nervous, impressionable man, suffering from ill-health, bowed down with the weight of his great responsibility. His father died in his arms, broken-hearted, bequeathing him an empire invaded by the armies of five European nations, hated of all the world, despised of all mankind. Even to-day there is a sinister sound in the very name of Russian. Men turn to look twice at one who comes from that stupendous empire. It is said that an hereditary melancholy broods beneath the weightiest earthly crown. History tells that none wearing it has ever reached a hale old age. Soldiers still hearty, still wearing the sword they have carried through half a dozen campaigns, bow to-day in the Winter Palace before their sovereign, having taken the oath of allegiance to four successive Czars.

Half in, half out of Europe, Alexander II. awoke with his own hand the great nation still wrapped in the sleep of the Middle Ages, only to find that he had stirred a slumbering power whose movements were soon to prove beyond control. He poured out education like water upon the surface of a vast field full of hidden seed, which must inevitably spring up wheat or tares—a bountiful harvest of good or a terrific growth of evil. He made reading and writing compulsory to the whole of his people. With a stroke of the pen he threw aside the last prop to despotic rule. Yet he hoped to continue Czar of All the Russias. This tall, pale, gentle, determined man was a man of courage. When the time came he faced the consequence of his own temerity with an unflinching eye.

"What do you want of me?" he asked, the very moment after he had been saved almost by a miracle from assassination.

For he knew that he was giving more than was wise. It is said that he was puzzled and thoughtful after each attempt upon his life.

The war with Turkey was the first sign that Russia was awakening—that the soldiers knew how to read and write. It was the first time in history that the nation forced a Czar to declare war, and Servia was full of Russian volunteers fighting for Christian Slavs before the Emperor realized that he must fight—and fight alone, for no nation in Europe would help him. He had taught Russia to read; had raised the veil of ignorance that hung between his people and the rest of civilization. They had read of the Bulgarian atrocities, and there was no holding them.

To rule autocratically what was then the vastest empire in the world was in itself more than one brain could compass. But in addition to his own internal troubles, Alexander II. was surrounded by European difficulties. England, his steady, deadly enemy, despite a declaration of neutrality, was secretly helping Turkey. Austria, as usual, the dog waiting on the threshold, was ready to side with the winner—for a consideration. No wonder this man was always weary. It is said that all through his reign he received and despatched telegrams at any hour of the night.

No wonder that his heart was hardened towards Poland. The most liberal-minded Czar had his mean point, as every man must have. There are many great and good men who will write a check readily enough and look twice at a penny. There are many who will give generously with one hand while grasping with the other that which is really the property of their neighbor. Alexander's mean point was Poland.

On the occasion of his first imperial visit to Warsaw he said, in the cold, calm voice which was so hated and feared: "Gentlemen, let us have no more dreams." Eleven years later he reminded an influential deputation of Polish nobles of the unforgiven and unforgotten words, commending the caution to their attention again. He paid frequent visits to Warsaw on one excuse or another. This dreamer would have no dreaming in his dominion. This mean man must ever be looking at his hoard. The chief interest in the study of a human life lies around the inexplicable. If we were quite consistent we should be entirely dull. No one knows why this liberal autocrat was mean to Poland.

From Warsaw, the city which has been commanded to stand still, Cartoner travelled across the plains of endless snow towards the north. He found as he progressed a hundred signs of the awakening. The very faces of the people had changed since he last looked upon them only a few years earlier. These people were now a nation, conscious of their own strength. They had fought in a great and victorious war, not because they had been commanded to fight, but because they wanted to. They had followed with understanding the diplomatic warfare that succeeded the signing of the treaty of San Stefano. They had won and lost. They were men, and no longer driven beasts.

It was evening when Cartoner arrived at St. Petersburg. The long northern twilight had begun, and the last glow of the western sky was reflected on the golden dome of St. Isaac's, while the arrowy spire of the Admiralty shot up into a cloudless sky.

The Warsaw Railway Station is in a quiet part of the town, and the streets through which Cartoner drove in his hired sleigh were almost deserted. It was the hour of the promenade in the Summer Garden, or the drive in the Newski Prospect, so that all the leisured class were in another quarter of the town. St. Petersburg is, moreover, the most spacious capital in the world, where there is more room than the inhabitants can occupy, where the houses are too large and the streets too wide. The Catherine Canal was, of course, frozen, and its broken surface had a dirty, ill-kept air, while the snow was spotted with rubbish and refuse, and trodden down into numberless paths and crossings. Cartoner looked at it indifferently. It had no history yet. The streets were silent beneath their cloak of snow. All St. Petersburg is silent for nearly half the year, and is the quietest city in the world, excepting Venice.

The sleigh sped across the Nicholas Bridge to the Vasili Island. The river showed no signs of spring yet. The usual pathways across it were still in use. The Vasili Ostrov is less busy than that greater part of the city which lies across the river. Behind the academy of Arts, and leading out of the Bolshoi Prospect, are a number of parallel streets where quiet people live—lawyers and merchants, professors at the university or at one or other of the numerous schools and colleges facing the river and looking across it towards the English Quay.

It was to one of these streets that Cartoner had told his driver to proceed, and the man had some difficulty in finding the number. It was a house like any other in the street—like any other in any other street. For St. Petersburg is a monstrous town, showing a flat face to the world, exhibiting to the sky a flat expanse of roof broken here and there by some startling inequality, the dagger-like spire of St. Peter and St. Paul, the great roof of the Kasan Cathedral, the dome of St. Isaac's— the largest cathedral in the world.

When the sleigh at length drew up with a shrill clang of bells the door-keeper came from beneath the great porch without enthusiasm. His was a quiet house, and he did not care for strangers, especially at this time, when every man looked askance at a new-comer and the police gave the dvorniks no peace. He seemed to recognize Cartoner, however, for he raised his hand to his peaked cap when he answered that the gentleman asked for was within.

"On the second floor. You will remember the door," he said, over his shoulder, as Cartoner, having paid the driver, hurried towards the house, leaving the dvornik to bring the luggage.

Cartoner's summons at the door on the second floor was answered by a clumsy Russian maid-servant, who smiled a broad, good-natured recognition when she saw him, and, turning without a word, led the way along a narrow passage. The smell of tobacco smoke and a certain bareness of wall and floor suggested a bachelor's home. The maid opened the door of a room and stood aside for Cartoner to pass in.

Seated near an open wood-fire was a man with grizzled hair and a short, brown beard, which had the look of concealing a determined chin. He was in the act of filling a wooden pipe from a jar on the table, and he stood up, pipe in hand, to greet the new-comer.

"Ah!" he said. "I was wondering if you would come, or if you had got other work to do."

"No, I am at the same work. And you?"

"As you see," replied the bearded man, dragging forward a chair with his foot and seating himself again before the fire. "I am here still, where you left me"—he paused to make a brief calculation—"five years ago. I stayed here all through the war—all through the Berlin Congress, when it was not good to be an Englishman in Petersburg. But I stayed.

Tallow! It does not sound heroic, but the world must have its tallow. And there is a simplicity about commerce, you know."

He gave a short laugh—the laugh of a man who had tried something and failed. Something that was not commerce, for his voice and speech had a ring of other things.

"Can you put me up?" asked Cartoner. "Only for a few days, perhaps."

"As long as you stay in Petersburg you stay in these rooms," replied the other, gravely.

Cartoner nodded his thanks and sat down. Their attitude towards each other had the repose which is only existent in a friendship that has lasted since childhood.

"Well?" he inquired.

"Gad!" exclaimed the other, "we are in a queer way. I went to the opera the other evening. He showed his face in the imperial box and the house was empty in half an hour. He always drives alone in his sleigh now, so that only one royal life may go at a time. They'll get him—they'll get him! And he knows it."

"Fools!" said Cartoner.

"They are worse than fools," answered the other. "The man is down, and they strike him. His asthma is worse. He has half a dozen complaints. His policy has failed. It was the finest policy ever tried in Russia. He is the finest Czar they have ever had. He gave them trial by jury; he abolished corporal punishment. Fools! they are the scum of this earth, Cartoner!"

"I know," replied Cartoner, in his gentle way, "students who cannot learn—workmen who will not work—women whom no one will marry."

"Yes, the sons and daughters of the serfs that he emancipated. It makes one sick to talk of them. Let me hear about yourself."

"Well," answered Cartoner, "I have had nothing to eat since breakfast."

"That is all you have to tell me about yourself?"

"That is all."

XXXI

THE PAYMENT

It was on every gossip's tongue in St. Petersburg that Jeliaboff had been arrested.

"It is the beginning of the end," men said. "They will now catch the others. The new reign of terror is over."

But Jeliaboff himself—a dangerous man (one of the Terrorists), the chief of the plot to blow up the imperial train at the Alexandroff Station—said that it was not so. This also, the mere bravado of an arrested criminal, was bandied from mouth to mouth.

For two years the most extraordinary agitation of modern days had held Russian society within its grip. All the world seemed to whisper. Men walking in the streets turned to glance over their shoulders at the approach of a step, at the sound of a sleigh-bell. The women were in the secret, too; and when the women touch politics they are politics no longer. For there should be no real emotion in politics; only the stimulated emotion of the platform.

For two years the Czar had been slowly and surely ostracized by a persecution which was as cruel as it was unreasoning.

Henry Seton Merriman

In former days the curious, and the many who loved to look on royalty, had studied his habits and hours to the end that they might gain a glimpse of him or perhaps a bow from the courteous Emperor. Now his habits and his daily life were watched for quite another purpose. If it was known that he would pass through a certain street, he was now allowed a monopoly of that thoroughfare. None passed nearer to the Winter Palace than he could help. If the Czar was seen to approach, men hurried in the opposite direction; women called their children to them. He was a leper among his own people.

"Do not go to the opera to-morrow," one lady would say to another. "I have heard that the Czar is to be there."

"Do not pass through the Little Sadovaia," men said to one another; "the street is mined. Do not let your wife linger in the Newski Prospect; it is honeycombed by mines."

The Czar withdrew himself, as a man must who perceives that others shrink from him; as the leper who sees even the pitiful draw aside his cloak. But some ceremonies he would not relinquish; and to some duties he remained faithful, calmly facing the risk, which he fully recognized.

He went to the usual Sunday review on the 12th of March, as all the world knows. It was a brilliant, winter morning. The sun shone from a cloudless sky upon streets and houses buried still beneath their winter covering of snow. The houses always look too large for their inmates, the streets too wide for those that walk them. St. Petersburg was planned on too large a scale by the man who did everything largely, and made his window looking out upon Europe a bigger window than the coldness of his home would allow.

The review passed off successfully. The Czar, men said, was

in good spirits. He had that morning signed a decree which was now in the hands of Loris Melikoff, and would to-morrow be given to the world, proving even to the most sceptical for the hundredth time that he had at heart the advance of Russia—the greater liberty of his people.

Instead of returning direct to the Winter Palace, the Czar paid his usual visit to his cousin, the Grand Duchess Catherine. He quitted her palace at two o'clock in his own carriage, accompanied by half a dozen Cossacks. His officers followed in two sleighs. It was never known which way he would take. He himself gave the order to the coachman. He knew the streets as thoroughly as the driver himself; for he had always walked in them unattended, unheeded, and unknown—had always mixed with his subjects. This was no French monarch living in an earthly heaven above his people. He knew—always had known—what men said to each other in the streets.

He gave the order to go to the Winter Palace by way of the Catherine Canal, which was not the direct way. Had he passed down the Newski Prospect half of that great street would have been blown to the skies. The road running by the side of the Catherine Canal was in 1881 a quiet enough thoroughfare, with large houses staring blankly across the frozen canal. The canal itself was none too clean a sight, for the snow was old and soiled and strewed with refuse. In some places there were gardens between the road and the waterways, but most of its length was bounded by a low wall and a railing.

The road itself was almost deserted. The side streets of St. Petersburg are quieter than the smaller thoroughfares of any other city in the world. A confectioner's boy was alone on the pavement, hurrying along and whistling as he went on his Sunday errand of delivery. He hardly glanced at the carriage that sped past him. Perhaps he saw a man looking over the low wall at the approach of the cavalcade. Perhaps he saw the bomb thrown and heard the deafening report. Though none can say what he heard or saw at that minute, for he was dead the next.

The bomb had fallen under the carriage at the back. A Cossack and his horse, following the imperial conveyance, were instantly killed. The Czar stepped out from amid the debris on to the torn and riven snow. He stumbled, and took a proffered arm. They found blood on the cushions afterwards. At that moment the only thought in his mind seemed to be anger, and he glanced at the dying Cossack—at the dead baker-boy. The pavement and the road were strewn with wounded—some lying quite still, others attempting to lift themselves with numbed and charred limbs. It was very cold.

Ryssakoff, who had thrown the bomb, was already in the hands of his captors. Had the crowd been larger, had the official element been weaker, he would have been torn to pieces then and there. The Czar went towards him. Some say that he spoke to him. But no clear account of those few moments was ever obtained. The noise, the confusion, the terror of it seemed to have deadened the faculties of all who took part in this tragedy, and they could only act mechanically, as men who were walking in their sleep.

Already a crowd had collected. Every moment added to its numbers.

"Stand back! Stand back! A second bomb is coming!" cried more than one voice. There are a hundred witnesses ready to testify that they heard this strange warning. But no man seemed to heed it. There are moments in the lives of men when their contempt for death raises them at one bound to the heights of immortality.

Those around the Czar urged him to quit the spot at once. In such a crowd of people there must be some enemies. At last he turned and went towards the sleigh which had been brought forward to take the place of the shattered carriage. He was pale now, and walked with an effort.

The onlookers stood aside to make a passage for him. Many raised their hats, and made silent manifestations of their respect and pity.

One man, alone, stood with folded arms, hat on head, and watched the Czar. He was on the pavement, with his back to the iron gate leading to the canal. The pavement was not six feet wide, and the Czar came along it towards him. For a moment they faced each other. Then the freed son of the serf raised both hands and threw his missile on the stones between them—at the feet of the man who had cut the chain of his slavery.

It was the serf who shrieked. The Emperor uttered no plaint. A puff of white-gray smoke rose to heaven. And those who watched there no doubt took note of it.

A shower of snow and human debris was thrown into the air. The very stones of the pavement were displaced.

The Emperor was on the ground against the railings. He was blind. One leg was gone, the other torn and mutilated to the hip. It was pitiful. He uttered no sound, but sought to move his bare limbs on the snow.

This was the end—the payment. He discharged his debt without a murmur. He had done the right—against the counsel of the wise, against his crown and his own greatness, against his purse and his father's teaching. He had followed the dictates of his own conscience. He had done more than any other Czar, before or since, for the good of Russia. And this was the payment!

The other—the man who had thrown the bomb—was already dead. The terrific explosion had sent his soul hard after the puff of white smoke, and in the twinkling of an eye he stood at the bar of the Great Assize. It is to be hoped that he made a good defence there, and did not stammer in the presence of his Judge.

The Czar's gentlemen in attendance were all killed or wounded. He was left to the care of his Cossack escort, who were doing what they could to succor him—though, being soldiers, they knew that he had passed beyond all human aid. The crowd parted to make way for a tall man who literally threw aside all who stood in his path. It was the Emperor's brother, the Grand Duke Michael, brought hither by the sound of the first explosion. He knelt on the blood-stained snow and spoke to the dying man.

The sleigh towards which he had been walking was now brought forward again, and the Czar was lifted from the snow. There was no doctor near. The mob drew back in dumb horror. In the crowd stood Cartoner, brought hither by that instinct which had made him first among the Vultures— the instinct that took him to the battle-field, where he was called upon to share the horror and reap none of the glory.

His quiet eyes were ablaze for once with a sudden, helpless anger. He could not even give way to the first and universal impulse to kill the killer.

He stood motionless through the brief silence that succeeded to the second explosion. There is a silence that follows those great events brought about by a man which seems to call aloud for a word from God.

Then, because it was his duty to draw his buzzing thoughts together, to be watchful and quick, to think and act while others stood aghast, he took one last look at the dying Emperor, and turned to make his way from the crowd while yet he could. He had pieced together, with the slow accuracy that Deulin envied him, the small scraps of information obtained from one source or another in Warsaw, in London from Captain Cable, in St. Petersburg from half a dozen friends. This was Poland's opportunity. A sudden inspiration had led him to look for the centre of the evil, not in Warsaw, but in St. Petersburg. And that which other men called his luck had brought him within sound of the first explosion by the side of the Catherine Canal.

He passed through a back street and out into wider thoroughfares. He hurried as much as was prudent, and in a few moments was beyond the zone, as it were, of alarm and confusion. A sleigh came towards him. The driver was half asleep, and looked about him with a placid, stupid face. Here was a man who had heard nothing.

Cartoner called him, and did not wait for him to descend to unhook the heavy leather apron.

"The telegraph office," he said.

And when the driver had settled down to his usual breakneck speed, he urged him to go faster. The passers on the pavement were going about their ordinary business now, bent on paying Sunday calls or taking Sunday exercise. None knew yet what had taken place a few hundred yards away.

Cartoner sat with clenched teeth and thought. He had a

strong grasp over his own emotions, but his limbs were shaking inside his thick furs. He made a supreme effort of memory. It was a moment in a lifetime, and he knew it. Which is not always the case, for great moments often appear great only when we look back at them.

He had not his code-books with him. He dared not carry them in the streets of St. Petersburg, where arrest might meet him at any corner by mistake or on erroneous suspicion. His head was stored with a thousand things to be remembered. Could he trust his memory to find the right word, or the word that came nearest to the emergency of this moment? Could he telegraph that the Emperor was dead when he had last seen him living, but assuredly feeling his way across the last frontier? The Czar must assuredly be dead before a telegram despatched now could reach England. It was a risk. But Cartoner was of a race of men who seem to combine with an infinite patience the readiness to take a heavy risk at a given moment.

The telegraph office was quiet. The clerks were dignified and sedate behind their caging—stiff and formal within their semi-military uniform. They knew nothing. As soon as the news reached them the inexorable wire windows would be shut down, and no unofficial telegrams could be despatched from Russia.

Cartoner had five minutes' start, perhaps, in front of the whole world. Five minutes might suffice to flash his news beyond the reach of recall.

The sense of discipline was strong in him. His first message was to London—a single word from the storehouse of his infallible memory.

He sent a second telegram to Deulin, in Warsaw, which was

no longer. The first message might reach its destination. The chances of the second were not so good, and the second might mean life or death to Wanda. He walked slowly back towards the double doors. He might even gain a minute there, he thought, by simulating clumsiness with the handle should any one wish to enter in haste. He was at the outer door when a man hurried up the steps. This was a small man, with a pale and gentle face, and eyes in which a dull light seemed to smoulder.

Cartoner detained him on the step for quite half a minute by persistently turning the handle the wrong way. When at length he was allowed to enter, he swore at the Englishman in a low voice as he passed, which Captain Cable would have recognized had he heard it. The two men looked at each other in the twilight between the doors. Each knew that the other knew. Then the little man passed in. The front of his black coat had a white stain upon it, as if he had been holding a loaf of bread under his arm. Cartoner noticed it, and remembered it afterwards, when he learned that the bombs which seem to have been sown broadcast in the streets of St. Petersburg that day were painted white.

He crossed the square to the Winter Palace, and stood with the silent crowd there until the bells told all Petersburg the news that the mightiest monarch had been called to stand before a greater than any earthly throne.

Henry Seton Merriman

XXXII

A LOVE-LETTER

The next morning Miss Netty Cahere took her usual walk in the Saski Gardens. It was much warmer at Warsaw than at St. Petersburg, and the snow had melted, except where it lay in gray heaps on either side of the garden walks. The trees were not budding yet, but the younger bark of the small branches was changing color. The first hidden movements of spring were assuredly astir, and Netty felt kindly towards all mankind.

She wished at times that there were more people in Warsaw to be kind to. It is dull work being persistently amiable to one's elderly relatives. Netty sometimes longed for a little more excitement, especially, perhaps, for the particular form of excitement which leads one-half of the world to deck itself in bright colors in the spring for the greater pleasure of the other half.

She wished that Cartoner would come back; for he was an unsolved problem to her, and there had been very few unsolved male problems in her brief experience. She had usually found men very easy to understand, and the failure to achieve her simple purpose in this instance aroused, perhaps, an additional attention. She thought it was that, but she was not quite sure. She had not arrived at a clear definition in her own mind as to what she thought of Cartoner. She was quite sure, however, that he was different from other men.

She had not seen Kosmaroff again, and the memory of her strange interview with him had lost sharpness. But she was conscious of a conviction that he had merely to come again, and he would regain at once the place he had so suddenly and violently taken in her thoughts. She knew that he was in the background of her mind, as it were, and might come forward at any moment. She often walked down the Bednarska to the river, and displayed much interest in the breaking up of the ice.

As to Prince Martin Bukaty, she had definitely settled that he was nice. It is a pity that the word nice as applied to the character of a young man dimly suggests a want of interest. He was so open and frank that there was really no mystery whatever about him. And Netty rather liked a mystery. Of course it was most interesting that he should be a prince. Even Aunt Julie, that great teacher of equality, closed her lips after speaking of the Bukatys, with an air of tasting something pleasant. It was a great pity that the Bukatys were so poor. Netty gave a little sigh when she thought of their poverty.

In the mean time, Martin was the only person at hand. She did not count Paul Deulin, who was quite old, of course, though interesting enough when he chose to be. Netty walked backward and forward down the broad walk in the middle of those gardens, which the government have so frequently had to close against public manifestations, and wondered why Martin was so long in coming. For the chance meetings had gradually resolved themselves into something very much like an understanding, if not a distinct appoint-ment. All people engaging in the game of love should be warned that it is a game which never stands still, but must move onward or backward. You may play it one day in jest, and find that it must be played in earnest next time. You may never take it up just where you left it, for the stake must always be either increasing or diminishing. And this is what makes it rather an interesting game. For you may never tell what it may grow to, and while it is in progress, none ever believe that it will have an end.

Netty liked Martin very much. Had he been a rich prince instead of a poor one, she would, no doubt, have liked him very much better. And it is a thousand pities that more young persons have not their affections in such practical and estimable control. Though, to be strictly just, it is young men who are guilty in this respect, much more than the maidens with whom they fall in love. It is rare, in fact, that a young girl is oblivious to the practical side of that which many mothers teach them to be the business of their lives. But then it is very rare that a girl is in love with the man she marries. Sometimes she thinks she is. Sometimes she does not even go so far as that.

Netty was, no doubt, engaged in these and other golden dreams of maidenhood as she walked in the Saski Gardens this March morning. The faces of those who passed her were tranquil enough. The news of yesterday's doings in St. Petersburg had not reached Warsaw, or, at all events, had not been given to the public yet. Even rumor is leaden-footed in this backward country.

Presently Netty sat down. Martin had never kept her waiting, and she felt angry and rather more anxious to see him, perhaps, than she had ever been before. The seats were, of course, deserted, for the air was cold. Down the whole length of the gardens there was only one other occupant of the polished stone benches—an old man, sitting huddled up in his shabby sheepskin coat. He seemed to be absorbed in thought, or in the dull realization of his own misery, and took no note of the passers.

Netty hardly glanced at him. She was looking impatiently towards the Kotzebue gate, which was the nearest to the Bukaty Palace of all the entrances to the Saski Gardens. At length she saw Martin, not in the gardens, but in the Kotzebue Street itself. She recognized his hat and fair hair through the railings. He was walking with some one who might almost have been Kosmaroff, better dressed than usual. But they parted hurriedly before she could make sure, and Martin came towards the gate of the gardens. He had evidently seen her and recognized her, but he did not come to her with his usual joyous hurry. He paused, and looked all ways before quitting the narrower path and coming out into the open.

Netty was at the lower end of the central avenue, close to the old palace of the king of Saxony, where there is but little traffic; for the two principal thoroughfares are at the farther corner of the gardens, near to the two market-places and the Jewish quarter.

It thus happened that there was no one in Netty's immediate vicinity except the old man, huddled up in his ragged coat. Martin paused to satisfy himself that he was not followed, and then came towards her, but Netty could see that he did not intend to stop and speak. He did not even bow as he approached, but passing close by her he dropped a folded note at her feet, and walked on without looking round.

There were others passing now in either direction, but Netty seemed to know exactly how to act. She sat with her foot on the note until they had gone. Then she stooped and picked up the paper. The precautions were unnecessary, it seemed, for no one was even looking in her direction.

"I must not speak to you," Martin wrote, "for there is danger in it—not to me, but to yourself. That of which you will not let me tell you is for to-night. Whatever you hear or see, do not leave your rooms at the Europe. I have already provided for your safety. There is great news, but no one knows it yet. Whatever happens, I shall always be thinking of you, and— no! I must not say that. But to-morrow I may be able to say it—who knows! I shall walk to the end of the garden and back again; but I must not even bow to you. If you go away before I pass again, leave something on the seat that I may keep until I see you again—your glove or a flower, to be my talisman."

Netty smiled as she read the letter, and glanced at Martin down the length of the broad walk, with the tolerant softness still in her eyes. She rather liked his old-fashioned chivalry, which is certainly no longer current to-day, and would, perhaps, be out of place between two young persons united fondly by a common sport or a common taste in covert-coating.

Martin was at the far end of the gardens now, and in a minute would turn and come towards her again. She had not long in which to think and to make up her mind. She had, as Martin wrote, prevented him from telling her of those political matters in which he was engaged. But she knew that events were about to take place which might restore the fortunes of the Bukatys. Should these fortunes be restored she knew that the prince would be the first man in Poland. He might even be a king. For the crown had gone by ballot in the days when Poland was a monarchy.

Netty had some violets pinned in the front of her jacket. She thoughtfully removed them, and sat looking straight in front of her—absorbed in maiden calculations. If Prince Bukaty should be first in Poland, Prince Martin must assuredly be second. She laid the violets on the stone seat. Martin had turned now though he was still far away. She looked towards him, still thinking rapidly. He was a man of honor. She knew that. She had fully gauged the honor of more than one man; had found it astonishingly reliable. The honor of women was quite a different question. That which Prince Martin said in the day of adversity he would assuredly adhere to in other circumstances. "Besides—" And she smiled a thoughtful smile of conscious power as she bent her head to rebutton her jacket and arrange her furs.

She tore the letter into small pieces and threw it behind the heap of snow at the back of the seat upon which she sat. Then she rose, looked at the bunch of violets still lying where she had laid them, and walked slowly away. She glanced over her shoulder at the old man sitting beneath the leafless trees at the other side of the broad avenue. He sat huddled within the high collar of his coat and heeded nothing. There was no one near to the seat that she had just vacated, and Martin was now going towards it. She hurried to the Saxon Palace, and as she passed beneath its arches turned just in time to see Martin bend over the stone seat and take up his talisman. He did it without disguise or haste. Any one may pick up a flower, especially one that has been dropped by a pretty girl.

Martin walked on, and turned to the left down the path that leads to the Kotzebue gate.

Then the old man on the seat nearly opposite to that upon which Netty had been sitting seemed to arouse himself from the lethargy of misery. He turned his head within his high collar, and watched Martin until he was out of sight. Netty had disappeared almost at once beneath the arches of the

Henry Seton Merriman

covered passages of the palace.

After a pause the old man rose, and crossing the pathway, sat down on the seat vacated by Netty. He waited there a few minutes until the passers-by had their backs turned towards him, and there was no one near enough to notice his movements. Then he stepped, nimbly enough, across the bank of gray snow, and collected the pieces of the letter which Netty had thrown there. He brought them back to the stone seat and spread them out there, like parts of a puzzle. He was, it seemed, an expert at such things; for in a moment he had them in order, and had pieced together the upper half of the paper. Moreover, he must have been a linguist; the note was written in English, and this Warsaw waif of the public gardens seemed to read it without difficulty.

"That of which you will not let me tell you is for to-night," he read, and instantly felt for his watch within the folds of his ancient clothing. It was not yet mid-day. But the man seemed suddenly in a flurry, as if there were more to be done before nightfall than he could possibly compass.

He collected the papers and placed them carefully inside a shabby purse. Then he rose and departed in the direction of the governor-general's palace. He must have been pressed for time, for he quite forgot to walk with the deliberation that would have beseemed his apparent years.

Netty walked round the outside of the gardens, and ultimately turned into the Senatorska, the street recommended to her by her uncle as being composed of the best shops in the town. Oddly enough, she met Joseph Mangles there—not loitering near the windows, but hurrying along.

"Ah!" he said, "thought I might meet you here."

He was, it appeared, as simple as other old gentlemen, and leaped to the conclusion that if Netty was out-of-doors she must necessarily be in the Senatorska. He suited his pace to hers. His head was thrust forward, and he appeared to have something to think about, for he offered no remark for some minutes.

"The mail is in," he then observed, in his usual lugubrious tone, as if the post had brought him his death-warrant.

"Ah!" answered Netty, glancing up at him. She was sure that something had happened. "Have you had important news?"

"Had nothing by the mail," he answered, looking straight in front of him. And Netty asked no more questions.

"Your aunt Jooly," he said, after a pause, "has had an interesting mail. She has been offered the presidency—"

"Of the United States?" asked Netty, with a little laugh, seeing that Joseph paused.

"Not yet," he answered, with deep gravity. "Of the Massachusetts Women Bachelors' Federation."

"Oh!"

"She'll accept," opined Joseph P. Mangles, lugubriously.

"Is it a great honor?"

"There are different sorts of greatness," Joseph replied.

"What is the Massachusetts Women Bachelors' Federation?"

Joseph Mangles did not reply immediately. He stepped out

into the road to allow a lady to pass. He was an American gentleman of the old school, and still offered to the stronger sex that which they intend to take for themselves in the future.

"Think it is like the blue-ribbon army," he said, when he returned to Netty's side. "The sight of the ribbon induces the curious to offer the abstainer drink. The Massachusetts Bachelor Women advertise their membership of the Federation, just to see if there is any man around who will induce 'em to resign."

"Is Aunt Julie pleased?" asked Netty.

"Almighty," was the brief reply. "And she will accept it. She will marry the paid secretary. They have a paid secretary. President usually marries him. He is not a bachelor-woman. They're mostly worms—the men that help women to make fools of themselves."

This was very strong language for Uncle Joseph, who usually seemed to have a latent admiration for his gifted sister's greatness. Netty suspected that he was angry, or put out by something else, and made the Massachusetts Women Bachelors bear the brunt of his displeasure.

"She is a masterful woman is Aunt Jooly," he said; "she'll give him his choice between dismissal and—and earthly paradise."

Netty laughed soothingly, and glanced up at him again. He was walking along with huge, lanky strides, much more hurriedly than he was aware of. His head was thrust forward, and his chin went first as if to push a way through a crowded world.

And it was borne in upon Netty that Uncle Joseph had received some order; that he was pluming his ragged old wings for flight.

Henry Seton Merriman

XXXIII

THIN ICE

It was not yet mid-day when Paul Deulin called at the Bukaty Palace.

"Is the prince in?" he asked. "Is he busy?" he added, when the servant had stood back with a gesture inviting him to enter. But the man only shrugged his shoulders with a smile. The prince, it appeared, was never busy. Deulin found him, in fact, in an arm-chair in his study, reading a German newspaper.

The prince looked at him over the folded sheet. They had known each other since boyhood, and could read perhaps more in each other's wrinkled and drawn faces than the eyes of a younger generation were able to perceive. The prince pointed to the vacant arm-chair at the other side of the fireplace. Deulin took the chair with that leisureliness of movement and demeanor of which Lady Orlay, and Cartoner, and others who were intimate with him, knew the inner meaning. His eyes were oddly bright.

They waited until the servant had closed the door behind him, and even then they did not speak at once, but sat looking at each other in the glow of the wood-fire. Then

Deulin shrugged his shoulders, and made, with both hands outspread, a gesture indicative of infinite pity.

"Do you know?" said the prince, grimly.

"I knew at eight o'clock this morning. Cartoner advised me of it by a cipher telegram."

"Cartoner?" said the prince, interrogatively.

"Cartoner is in Petersburg. He went there presumably to attend this—pleasing denouement."

The prince gave a short laugh.

"How well," he said, folding his newspaper, and laying it aside reflectively—"how well that man knows his business. But why did he telegraph to you?"

"We sometimes do each other a good turn," explained Deulin, rather curtly. "It must have happened yesterday afternoon. One can only hope that—it was soon over."

The prince laughed, and looked across at the Frenchman with a glitter beneath his shaggy brows.

"My friend," he said, "you must not ask me to get up any sentiment on this occasion. Do not let us attempt to be anything but what God made us—plain men, with a few friends, whom one would regret; and a number of enemies, of whose death one naturally learns with equanimity. The man was a thief. He was a great man and in a great position, which only made him the greater thief."

The prince moved his crippled legs with an effort and contemplated the fire.

"He is dead," he went on, after a pause, "and there is an end to it. I do not pray that he may go to eternal punishment. I only want him to be dead; and he is dead. Voila! It is a matter of rejoicing."

"You are a ruffian; I always said you were a ruffian," said Deulin, gravely.

"I am a man, my friend, who has an object in life. An object, moreover, which cannot take into consideration a human life here or there, a human happiness more or less. You see, I do not even ask you to agree with me or to approve of me."

"My friend, in the course of a long life I have learned only one effective lesson—to judge no man," put in Deulin.

"Remember," continued the prince, "I deplore the method. I understand it was a bomb. I take no part in such proceedings. They are bad policy. You will see—we shall both see, if we live long enough—that this is a mistake. It will alienate all sympathies from the party. They have not even dared to approach me with any suggestion of co-operation. They have approached others of the Polish party and have been sent about their business. But—well, one would be a fool not to take advantage of every mishap to one's enemy."

Deulin help up one hand in a gesture imploring silence.

"Thin ice!" he said, warningly.

"Bah!" laughed the other. "You and your thin ice! I am no diplomatist—a man who is afraid to look over a wall."

"No. Only a man who prefers to find out what is on the other side by less obvious means," corrected the Frenchman. "One must not be seen looking over one's neighbor's wall—that is the first commandment of diplomacy."

"Then why are you here?" asked the prince, abruptly, with his rough laugh.

And Paul Deulin suddenly lost his temper. He sat bolt upright in his chair, and banged his two hands down on the arms of it so that the dust flew out. He glared across at the prince with a fierceness in his eyes that had not glittered there for twenty years.

"You think I came here to pry into your affairs—to turn our friendship into a means for my own aggrandizement? You think that I report to my government that which you and I may say to each other, or leave unsaid, before your study fire? Was it not I who cried 'Thin ice'?"

"Yes—yes," answered the prince, shortly. And the two old friends glared at each other gleams of the fires that had burned fiercely enough in other days. "Yes—yes! but why are you here this morning?"

"Why am I here this morning? I will tell you. I ask you no questions, I want to know nothing of your schemes and plans. You can run your neck into a noose if you like. You have been doing it all your life. And—who knows?—you may win at last. As for Martin, you have brought him up in the same school. And, bon Dieu! I suppose you are Bukatys, and you cannot help it. It is your affair, after all. But you shall not push Wanda into a Russian prison! You shall not get her to Siberia, if I can help it!"

"Wanda!" said the prince, in some surprise—"Wanda!"

"Yes. You forget—you Bukatys always have forgotten—the women. Warsaw is no place for Wanda to-day. And to-day's work—to-night's work—is no work for Wanda!"

"To-night's work! What do you mean?"

The prince sat forward and looked hard at his friend.

"Oh, you need not be alarmed. I know nothing," was the answer. "But I am not a complete fool. I put two and two together at random. I only guess, as you know. I have guessed all my life. And as often as not I have guessed right, as you know. Ah! you think I am interfering in that which is not my business, and I do not care a snap of the finger what you think!"

And he illustrated this indifference with a gesture of his finger and thumb.

The prince laughed suddenly and boisterously.

"If I did not know that you had broken your heart—more than once—long ago," he began. But Deulin interrupted him.

"Only once," he put in, with a short, hard laugh.

"Well, only once, then. I should say that you had fallen in love with Wanda."

"Ah!" said Deulin, lightly, "that is an old affair. That happened when she used to ride upon my shoulder. And one keeps a tenderness for one's old loves, you know."

"Well, and what do you propose to do? I tell you honestly I have had no time to think of my own affairs. I have had no courage to think of them, perhaps. I have been at work all night. Yes, yes! I know! Thin ice! You ought to know it when you see it. You have been on it all your life, and through it—"

"Only once," repeated Deulin. "I propose what any other young lover would propose to do—to run away with her from Warsaw."

"When?"

Deulin looked at his watch.

"In half an hour. Think of the risks, Bukaty—a young girl."

And he saw a sudden fierceness in the old man's eyes. The point was gained.

"I could take her to Cracow this evening. Your sister there will take her in."

"Yes, yes! But will Wanda go?"

"If you tell her to go she will. I think that is the only power on earth that can make her do it."

The prince smiled.

"You seem to know her failings. You are no lover, my friend."

"That is a question in which we are both beyond our depth. You will do this thing for me. I come back in half an hour."

"What about the passport, and the difficulties of getting away from Warsaw to-day?" asked the prince. "What we know others must know now."

"Leave those matters to me. You can safely do so. Please do

not move. I will find my way to the door, thank you."

"If you see Wanda as you go," called out the prince, as Deulin closed the door behind him, "send her to me."

Deulin did see Wanda. He had always intended to do so. He went to the drawing-room and there found her, busy over some household books. He held out beneath her eyes the telegram he had received that morning.

"A telegram," she said, looking at it. "But I cannot make out its meaning. I never saw or heard of that word before."

"Nevertheless the news it contains will stir the blood of men till the end of time," answered Deulin, lightly. "It is from a reliable source. Cartoner sent it. Upon that news your father is basing that which he wishes to say to you in his study now."

"Ah!" said Wanda, with a ring of anxiety in her voice.

"It is nothing!" put in Deulin, quickly, at the sight of her face. "Nothing that need disturb your thoughts or mine. It is only a question of empires and kingdoms."

With his light laugh, he turned away from her, and was gone before she could ask him a question.

In half an hour he returned. He had a cab waiting at the door, and the passport difficulty had been overcome, he said.

"The man in the street," he added, turning to the prince, sitting beside Wanda, who stood before the study fire in her furs, ready to go—"the man in the street and the innumerable persons who carry swords in this city know nothing."

"They will know at the frontier," answered the prince, "and it is there that you will have difficulties."

"Then it is there that we shall overcome them," he replied, gayly. "It is there also, I hope, that we shall dine. For I have had no lunch. No matter; I lunched yesterday. I shall eat things in the train, and Wanda will hate me. I always hate other people's crumbs, while for my own I have a certain tenderness. Yes. Now let us say good-bye and be gone."

For Paul Deulin's gayety always rose to the emergency of the moment. He came of a stock that had made jests on the guillotine steps. He was suddenly pressed for time, and had scarcely a moment in which to bid his old friend good-bye, and no leisure to make those farewell speeches which are nearly always better left unsaid.

"I must ask you," he said to Wanda, when they were in the cab, "to drive round by the Europe, and keep you waiting a few moments while I run up-stairs and put together my belongings. I shall give up my room. I may not come back. One never knows."

And he looked curiously out of the cab window into the street that had run with blood twice within his own recollection. He peered into the faces of the passers-by as into the faces of men who were to-day, and to-morrow would be as the seed of grass.

In the Cracow Faubourg all seemed to be as usual. Some were going about their business without haste or enthusiasm, as the conquered races always seem to do, while others appeared to have no business at all beyond a passing interest in the shop-windows and a leisurely sense of enjoyment in the sunshine. The quieter thoroughfares were quieter than usual, Deulin thought. But he made no comment, and Wanda seemed to be fully occupied with her own thoughts. The long expected, when it comes at last, is really more surprising than the unexpected itself.

It was the luncheon hour at the Hotel de l'Europe, but the entrance hall was less encumbered with hats and fur coats than was usual between twelve and two. The man in the street might, as he had said, know nothing; but others, and notably the better-born, knew now that the Czar was dead.

As Deulin was preparing to open the carriage door, Wanda spoke for the first time.

"What will you do about the Mangles?" she asked. "We cannot let them remain here unwarned."

Deulin reflected for a moment.

"I had forgotten them," he answered. "In times of stress one finds out one's friends, because the others are forgotten. I will say a word to Mangles, if you like."

"Yes," answered Wanda, sitting back in the cab so that on one should see her—"yes, do that."

"Odd people women are," said Deulin to himself, as he hurried up-stairs. He must really have been in readiness to depart, for he came down again almost at once, followed by a green-aproned porter carrying his luggage.

"I looked into Mangles's salon," he said to Wanda, when he was seated beside her again. "He remains here alone. The ladies have already gone. They must have taken the mid-day train to Germany. He is no fool—that Mangles. But this morning he is dumb. He would say nothing."

At the station and at the frontier there were, as the prince had predicted, difficulties, and Deulin overcame them with the odd mixture of good-humor and high-handedness which formed his method of ruling men. He seemed to be in good spirits, and always confident.

"They know," he said, when Wanda and he were safely seated in the Austrian railway carriage. "They all know. Look at their stupid, perturbed faces. We have slipped across the frontier before they have decided whether they are standing on their heads or their heels. Ah! what a thing it is to have a smile to show the world!"

"Or a grin," he added, after a long pause, "that passes for one."

XXXIV

FOR ANOTHER TIME

The thaw came that afternoon. Shortly before sunset the rain set in; the persistent, splashing, cold rain that drives northward from the Carpathians. In a few hours the roads would be impassable. The dawn would see the rise of the Vistula; and there are few sights in nature more alarming than the steady rise of a huge river.

There is to this day no paved road across the plain that lies to the south of Warsaw. From the capital to the village of Wilanow there are three roads which are sandy in dry weather, and wet in spring and autumn. During the rains the whole tracks, and not only the ruts, are under water. They are only passable and worthy of the name of road in winter, when the sleighs have pressed down a hard and polished track.

Along the middle road—which is the worst and the least frequented—a number of carts made their way soon after eight o'clock at night. The road is not only unmade, but is neglected and allowed to fall into such deep ruts and puddles as to make it almost impassable. It is bordered on either side by trees and a deep ditch. In the late summer it is used for the transit of the hay which is grown on the low-lying land. In winter it is the shortest road to Wilanow. In spring and autumn it is not used at all.

It was raining hard now, and the wind hummed drearily through the pollarded trees. Each of the four carts was dragged by three horses, harnessed abreast in the Russian fashion. They were the ordinary hay-carts of the country, to be encountered at any time on the more frequented road nearer to the hills, carrying produce to the city. The carts were going towards the city now, but they were empty.

Fifty yards in front of the caravan a man splashed along through the standing water, his head bent to the rain. It was Kosmaroff. He was in his working clothes, and the rain had glued his garments to his spare limbs. He walked with long strides, heedless of where he set his feet. He had reached that stage of wetness where whole water could scarcely have made him wetter. Or else he had such business in hand that mere outward things were of no account. Every now and then he turned his head, half impatiently, to make sure that the carts were following him. The wheels made no sound on the wet sand, but the heavy wood-work of the carts groaned and creaked as they rolled clumsily in the deep ruts.

At the cross-ways, where the shorter runs at right angles into the larger Wilanow road, Kosmaroff found a man waiting for him, on horseback, under the shadow of the trees, which are larger here. The horseman was riding slowly towards him from the town, and led a spare horse. He was in a rough peasant's overcoat of a dirty white cloth, drawn in at the waist, and split from heel to band, for use in the saddle. They wear such coats still in Poland and Galicia.

Kosmaroff gave a little cough. There is nothing so unmistakable as a man's trick of coughing. The horseman pulled up at once.

"You are punctual," he said. "I was nearly asleep in the saddle."

And the voice was that of Prince Martin Bukaty. He had another coat such as he was wearing thrown across the saddle in front of him, and he leaned forward to hand it down to Kosmaroff.

"You are not cold?" he asked.

"No; I feel as if I should never be cold again."

"That is good. Put on your coat quickly. You must not catch a chill. You must take care of yourself."

"So must you," answered Kosmaroff, with a little laugh.

Though one was dark and the other fair, there was a subtle resemblance between these two men which lay, perhaps, more in gesture and limb than in face. There also existed between them a certain sympathy which the French call *camaraderie*, which was not the outcome of a long friendship. Far back in the days of Poland's greatness they must have had a common ancestor. In the age of chivalry some dark, spare knight, with royal blood in his veins, had perhaps fallen in love with one of the fair Bukatys, whose women had always been beautiful, and their men always reckless.

Kosmaroff climbed into the saddle, and they stood side by side, waiting for the carts to come up. Martin's horse began to whinny at the sound of approaching hoofs, when its rider leaned forward in the saddle and struck it fiercely on the side of its great Roman nose, which sounded hollow, like a drum.

"I suppose you had little sleep last night," said Kosmaroff

when Martin yawned, with his face turned up to the sky.

"I had none."

"Nor I," said Kosmaroff. "We may get some—to-morrow."

The carts now came up. Each team had two drivers, one walking on either side.

"You know what to do," said Martin to these in turn. "Come to the iron-foundry, where you will find us waiting for you. When you are laden you are to go straight back as quickly as you can by this same road to the military earthworks, where you will find our friends drawn up in line. You are to turn to the left, down the road running towards the river on this side of the fortifications, and pass slowly down the line, dropping your load as directed by those who will meet you there. If you are stopped on the road by the police or a patrol, who insist on asking what you have in your carts, you must be civil to them, and show them; and while they are looking into your carts you must kill them quietly with the knife."

The drivers seemed to have heard these instructions before, for they merely nodded, and made no comment. One of them gave a low laugh, and that was all. He appeared to be an old man with a white beard, and had perhaps waited a long time for this moment. There was a wealth of promise in his curt hilarity.

Then Martin and Kosmaroff turned and rode on towards Warsaw at a trot. Before long they wheeled to the right, quitting the highway and taking to the quieter Czerniakowska, that wide and deserted road which runs by the river-side, skirting the high land now converted into a public pleasure-ground, under the name of the Lazienki Park.

In the daytime the Czerniakowska is only used by the sand-carts and the workmen going to and from the manufactories. To-night, in the pouring rain, no one passed that way.

Before the iron-foundry is reached the road narrows somewhat, and is bounded on either side by a high stone wall. On the left are the lower lands of the Lazienki Park; the yards and storehouses of the iron-foundry are on the right.

At the point where the road narrows Kosmaroff suddenly reined in his horse, and leaning forward, peered into the darkness. There are no lamps at the farther end of the Czerniakowska.

"What is it?" asked Martin.

"I thought I saw a glint under the wall," answered Kosmaroff. "There—there it is again. Steel. There is some one there. It is the gleam of those distant lights on a bayonet."

"Then let us go forward," said Martin, "and see who it is."

And he urged his horse, which seemed tired, and carried its head low beneath the rain. They had not gone ten paces when a rough voice called out:

"Who goes there?"

"Who goes there?" echoed Martin. "But this is a high-road." And he moved nearer to the wall. The man stepped from the shadow, and his bayonet gleamed again.

"No matter," he said; "you cannot pass this way."

"But, my friend—" began Martin, with a protesting laugh. But he never finished the sentence, for Kosmaroff had slipped out of the saddle on the far side, and interrupted him by pushing the bridle into his hand. Then the ex-Cossack ran round at the back of the horses.

The soldier gave a sharp exclamation of surprise, and the next moment his rifle rattled down against the wall. Both men were on the ground now in the water and the mud. There came to Martin's ears the sound of hard breathing, and some muttered words of anger; then a sharp cough, which was not Kosmaroff's cough.

After an instant of dead silence, Kosmaroff rose to his feet.

"First blood," he said, breathlessly. He went to his horse and wiped his hands upon its mane.

"Bah!" he exclaimed, "how he smelled of bad cigarettes!"

Martin was leaning in the saddle, looking down at the dark form in the mud.

"Oh, he is dead enough," said Kosmaroff. "I broke his neck. Did you not hear it go?"

"Yes—I heard it. But what was he doing here?"

"That is yet to be found out," was the reply, in a sharp, strained voice. "This is Cartoner's work."

"I doubt it," whispered Martin. And yet in his heart he could scarcely doubt it at that moment. Nothing was further from his recollection than the note he had given to Netty in the Saski Gardens ten hours ago.

"What does it mean?" he asked, with a sudden despair in his voice. He had always been lucky and successful.

"It means," answered the man who had never been either, "that the place is surrounded, of course. They have got the arms, and we have failed—this time. Take the horses back towards the barracks—and wait for me where the water is across the road. I will go forward on foot and make sure. If I do not return in twenty minutes it will mean that they have taken me."

As he spoke he took off his white overcoat, which was all gray and bespattered with mud, and threw it across the saddle. His working clothes were sombre and dirty. He was almost invisible in the darkness.

"Wait a moment," he said. "I will get over the wall here. Bring your horse against the wall."

Martin did so, avoiding the body of the sentry, which lay stretched across the foot-path. The wall was eighteen feet high.

"Stand in your stirrups," said Kosmaroff, "and hold one arm up rigid against the wall."

He was already standing on the broad back of the charger, steadying himself by a firm grip of Martin's collar. He climbed higher, standing on Martin's shoulders, and steadying himself against the wall.

"Are you ready? I am going to spring."

He placed the middle of his foot in Martin's up-stretched palm, gave a light spring and a scramble, and reached the summit of the wall. Martin could perceive him for a moment against the sky.

"All right," he whispered, and disappeared.

Martin had not returned many yards along the road they had come when he heard pattering steps in the mud behind him. It was Kosmaroff, breathless.

"Quick!" he whispered. "Quick!"

And he scrambled into the saddle while the horse was still moving. He was, it must be remembered, a trained soldier. He led the way at a gallop, stooping in the saddle to secure the swinging stirrups. Martin had to use his spurs to bring his horse alongside. Shoulder to shoulder they splashed on in the darkness.

"I went right in," gasped Kosmaroff. "The arms are gone. The place is full of men. There is a sotnia drawn up in the yard itself. It is an ambuscade. We have failed—failed—this time!"

"We must stop the carts, and then ride on and disperse the men," said Martin. "We may do it. We may succeed. It is a good night for such work."

Kosmaroff gave a short, despairing laugh.

"Ah!" he said. "You are full of hope—you."

"Yes—I am full of hope—still," answered Martin. He had more to lose than his companion. But he had also less to gain.

They rode hard until they met the carts, and turned them back. So far as these were concerned, there was little danger in going away empty from the city.

Then the two horsemen rode on in silence. They were far out in the marsh-lands before Kosmaroff spoke.

"I am sure," he then said, "that I was seen as I climbed back over the wall. I heard a stir among the rifles. But they could not recognize me. It is just possible that I may not be suspected. For you it is different. If they knew where the arms were stored, they must also know who procured them. You will never be able to show yourself in Warsaw again."

"I may be able to make myself more dangerous elsewhere," said Martin, with a laugh.

"I do not know," went on Kosmaroff, "if they will have arrested your father and sister; but I am quite sure that they will be in the palace now awaiting your return there. We must get away to-night."

"Oh," answered Martin gayly, "it does not matter much about that. What I am thinking of are these four thousand men waiting out here in the rain. How are we to get them to their homes in Warsaw?"

And Kosmaroff had no answer to this question.

Beneath the trees on the low, wet land inside the fortifications they found their men drawn up in a double line. There were evidences of military organization and training in their bearing and formation. If the arms had been forthcoming, these would have been dangerous soldiers; for they were desperate men, and had each in his heart a grievance to be wiped out. They were only the nucleus of a great rising, organized carefully and systematically—the brand to be thrown amid the straw. They were to surprise and hold the two strongholds in Warsaw, while the whole country was set in a blaze, while the foreign powers and the parties to the treaty which Russia had systematically broken were appealed to and urged to assist. It was a wild scheme, but not half so wild as many that have succeeded.

The four thousand heroically waiting the word that was to send them on their forlorn hope heard the news in silence, and all silently moved away.

"It is for another time—it is for another time!" said Kosmaroff and Martin repeatedly and confidently, as the men moved past them in the darkness.

In Warsaw there was a queer silence, and every door was shut. The streets had been quite deserted, and they were now full of soldiers, who, at a given word, had moved out from the barracks to line the streets.

At midnight they were still at their posts, when the first stragglers came in from the south, silent, mud-bespattered, bedraggled men, who shuffled along in their dripping clothes in the middle of the street in groups of two and three. They hung their heads and crept to their houses. And the conquerors watched them without sympathy, without anger.

It was a miserable fiasco.

XXXV

ACROSS THE FRONTIER

Those who listened at their open windows that night for the sound of firing heard it not. They heard, perhaps, the tread of slipshod feet hurrying homeward. They could scarcely fail to hear the Vistula grinding and grumbling in its new-found strength. For the ice was moving and the water rising. The long sleep of winter was over, and down the great length of the river that touches three empires men must needs be on the alert night and day.

Between the piers of the bridge the ice had become blocked, and the large, flat floes sweeping down on the current were pushing, hustling, and climbing on each other with grunts and squeaks as if they had been endowed with some low form of animal life. The rain did not cease at midnight, but the clouds lifted a little, and the night was less dark. The moon above the clouds was almost full.

"There is only one chance of escape," Kosmaroff had said— "the river. Meet me on the steps at the bottom of the Bednarska at half-past twelve. I will get a boat. Have you money?"

"I have a few roubles—I never had many," answered Martin.

"Get more if you can—get some food if you can—a bottle of vodka may make the difference between life and death. Keep your coat."

And they parted hurriedly on the hill where the road rises towards the Mokotow. Kosmaroff turned to the right and went to the river, where he earned his daily bread, where his friends eked out their toilsome lives. Martin joined the silent, detached groups hurrying towards the city. He passed down the whole length of the Marszalkowska with the others slouching along the middle of the street beneath the gaze of the soldiers, brushing past the horses of the Cossacks stationed at the street corners. And he was allowed to pass, unrecognized.

A group of officers stood in the wide road opposite to the railway station, muffled in their large cloaks. They were talking together in a low voice. One of them gave a laugh as Martin passed. He recognized the voice as that of a friend—a young Cossack officer who had lunched with him two days earlier.

Soon after midnight he made his way down the steep Bednarska. He had found out that the Bukaty Palace was surrounded; had seen the light filtering through the dripping panes of the conservatory. His father was probably sitting in the great drawing-room alone, before the wood-fire, meditating over the failure which he must have realized by now from a note hurriedly sent by one of the few servants whom they could trust. Martin knew that Wanda had gone. He also knew the address that would find her. This was one of the hundred details to which the prince himself had attended. He had been a skilled organizer in the days when he had poured arms and ammunition into Poland across the Austrian frontier, and his hand had not lost its cunning. All Poland was seamed by channels through which information

Henry Seton Merriman

could be poured at any moment day or night, just as water is distributed over the land of an irrigated farm.

Martin had procured money. He carried some large round loaves of gray bread under his arm. The neck of a bottle protruded from the pocket of his coat. Among the lower streets near the river these burdens were more likely to allay than to arouse suspicion.

Between the Bednarska and the bridge which towers above the low-roofed houses fifty yards farther down the river are the landing-stages for the steamers that ply in summer. There is a public bath, and at one end of this floating erection a landing-stage for smaller boats, where as often as not Kosmaroff found work. It was to this landing-stage that Martin directed his steps. In summer there were usually workers and watchers here night and day; for the traffic of a great river never ceases, and those whose daily bread is wrested from wind, water, and tide must get their sleep when they can.

To-night there were a few men standing at the foot of the street where the steps are—river-workers who had property afloat and imprisoned by the ice, dwellers, perhaps, in those cheap houses beneath the bridge which are now gradually falling under the builder's hammer, who took a sleepless interest in the prospects of a flood.

Martin went out onto the landing-stage, and looked about him as if he also had a stake in this, one of nature's great lotteries. There he had a fit of coughing, such as any man might have on such a night, and at the most deadly time of the year. He waited ten minutes, perhaps, coughing at intervals, and at length Kosmaroff came to him, not from the land, but across the moving floes from the direction of the bridge.

"The water is running freely," he said, "through the middle arch. I have a boat out there on the ice. Come!"

And he took the bread from Martin's arms, and led the way on to the river that he knew so well in all its varying moods. The boat was lying on the ice a few yards above the massive pier of the bridge, almost at the edge of the water, which could be heard gurgling and lapping as it flowed towards the sea with its burden of snow and ice. It was so dark that Martin, stumbling over the chaos of ice, fell against the boat before he saw it. It was one of the rough punts of a primeval simplicity of build used by the sand-workers of the Vistula.

Kosmaroff gave his orders shortly and sharply. He was at home on the unstable surface, which was half water, half ice. He was commander now, and spoke without haste or hesitation.

"Help me," he said, "to carry her to the edge, but do not stand upright. We can easily get away unseen, and you may be sure that no one will come out on the ice to look for us. We must be twenty miles away before dawn."

The boat was a heavy one, and they stumbled and fell several times; for there was no foothold, and both were lightly made men. At last they reached the running water and cautiously launched into it.

"We must lie down in the bottom of the boat," said Kosmaroff, "and take our chances of being crushed until we are past the citadel."

As he spoke they shot under the bridge. Above them, to the left, towered the terrace of the castle, and the square face of that great building which has seen so many vicissitudes. Every window was alight. For the castle is used as a barracks now, and the soldiers, having been partially withdrawn from the streets, were going to bed. Soon these lights were left behind, and the outline of the citadel, half buried in trees, could be dimly seen. Then suddenly they left the city behind, and were borne on the breast of the river into the outer darkness beyond.

Kosmaroff sat up.

"Give me a piece of bread," he said. "I am famished."

But he received no answer. Prince Martin was asleep.

The sky was beginning to clear. The storm was over, but the flood had yet to come. The rain must have fallen in the Carpathians, and the Vistula came from those mountains. In twenty-four hours there would be not only ice to fear, but uprooted trees and sawn timber from the mills; here and there a mill-wheel torn from its bearings, now and then a dead horse; a door, perhaps, of a cottage, or part of a roof; a few boats; a hundred trophies of the triumph of nature over man, borne to the distant sea on muddy waters.

Kosmaroff found the bread and tore a piece off. Then he made himself as comfortable as he could in the stern of the boat, using one oar as a rudder. But he could not see much. He could only keep the boat heading down stream and avoid the larger floes. Then—wet, tired out, conscious of failure, sick at heart—he fell asleep, too, in the hands of God.

When he awoke he found Martin crouching beside him, wide awake. The prince had taken the oar and was steering. The clouds had all cleared away, and a full moon was high above them. The dawn was in the sky above the level land. They were passing through a plain now, broken here and there by pollarded trees, great spaces of marsh-land, with big, low-roofed farms standing back on the slightly rising ground. It was almost morning.

Kosmaroff sat up, and immediately began to shiver. Martin was shivering too, and handed him the vodka-bottle with a laugh. His spirits were proof even against failure and a hopeless dawn and bitter cold.

"Where are we?" he asked.

Kosmaroff stood up and looked round. They were travelling at a great pace in the company of countless ice-floes, some white with snow, others gray and muddy.

"I know where we are," he answered, after a pause. "We have passed Wyszogrod. We are nearing Plock. We have come a great distance. I wish my teeth wouldn't chatter."

"I have secured mine with a piece of bread," mumbled Martin.

Kosmaroff was looking uneasily at the sky.

"We cannot travel during the day," he said, after a long examination of the little clouds hanging like lines across the eastern sky. "We shall not be able to cross the frontier at Thorn with this full moon, and I am afraid we are going to have fine weather. We shall soon come to some large islands on this side of Plock. I know a farmer there. We must wait with him until we have promise of a suitable night to pass through Thorn."

Before daylight they reached the islands. There was no pack now; the ice was afloat and moving onward. All Kosmaroff's skill, all the little strength of both was required to work the boat through the floes towards the land. The farmer took them in willingly enough, and boasted that they could not have found a safer hiding-place in all Poland, which, indeed, seemed true enough. For none but expert and reckless boatmen would attempt to cross the river now.

Nevertheless, Kosmaroff made the passage to the mainland before mid-day, and set off on foot to Plock. He was going to communicate with the prince at Warsaw, and ask him to provide money or means of escape to await them at Dantzic. In two days a reply came, telling them that their escape was being arranged, but they must await further instructions before quitting their hiding-place. After the lapse of four days these further orders came by the same sure channel, which was independent of the Russian post-offices.

The fugitives were to proceed cautiously to Dantzic, to pass through that town at night to the anchorage below Neufahrwasser. Here they would find Captain Cable, in the *Minnie*, anchored in the stream ready for sea. The instructions were necessarily short. There were no explanations whatever. There was no news.

At Plock, Kosmaroff could learn nothing, for nothing was known there. The story of the great plot had been hushed up by the authorities. There are persons living in Warsaw who do not know of it to this day. There are others who know of it and deny that it ever existed. The arms are in use in Central Asia at the present time, though their pattern is already considered antiquated. Any one who may choose to walk along the Czerniakowska will find to-day on the left-hand side of it a large building, once an iron-foundry, now deserted and falling into disrepair. If it be evening-time, he will, as likely as not, meet the patrol from the neighboring hussar barracks, which nightly guards this road and the river-side.

After receiving their final instructions, Kosmaroff and Martin had to wait two days until the weather changed—until the moon, now well on the wane, did not rise before midnight.

At last they set out, in full daylight, on a high river still encumbered by ice. It was much warmer during the day now; but the evenings were cold, and a thick mist usually arose from the marsh-lands. This soon enveloped them, and they swept on unseen. None could have followed them into the mist, for none had Kosmaroff's knowledge of the river.

The frontier-line is some miles above the ancient city of Thorn. It is strictly guarded by day and night. The patrol-boats are afloat at every hour. Kosmaroff had arranged to arrive at this spot early in the night, before the mists had been dispelled by the coming of the moon.

Even he could only guess at their position. Once they dared to approach the shore in order to discover some landmark. But they navigated chiefly by sound. The whistle of a distant train, the sound of church clocks, the street cries of a town—these were Kosmaroff's degrees of latitude.

"We are getting near," he said, in little more than a whisper. "What is the time?"

It was nearly eleven o'clock. If they got past the frontier they would sweep through Thorn before mid-night. The river narrows here, and goes at a great pace. It is still of a vast width—one of the largest rivers in Europe.

The mist was very thick here.

"Listen!" whispered Kosmaroff, suddenly. And they heard the low, regular thud of oars. It was the patrol-boat.

Almost immediately a voice, startlingly near, called upon them to halt. They crouched low in the boat. In a mist it is very difficult to locate sound. They looked round in all directions. The voice seemed to have come from above. It was raised again, and seemed to be behind them this time.

"Stop, or we fire!" it said, in Russian. Then followed a sharp whistle, which was answered by two or three others. There were at least three boats close at hand, seeking to locate each other before they fired.

Immediately afterwards the firing began, and was taken up by the more distant boats. A bullet splashed in the water close behind Kosmaroff's oar, with a sharp spit like that of an angry cat. Martin gave a suppressed laugh. Kosmaroff only smiled.

Then two bullets struck the boat simultaneously, one on the stern-post, fired from behind, the other full on the side amidships, where Martin lay concealed.

Neither of the two men moved or made a sound. Kosmaroff leaned forward and peered into the fog. The patrol-boats were behind now, and the officers were calling to each other.

"What was it—a boat or a floating tree?" they heard them ask each other.

Kosmaroff was staring ahead, but he saw Martin make a quick movement in the bottom of the boat.

"What is it?" he whispered.

"A bullet," answered Martin. "It came through the side of the boat, low down. It struck me in the back—the spine. I cannot move my legs. But I have stopped the water from coming in.

I have my finger in the hole the bullet made below the water-line. I can hold on till we have passed through Thorn."

He spoke in his natural voice, quite cheerfully. They were not out of danger yet. Kosmaroff could not quit the steering-oar. He glanced at Martin, and then looked ahead again uneasily.

Martin was the first to speak. He raised himself on his elbow, and with a jerk of the wrist threw something towards Kosmaroff. It was an envelope, closed and doubled over.

"Put that in your pocket," he said. And Kosmaroff obeyed.

"You know Miss Cahere, who was at the Europe?" asked Martin, suddenly, after a pause.

Kosmaroff smiled the queer smile that twisted his face all to one side.

"Yes, I know her."

"Give her that, or get it to her," said Martin.

"But—"

"Yes," said Martin, answering the unasked question, "I am badly hit, unless you can do something for me after we are past Thorn."

And his voice was still cheerful.

XXXVI

CAPTAIN CABLE SOILS HIS HANDS

Cartoner was preparing to leave St. Petersburg when he received a letter from Deulin. The Frenchman wrote from Cracow, and mentioned in a rather rambling letter that Wanda was staying with a relative in that ancient city. He also thought it probable that she would make a stay in England pending the settlement of certain family affairs.

"I suppose," wrote Deulin, "that you will soon be on your way home. I think it likely we shall both be sent to Madrid before long. At all events, I hope we may meet somewhere. If you are passing through Dantzic on your homeward journey, you will find your old friend Cable there."

This last sentence was partly disfigured by a peculiar-shaped blot. The writer had evidently dropped his pen, all laden with ink, upon the letter as he wrote it. And Cartoner knew that this was the kernel, as it were, of this chatty epistle. He was bidden to make it convenient to go to Dantzic and to see Captain Cable there.

He arrived in Dantzic early in the morning, and did not go to a hotel. He left his luggage at the station and walked down to the Lange Brucke, where the river steamers start for Neufahrwasser.

The boats ran every hour, and Cartoner had not long to wait. He was not pressed for time, however, on his homeward journey, as he was more or less his own master while travelling, and could break his journey at Dantzic quite as easily as at Berlin.

Neufahrwasser is slowly absorbing the commerce of Dantzic, and none but small vessels go up the river to the city now. Captain Cable was deeply versed in those by-paths of maritime knowledge which enable small vessels to hold their own in these days of monopoly.

Cartoner knew that he would find the *Minnie* not in dock, but in one of the river anchorages, which are not only cheaper, but are more convenient for a vessel wanting to go to sea at short notice. And Captain Cable had a habit of going to sea at short notice.

Cartoner was not far wrong. For his own steamer passed the *Minnie* just above Neufahrwasser, where the river is broad and many vessels lie in mid-stream. The *Minnie* was deeply laden and lay anchored bow and stern, with the rapid tide rustling round her chains. She was ready for sea. Cartoner could see that. But she flew no bluepeter nor heralded her departure, as some captains, and especially foreigners, love to do. It adds to their sense of importance, and this was a modern quality little cultivated by Captain Cable. Neither was his steam aggressively in evidence. The *Minnie* did not catch the eye of the river-side idler, but conveyed the impression that she was a small, insignificant craft minding her own business, and would be much obliged if you would mind yours.

Cartoner had to walk back by the river-side and then take a

boat from the steps opposite to the anchorage. He bade the boatman wait while he clambered on board. Captain Cable had been informed of the approach of a shore boat, and was standing squarely on his own iron main-deck when Cartoner put his leg across the rail.

"Come below," he said, without enthusiasm. "It wasn't you that I was expecting. I tell you that."

Cartoner followed the captain into the little, low cabin, which smelled of petroleum, as usual. The *Minnie* was a hospitable ship, according to her facilities, and her skipper began by polishing a tumbler with a corner of the table-cloth. Then he indicated the vacant swing-back bench at the far side of the table, and sat down opposite to Cartoner himself.

"Was up the Baltic," he explained. "Pit props. Got a full cargo on board. Got an offer such as a poor sailorman couldn't afford to let slip to come to Dantzic and wait here till two gents came aboard. That's all I'm going to tell you."

"That's all I want to know," answered Cartoner.

"But, dammy, it's not all I want to know!" shouted Cable, suddenly, with a bang of his little, thick fist on the table. "I've been thinking since I lay here—been sleeping badly, and took the anchor watch meself—what I want to know is whether I'm to be treated gentlemanly!"

"In what way?" inquired Cartoner, gently. And the sound of his voice seemed to pacify the captain.

"Of course," he admitted, "I'm not a gentleman, I know that; but in seafaring things I'll be treated as such. Truth is, I'm afraid it's something to do with this news from St. Petersburg. And I don't take any bombmen on board my ship, and that's flat."

"I think I can assure you on that point," said Cartoner. "Nobody who had to do with the assassination of the Czar is likely to be in Dantzic. But I do not know whom you are to take on board here."

"May be as you can guess," suggested the captain.

"Yes, I think I can guess," admitted Cartoner, with his slow smile.

"But you won't tell me?"

"No. When do you expect them?"

"I'll answer that and ask you another," said Captain Cable, getting a yellow decanter from a locker beneath the table. "That's port—ship-chandler's port. I won't say it's got a bokay, mind."

For Captain Cable's hospitality was not showy or self-sufficient.

"I'll answer that and ask you another. I expected them last night. They'll likely come down with the tide, soon after midnight to-night. And now I'll ask you, what brought you aboard this ship, here in Dantzic River, Mr. Cartoner?"

"A letter from a Frenchman you know as well as I do—Paul Deulin. Like to read it?"

And Cartoner laid the letter before Captain Cable, who smiled contemptuously. He knew what was expected of a gentleman better than even to glance at it as it lay before him in its envelope.

"No, I wouldn't," he answered. He scratched his head reflectively, and looked beneath his bushy brows at Cartoner as if he expected the ship-chandler's port to have an immediate effect of some sort.

"Got your luggage in the boat alongside?" he asked, at length.

"No. It's at the station."

"Then let me send a hand ashore for it. Got three Germans furard. You'll come aboard and see this thing through, I hope."

"Thank you," answered Cartoner. He handed Captain Cable the ticket for his luggage.

"Mate's receipt?" inquired the captain.

And Cartoner nodded. The captain pushed the decanter towards his guest as he rose to go and give the necessary orders.

"No stint of the wine," he said, and went out on deck.

When he came back he laid the whole question aside, and devoted himself to the entertainment of his guest. They both slept in the afternoon. For the captain had been up all night, and fully expected to see no bed the following night.

"If they come down with the tide we'll go to sea on the same ebb," he said, as he lay down on his state-room locker and composed himself to sleep.

He sent the hands below at ten o'clock, saying he would keep the anchor watch himself. He wanted no forecastle gossip, he said to Cartoner, and did not trouble to explain that he had kept the watch three nights in succession on that account. Cartoner and he walked the deck side by side, treading softly for the sake of the sleepers under deck. For the same reason, perhaps, they were silent.

Once only Captain Cable spoke in little more than a whisper.

"Hope he is pleased with himself," he said, as he stood at the stern rail, looking up river, as it happened, towards Cracow. "For it is his doing, you and me waiting his orders here this cold night. They're tricky—the French. He's a tricky man."

"Yes," admitted Cartoner, who knew that the captain spoke of Deulin, "he is a tricky man."

After this they walked backward and forward for an hour without speaking. Then Captain Cable suddenly raised his hand and pointed into the night.

"There's a boat yonder," he said, "coming down quiet, under the lee of the land."

They stood listening, and presently heard the sound of oars used with great caution. A boat was crossing the river now and coming towards them. Captain Cable went forward and took a coil of rope. He clambered laboriously to the rail and stood there, watching the shadowy shape of the boat, which was now within hail. It was swinging round on the tide with perfect calculation and a most excellent skill.

"Stand by," said Captain Cable, gruffly, and the coils of his rope uncurled against the sky, to fall in a straight line across the boat.

Cartoner could see a man catch the rope neatly and make it

fast with two turns. In a moment the boat came softly nestling against the steamer as a kitten may nestle against its mother.

The man, who seemed to be the sole occupant, stood up, resting his hand on the rail of the *Minnie*. His head came up over the rail, and he peered into Cartoner's face.

"You!" he exclaimed.

"Yes," answered Cartoner, watching his hands, for there was a sort of exultation in Kosmaroff's voice, as if fate had offered him a chance which he never expected.

Cable came aft and stood beside Cartoner.

"I want to go to sea this tide," he said. "Where is the other man?"

"The other man is Prince Martin Bukaty," was the answer. "Help me to lift him on board."

"Why can't he come on board himself?"

"Because he is dead," answered Kosmaroff, with a break in his voice. And he lurched forward against the rail. Cartoner caught him by one arm and held him up.

"I am so weak!" he murmured, "so weak! I am famished!"

Cartoner lifted him bodily over the rail, and Cable received him, half fainting, in his arms. The next moment Cartoner was kneeling in the boat that rode alongside. He slowly raised Martin, and with an effort held him towards the captain, who was sitting astride on the rail. Thus they got him on board and carried him to the cabin. They passed through it to that which was grandly called the captain's state-room. They laid him on the locker which served for a bed, while Kosmaroff, supporting himself against the bulkhead, watched them in silence.

The captain glanced at Martin, and then, catching sight of Kosmaroff's face, he hurried to the cabin, to return in a minute with the inevitable decanter, yellow with age and rust.

"Here," he said, "drink that. Eat a bit o' biscuit. You're done."

Kosmaroff did as he was told. His eyes had the unmistakable glitter of starvation and exhaustion. They were fixed on Cartoner's face, with a hundred unasked questions in them.

"How did it happen?" asked Cartoner, at length.

"They fired on us crossing the frontier, and hit him. Pity it was not me. He is a much greater loss than I should have been. That was the night before last. He died before the morning."

"Tut! tut!" muttered Captain Cable, with an unwritable expression of pity. "There was the makings of a man in him," he said—"the makings of a man!"

And what Captain Cable held worthy of the name of man is not so common as to be lost to the world with indifference. He stood reflecting for a moment while Kosmaroff ate the ship's biscuit offered to him in the lid of a box, and Cartoner stared thoughtfully at the flickering lamp.

"I'll take him out to sea and bury him there," said Cable, at length, "if so be as that's agreeable to you. There's many a good man buried at sea, and when my time comes I'll ask for no better berth."

"That is the only thing to be done," said Cartoner.

Kosmaroff glanced towards the bed.

"Yes," he said, "that will do. He will lay quiet enough there."

And all three, perhaps, thought of all that they were to bury beneath the sea with this last of the Bukatys.

Captain Cable was the first to move. He turned and glanced at the clock.

"I'll turn the hands out," he said, "and we'll get to sea on the ebb. But I'll have to send ashore for a pilot."

"No," answered Kosmaroff, rising and finishing his wine, "you need not do that. I can take you out to sea."

The captain nodded curtly and went on deck, leaving Kosmaroff and Cartoner alone in the cabin in the silent presence of the man who had been the friend of both.

"Will you answer me a question?" asked Kosmaroff, suddenly.

"If I can," was the reply, economical of words.

"Where were you on the 13th of March?"

Cartoner reflected for a moment, and then replied:

"In St. Petersburg."

"Then I do not understand you," said Kosmaroff. "I don't

understand how we failed. For you know we have failed, I suppose?"

"I know nothing," answered Cartoner. "But I conclude you have failed, since you are here—and he is there."

And he pointed towards Martin.

"Thanks to you."

"No, I had nothing to do with it," said Cartoner.

"You cannot expect me to believe that."

"I do not care," replied the English diplomat, gently, "whether you believe it or not."

Kosmaroff moved towards the door. He carefully avoided passing near Cartoner, as if too close a proximity might make him forget himself.

"I will tell you one thing," he said, in a hard, low voice. "It will not do for you to show your face in Poland. Don't ever forget that I will take any chance I get to kill you! There is not room for you and me in Poland!"

"If I am sent there I shall go," replied Cartoner. And there crept to one side of Kosmaroff's face that slow smile which seemed to give him pain.

"I believe you will."

Then he went to the door. For Captain Cable could be heard on deck giving his orders, and already the winches were at work. But the Pole paused on the threshold and looked back. Then he came into the cabin again with his hand in the pocket of his threadbare workman's jacket.

"Look here," he said, bringing out a folded envelope and laying it on the cabin-table between them. "A dead man's wish. Get that to Miss Cahere. There is no message."

Cartoner took up the envelope and put it in his pocket.

"I shall not see her, but I will see that she gets it," he said.

The dawn was in the sky before the *Minnie* swept out past the pier-head light of Neufahrwasser. It was almost daylight when she slowed down in the bay to drop her pilot. Kosmaroff's boat was towing astern, jumping and straining in the wash of the screw. They hauled it up under the quarter, and in the dim light of coming day Cable and Cartoner drew near to the Pole, who had just quitted the wheel.

The three men stood together for a moment in silence. There was much to be said. There was a multitude of questions to be asked and answered. But none of the three had the intention of doing either one or the other.

"If you want a passage home," said Cable, gruffly, "cut your boat adrift. You're welcome."

"Thank you," was the answer. "I am going back to Poland to try again."

He turned to Cartoner, and peered in the half-light into the face of the only man he had had dealings with who had not been afraid of him. "Perhaps we shall meet again soon," he said, "in Poland."

"Not yet," replied Cartoner. "I am under orders for Madrid."

Kosmaroff stood by the rail for a moment, looking down into his boat. Then he turned suddenly to Cartoner, and made him a short, formal bow.

"Good-bye," he said.

Cartoner nodded, and said nothing.

Kosmaroff then turned towards Cable, who was standing with his hands thrust into his jacket-pockets, looking ahead towards the open sea.

"Captain," he said, and held out his hand so that Cable could not help seeing it. The captain hesitated, and at length withdrew his hand from the shelter of his pocket.

"Good-bye, mister," he said.

Then Kosmaroff climbed down into his boat. They cut the rope adrift, and he sat down to the oars.

There was a lurid streak of dawn low down in the sky, and Kosmaroff headed his boat towards it across the chill, green waters. Above the promise of a stormy day towered a great bank of torn clouds hanging over Poland.

XXXVII

THE PARTING OF THE WAYS

Paul Deulin happened to be in Lady Orlay's drawing-room, nearly a month later, when Miss Cahere's name was announced. He made a grimace and stood his ground.

Lady Orlay, it may be remembered, was one of those who attempt to keep their acquaintances in the right place—that is to say, in the background of her life. With this object in view, she had an "at home" day, hoping that her acquaintances would come to see her then and not stay too long. To-day was not that day.

"I know I ought not to have come this afternoon," explained Netty, with a rather shy haste, as she shook hands. "But I could not wait until next Tuesday, because we sail that day."

"Then you are going home again?"

Netty turned to greet Deulin, and changed color very prettily.

"Yes," she said, looking from one to the other with the soft blush still in her cheeks—"yes, and I am engaged to be married."

"Ah!" said Deulin. And his voice meant a great deal, while his eyes said nothing.

"Do we know the—gentleman?" asked Lady Orlay kindly. She was noting, with her quick and clever eyes, that Netty seemed happy and was exquisitely dressed. She was quite ready to be really interested in this idyl.

"I do not know," answered Netty. "He is not unknown in London. His name is Burris."

"Oh!" said Lady Orlay, "the comp—" Then she remembered that to call a fellow-creature a company promoter is practically a libel. "The millionaire?" she concluded, rather lamely.

"I believe he is very rich," admitted Netty, "though, of course—"

"No, of course not," Lady Orlay hastened to say. "I congratulate you, and wish you every happiness."

She turned rather abruptly towards Deulin, as if to give the next word to him. He took it promptly.

"And I," he said, with his old-world bow and deprecatory outspreading of the hands—"I wish you all the happiness—that money can buy."

Then he walked towards the fireplace, and stood there with his shoulder turned towards them while the two ladies discussed that which was to be Netty's future life. Her husband would be old enough to be her father, but he was a millionaire twice over—in London and New York. He had, moreover, a house in each of those great cities, of which details appeared from time to time in the illustrated monthly magazines.

"So I shall hope to be in London every year," said Netty, "and to see all the friends who have been so kind to us—you and Lord Orlay and Mr. Deulin."

"And Reginald Cartoner," suggested Deulin, turning to look over his shoulder for the change which he knew would come into Netty's eyes. And it came.

"Yes," she said. She looked as if she would like to ask a question, but did not give way to the temptation. She did not know that Cartoner was in the house at that moment, and Wanda, too. She did not know that Deulin had brought Wanda to London to stay at Lady Orlay's until Martin effected his escape and joined his sister in England. She only knew what the world now knew—that Price Martin Bukaty had died and been buried at sea. It was very sad, she had said, he was so nice.

Deulin did not join in the conversation again. He seemed to be interested in the fire, and Lady Orlay glanced at him once or twice, seeking to recall him to a sense of his social obligations. He had taken an envelope from his pocket, and, having torn it in two, had thrown it on the fire, where it was smouldering now on the coals. It was a soiled and worn envelope, as if it had passed through vicissitudes; there seemed to be something inside it which burned and gave forth an aromatic odor.

He was still watching the fire when Netty rose and took her leave. When the door closed again Lady Orlay went towards the fire.

"What is that in which you are so deeply interested that you quite forgot to be polite?" she said to Deulin. "Is it a letter?"

"It is a love-token," answered the Frenchman.

"For Netty Cahere?"

"No. For the woman that some poor fool supposed her to be."

Lady Orlay touched the envelope with the toe of a slipper which was still neat and small, so that it fell into the glowing centre of the fire and was there consumed.

"Perhaps you have assumed a great responsibility," she said.

"I have, and I shall carry it lightly to heaven if I get there."

"It has a smell of violets," said Lady Orlay, looking down into the fire.

"They are violets—from Warsaw," admitted Deulin. "Wanda is in?" he asked, gravely.

"Yes; they are in the study. I will send for her."

"I have received a letter from her father," said Deulin, with his hand on the bell.

Wanda came into the room a few minutes later. She was, of course, in mourning for Martin now, as well as for Poland. But she still carried her head high and faced the world with unshrinking eyes. Cartoner followed her into the room, his thoughtful glance reading Deulin's face.

"You have news?"

"I have heard from your father at last."

The Frenchman took the letter from his pocket, and his manner of unfolding it must have conveyed the intimation that he was not going to give it to Wanda, but intended to read it aloud, for Lady Orlay walked to the other end of the long room, out of hearing. Cartoner was about to follow her, when Wanda turned and glanced at him, and he stayed.

"The letter begins," said Deulin, unconsciously falling into a professional preliminary—

"'I have received Cartoner's letter supplementing the account given by the man who was with Martin at the last. I remember Captain Cable quite well. When we met him at the Signal House, at Northfleet, I little thought that he would be called upon to render the last earthly service to my son. So it was he who read the last words. And Martin was buried in the Baltic. You, my old friend, know all that I have given to Poland. The last gift has been the hardest to part with. Some day I hope to write to Cartoner, but not now. He is not a man to attach much importance to words. He is, I think, a man to understand silence. At present I cannot write, as I am virtually a prisoner in my own house. From a high quarter I have received a gracious intimation that my affairs are under the special attention of a beneficent monarch, and that I am so far to be mercifully forgiven that a sentence of perpetual confinement within the barriers of Warsaw will be deemed sufficient punishment for—not having been found out. But my worst enemies are my own party. Nothing can now convince them that Martin and I did not betray the plot. Moreover, Cartoner's name is freely coupled with ours. So they believe. So it will go down to history, and nothing that we can say will make any difference. That I find myself in company with Cartoner in this error only strengthens the feeling of friendship, of which I was conscious when we first met. Beg him, for his own sake, never to cross this frontier again. Ask him, for mine, to avoid making any sign of friendship towards me or mine.'"

As fate ruled it, the letter required turning at this point, and Deulin, for the first time in his life, perhaps, made a mistake at a crucial moment. He allowed his voice to break on the next word, and had to pause for an instant before he could proceed.

"Then follow," he said, rather uneasily, "certain passages to myself which I need not read. Further on he proceeds: 'I am in good health. Better, indeed, than when I last saw you. I am, in fact, a very tough old man, and may live to give much trouble yet.'"

Deulin broke off, and laughed heartily at this conceit. But he laughed alone.

"So, you see, he seems very cheerful," he said, as if it was the letter that had laughed. He folded the paper and replaced it in his pocket. "He seems to be getting on very well without you, you perceive," he added, smiling at Wanda. But he lacked conviction. There was in his voice and manner a dim suggestion of the losing game, consciously played.

"May I read the letter for myself?" asked Wanda, holding out her slim, steady hand.

After a moment's hesitation, Deulin took the folded paper from his pocket and handed it to her. Lady Orlay had returned to the group standing near the fire. He turned and met her eyes, making an imperceptible movement of his eyebrows, as of one who had made an attempt and failed. They waited in silence while Wanda read the letter, and at length she handed it back to him.

"Yes," she said, "I read it differently. It is not only the world which appears differently to two different people, even a letter may have two meanings to two readers. You shed a sort of gayety upon that—"

She indicated the letter which he still held in his hand, and Deulin deprecated the suggestion by a shrug of the shoulders.

"—which is not really there. To me it is the letter of a broken-hearted man," she added slowly. There was an odd pause, during which Wanda seemed to reflect. She was at the parting of the ways. Even Deulin had nothing to say. He could not point out the path. Perhaps Cartoner had already done so by his own life, without any words at all.

"I shall go to Warsaw to-night," she said at last to Lady Orlay, "if you will not think me wanting in manners. Believe me, I do not lack gratitude. But—you understand?"

"Yes, dear, I understand," replied the woman who had known happiness. And she closed her lips quickly, as if she feared that they might falter.

"It is so clearly my duty, and duty is best, is it not?" said Wanda. As she spoke she turned to Cartoner. The question was asked of none other. It was unto his judgment that she gave her case; to his wisdom she submitted the verdict of her life. She wished him to give it before these people. As if she took a subtle pride in showing them that he was what she knew him to be. She was sure of her lover; which is, perhaps, happiness enough for this world.

"Duty is best, is it not?" she repeated.

"It is the only thing," he answered.

Deulin was the first to speak. He had strong views upon last words and partings. The mere thought of such things made him suddenly energetic and active. He turned to Wanda with his watch in his hand.

"Your mind is made up?" he asked. "You go to-night?"

"Yes."

"Then I must go at once to see to your passport and make arrangements for the journey. I take you as far as Alexandrowo. I cannot take you across the frontier, you understand?"

He turned to Cartoner.

"And you? When do you go to Spain?"

"To-night," was the answer.

"Then good-bye." The Frenchman held out his hand, and in a moment was at the door. Lady Orlay followed him out of the room and closed the door behind her. She followed him down-stairs. In the hall they stood and looked at each other in silence. There were tears in the woman's eyes. But Deulin's smile was sadder.

"And this is the end," he said—"the end!"

"No," said Lady Orlay; "it is not. It cannot be. I have never known a great happiness yet that was not built upon the wreckage of other happinesses. That is why happy people are never gay. It is not the end, Paul. Heaven is kind."

"Sometimes," answered Deulin, grudgingly. On the door-step he paused, and, facing her suddenly, he made a gesture indicating himself, commanding her attention to his long life and story. "Sometimes, milady."

Choose from Thousands of 1stWorldLibrary Classics By

A. M. Barnard
Ada Leverson
Adolphus William Ward
Aesop
Agatha Christie
Alexander Aaronsohn
Alexander Kielland
Alexandre Dumas
Alfred Gatty
Alfred Ollivant
Alice Duer Miller
Alice Turner Curtis
Alice Dunbar
Allen Chapman
Alleyne Ireland
Ambrose Bierce
Amelia E. Barr
Amory H. Bradford
Andrew Lang
Andrew McFarland Davis
Andy Adams
Angela Brazil
Anna Alice Chapin
Anna Sewell
Annie Besant
Annie Hamilton Donnell
Annie Payson Call
Annie Roe Carr
Annonaymous
Anton Chekhov
Archibald Lee Fletcher
Arnold Bennett
Arthur C. Benson
Arthur Conan Doyle
Arthur M. Winfield
Arthur Ransome
Arthur Schnitzler
Arthur Train
Atticus
B.H. Baden-Powell
B. M. Bower
B. C. Chatterjee
Baroness Emmuska Orczy
Baroness Orczy
Basil King
Bayard Taylor
Ben Macomber
Bertha Muzzy Bower
Bjornstjerne Bjornson

Booth Tarkington
Boyd Cable
Bram Stoker
C. Collodi
C. E. Orr
C. M. Ingleby
Carolyn Wells
Catherine Parr Traill
Charles A. Eastman
Charles Amory Beach
Charles Dickens
Charles Dudley Warner
Charles Farrar Browne
Charles Ives
Charles Kingsley
Charles Klein
Charles Hanson Towne
Charles Lathrop Pack
Charles Romyn Dake
Charles Whibley
Charles Willing Beale
Charlotte M. Braeme
Charlotte M. Yonge
Charlotte Perkins Stetson
Clair W. Hayes
Clarence Day Jr.
Clarence E. Mulford
Clemence Housman
Confucius
Coningsby Dawson
Cornelis DeWitt Wilcox
Cyril Burleigh
D. H. Lawrence
Daniel Defoe
David Garnett
Dinah Craik
Don Carlos Janes
Donald Keyhoe
Dorothy Kilner
Dougan Clark
Douglas Fairbanks
E. Nesbit
E. P. Roe
E. Phillips Oppenheim
E. S. Brooks
Earl Barnes
Edgar Rice Burroughs
Edith Van Dyne
Edith Wharton

Edward Everett Hale
Edward J. O'Biren
Edward S. Ellis
Edwin L. Arnold
Eleanor Atkins
Eleanor Hallowell Abbott
Eliot Gregory
Elizabeth Gaskell
Elizabeth McCracken
Elizabeth Von Arnim
Ellem Key
Emerson Hough
Emilie F. Carlen
Emily Bronte
Emily Dickinson
Enid Bagnold
Enilor Macartney Lane
Erasmus W. Jones
Ernie Howard Pie
Ethel May Dell
Ethel Turner
Ethel Watts Mumford
Eugene Sue
Eugenie Foa
Eugene Wood
Eustace Hale Ball
Evelyn Everett-green
Everard Cotes
F. H. Cheley
F. J. Cross
F. Marion Crawford
Fannie E. Newberry
Federick Austin Ogg
Ferdinand Ossendowski
Fergus Hume
Florence A. Kilpatrick
Fremont B. Deering
Francis Bacon
Francis Darwin
Frances Hodgson Burnett
Frances Parkinson Keyes
Frank Gee Patchin
Frank Harris
Frank Jewett Mather
Frank L. Packard
Frank V. Webster
Frederic Stewart Isham
Frederick Trevor Hill
Frederick Winslow Taylor

Friedrich Kerst
Friedrich Nietzsche
Fyodor Dostoyevsky
G.A. Henty
G.K. Chesterton
Gabrielle E. Jackson
Garrett P. Serviss
Gaston Leroux
George A. Warren
George Ade
Geroge Bernard Shaw
George Cary Eggleston
George Durston
George Ebers
George Eliot
George Gissing
George MacDonald
George Meredith
George Orwell
George Sylvester Viereck
George Tucker
George W. Cable
George Wharton James
Gertrude Atherton
Gordon Casserly
Grace E. King
Grace Gallatin
Grace Greenwood
Grant Allen
Guillermo A. Sherwell
Gulielma Zollinger
Gustav Flaubert
H. A. Cody
H. B. Irving
H. C. Bailey
H. G. Wells
H. H. Munro
H. Irving Hancock
H. R. Naylor
H. Rider Haggard
H. W. C. Davis
Haldeman Julius
Hall Caine
Hamilton Wright Mabie
Hans Christian Andersen
Harold Avery
Harold McGrath
Harriet Beecher Stowe
Harry Castlemon
Harry Coghill
Harry Houidini

Hayden Carruth
Helent Hunt Jackson
Helen Nicolay
Hendrik Conscience
Hendy David Thoreau
Henri Barbusse
Henrik Ibsen
Henry Adams
Henry Ford
Henry Frost
Henry James
Henry Jones Ford
Henry Seton Merriman
Henry W Longfellow
Herbert A. Giles
Herbert Carter
Herbert N. Casson
Herman Hesse
Hildegard G. Frey
Homer
Honore De Balzac
Horace B. Day
Horace Walpole
Horatio Alger Jr.
Howard Pyle
Howard R. Garis
Hugh Lofting
Hugh Walpole
Humphry Ward
Ian Maclaren
Inez Haynes Gillmore
Irving Bacheller
Isabel Cecilia Williams
Isabel Hornibrook
Israel Abrahams
Ivan Turgenev
J. G.Austin
J. Henri Fabre
J. M. Barrie
J. M. Walsh
J. Macdonald Oxley
J. R. Miller
J. S. Fletcher
J. S. Knowles
J. Storer Clouston
J. W. Duffield
Jack London
Jacob Abbott
James Allen
James Andrews
James Baldwin

James Branch Cabell
James DeMille
James Joyce
James Lane Allen
James Lane Allen
James Oliver Curwood
James Oppenheim
James Otis
James R. Driscoll
Jane Abbott
Jane Austen
Jane L. Stewart
Janet Aldridge
Jens Peter Jacobsen
Jerome K. Jerome
Jessie Graham Flower
John Buchan
John Burroughs
John Cournos
John F. Kennedy
John Gay
John Glasworthy
John Habberton
John Joy Bell
John Kendrick Bangs
John Milton
John Philip Sousa
John Taintor Foote
Jonas Lauritz Idemil Lie
Jonathan Swift
Joseph A. Altsheler
Joseph Carey
Joseph Conrad
Joseph E. Badger Jr
Joseph Hergesheimer
Joseph Jacobs
Jules Vernes
Julian Hawthrone
Julie A Lippmann
Justin Huntly McCarthy
Kakuzo Okakura
Karle Wilson Baker
Kate Chopin
Kenneth Grahame
Kenneth McGaffey
Kate Langley Bosher
Kate Langley Bosher
Katherine Cecil Thurston
Katherine Stokes
L. A. Abbot
L. T. Meade

L. Frank Baum
Latta Griswold
Laura Dent Crane
Laura Lee Hope
Laurence Housman
Lawrence Beasley
Leo Tolstoy
Leonid Andreyev
Lewis Carroll
Lewis Sperry Chafer
Lilian Bell
Lloyd Osbourne
Louis Hughes
Louis Joseph Vance
Louis Tracy
Louisa May Alcott
Lucy Fitch Perkins
Lucy Maud Montgomery
Luther Benson
Lydia Miller Middleton
Lyndon Orr
M. Corvus
M. H. Adams
Margaret E. Sangster
Margret Howth
Margaret Vandercook
Margaret W. Hungerford
Margret Penrose
Maria Edgeworth
Maria Thompson Daviess
Mariano Azuela
Marion Polk Angellotti
Mark Overton
Mark Twain
Mary Austin
Mary Catherine Crowley
Mary Cole
Mary Hastings Bradley
Mary Roberts Rinehart
Mary Rowlandson
M. Wollstonecraft Shelley
Maud Lindsay
Max Beerbohm
Myra Kelly
Nathaniel Hawthrone
Nicolo Machiavelli
O. F. Walton
Oscar Wilde
Owen Johnson
P.G. Wodehouse
Paul and Mabel Thorne

Paul G. Tomlinson
Paul Severing
Percy Brebner
Percy Keese Fitzhugh
Peter B. Kyne
Plato
Quincy Allen
R. Derby Holmes
R. L. Stevenson
R. S. Ball
Rabindranath Tagore
Rahul Alvares
Ralph Bonehill
Ralph Henry Barbour
Ralph Victor
Ralph Waldo Emmerson
Rene Descartes
Ray Cummings
Rex Beach
Rex E. Beach
Richard Harding Davis
Richard Jefferies
Richard Le Gallienne
Robert Barr
Robert Frost
Robert Gordon Anderson
Robert L. Drake
Robert Lansing
Robert Lynd
Robert Michael Ballantyne
Robert W. Chambers
Rosa Nouchette Carey
Rudyard Kipling
Saint Augustine
Samuel B. Allison
Samuel Hopkins Adams
Sarah Bernhardt
Sarah C. Hallowell
Selma Lagerlof
Sherwood Anderson
Sigmund Freud
Standish O'Grady
Stanley Weyman
Stella Benson
Stella M. Francis
Stephen Crane
Stewart Edward White
Stijn Streuvels
Swami Abhedananda
Swami Parmananda
T. S. Ackland

T. S. Arthur
The Princess Der Ling
Thomas A. Janvier
Thomas A Kempis
Thomas Anderton
Thomas Bailey Aldrich
Thomas Bulfinch
Thomas De Quincey
Thomas Dixon
Thomas H. Huxley
Thomas Hardy
Thomas More
Thornton W. Burgess
U. S. Grant
Upton Sinclair
Valentine Williams
Various Authors
Vaughan Kester
Victor Appleton
Victor G. Durham
Victoria Cross
Virginia Woolf
Wadsworth Camp
Walter Camp
Walter Scott
Washington Irving
Wilbur Lawton
Wilkie Collins
Willa Cather
Willard F. Baker
William Dean Howells
William le Queux
W. Makepeace Thackeray
William W. Walter
William Shakespeare
Winston Churchill
Yei Theodora Ozaki
Yogi Ramacharaka
Young E. Allison
Zane Grey

www.ingramcontent.com/pod-product-compliance
Lightning Source LLC
Chambersburg PA
CBHW032136270626
47172CB00008B/85